# Wheels and Deals

# Wheels and Deals

## The automotive industry in twentieth-century Australia

Robert Conlon
and
John Perkins

Routledge
Taylor & Francis Group

LONDON AND NEW YORK

First published 2001 by Ashgate Publishing

Reissued 2018 by Routledge
2 Park Square, Milton Park, Abingdon, Oxon OX14 4RN
711 Third Avenue, New York, NY 10017, USA

*Routledge is an imprint of the Taylor & Francis Group, an informa business*

Publisher's Note
The publisher has gone to great lengths to ensure the quality of this reprint but points out that some imperfections in the original copies may be apparent.

Disclaimer
The publisher has made every effort to trace copyright holders and welcomes correspondence from those they have been unable to contact.

Typeset in Times by N²productions

A Library of Congress record exists under LC control number: 2001018923

ISBN 13: 978-1-138-71272-0 (hbk)
ISBN 13: 978-1-138-71270-6 (pbk)
ISBN 13: 978-1-315-19929-0 (ebk)

# Contents

List of tables        vii

Acknowledgements        ix

1    Introduction: the Automobile Industry in Australia    1
        A century of auto industry policy

2    False Start: the Early Years of Motoring and Automotive
        Manufacturing    9
        The supply side
        The demand side
        The Model T Ford in Australia
        The tariff and the 'spoke-shave and hammer brigade'

3    Acceleration: the Accretion Model of Automotive Industry
        Development in Australia, 1919–1939    28
        Tariffs as a source of revenue
        The lobby
        The role of the bureaucracy
        Industry structure and performance
        Tariffs and the 'motorization' of society
        The outcome of interwar 'policy'

4    Stalled: Politics and Government Policies of the Later 1930s    50
        Trade diversion and the motor vehicle engine bounty proposal
        National interest or self interest? Conflict and cooperation
            among the leading firms
        Political conflict and the bounty scheme
        War and the Motor Vehicles Agreement Act
        A patriotic duty: Australian Consolidated Industries and the
            so-called monopoly
        The end of the affair
        Evaluation

5    The Canadian Connection    83
        Early development of the industry in Canada
        Market conditions
        Trade barriers and foreign ownership

Trade barriers, automobile production and exports
Evaluation

6 Britain and Empire 102
   Regaining the Australian market
   Australian trade policy in the 1930s
   British producers and Australian production

7 Post-Second World War 115
   From proposal to manufacture: the establishment of an industry
   The development of the industry in the 1950s
   The local content plans, 1964–1983

8 The 'Button' Car Plan and the Post-1992 Environment 136
   A selective look at the post-Button Plan industry

9 A Summing-up 158
   The 1990s and beyond
   How protection shaped the Australian automotive industry in
      the twentieth-century

Bibliography 170

Index 177

# Tables

| | | |
|---|---|---|
| 2.1 | Motor chassis and body imports by country of origin, 1911–1914 | 23 |
| 5.1 | Canada – automobile industry, 1918–1939 | 88 |
| 5.2 | Major countries – motor vehicle exports and production, 1918–1939 | 90 |
| 5.3 | Canada – motor vehicle manufacturing, 1918–1939 | 91 |
| 5.4 | Canada – auto parts and accessories, 1918–1939 | 92 |
| 5.5 | Australia – motor industry, 1919/20–1929/30 | 93 |
| 5.6 | Australia – motor industry, 1926/27–1938/39 | 94 |
| 5.7 | Australia – chassis imports, 1919/20–1938/39 | 95 |
| 6.1 | New car registrations in Australia, 1926–1939 | 105 |
| 6.2 | Sources of unassembled chassis imports, 1931/32–1938/39 | 110 |
| 7.1 | Australia – new passenger motor vehicle registrations, 1921–1998 | 133 |
| 8.1 | Australia – estimated passenger motor vehicle sales volumes and market shares, 1982–1998 | 138 |
| 8.2 | Australia – automotive exports, 1982–1998 | 140 |
| 8.3 | Australia – December quarter price indices, 1982–1998 | 142 |
| 8.4 | Average number of owner detected faults for Australian and imported cars, 1985–1998 | 144 |
| 8.5 | Australia – profits (losses) as a return on sales | 145 |
| 8.6 | Sources of profits – passenger motor vehicles | 147 |
| 8.7 | Australia – production volumes by passenger motor vehicle model lines, 1985–1998 | 149 |
| 8.8 | Australia – numbers employed in the automotive industry, 1983–1998 | 150 |

8.9    Australia – comparison of anticipated and actual investment
       in the automotive industry, 1986/89–1995/97                    151

9.1    Australia – sources of imported CBU passenger motor vehicles,
       1985–1998                                                      160

9.2    Major passenger motor vehicle producer countries – production,
       registrations, and exportable surplus, 1985, 1990–1996         162

## Figure

8.1    Australia – market characteristics, 1982–1998                  139

# Acknowledgements

Chapter 3

This chapter draws on material published in an earlier paper: 'Australian Governments and Automotive Manufacturing, 1919–1939', *Australian Journal of Politics and History*, Vol. 45, No. 3, September, 1999, 376–91. We are grateful to the Departments of Government and History, University of Queens and Blackwell Publishers Ltd for their permission to use the material.

Chapter 5

This chapter draws on material published in an earlier paper: 'Canada's Role in the Inter-War Development of the Automobile Industry in Australia', *Australian-Canadian Studies*, Vol. 17, No. 1, 1999, 81–103. We are grateful to the publishers of *Australian-Canadian Studies* for their permission to use the material.

# Modern Economic and Social History Series
## General Editor's Preface

Economic and social history has been a flourishing subject of scholarly study during recent decades. Not only has the volume of literature increased enormously but the range of interest in time, space and subject matter has broadened considerably so that today there are many sub-branches of the subject which have developed considerable status in their own right.

One of the aims of this series is to encourage the publication of scholarly monographs on any aspect of modern economic and social history. The geographical coverage is world-wide and contributions on non-British themes will be especially welcome. While emphasis will be placed on works embodying original research, it is also intended that the series should provide the opportunity to publish studies of a more general and thematic nature which offer a reappraisal or critical analysis of major issues of debate.

Derek H. Aldcroft

*Manchester Metropolitan University*

# 1   Introduction: the Automobile Industry in Australia

On 29 November 1948 'Australia's Own Car', the first Holden (Model 48-215) left the assembly line of the GM-H plant at Fishermen's Bend in Victoria. The Holden 48-215, the product of a joint American–Australian design team, was presented as a milestone in the history of Australian manufacturing and indeed it was – as the first 'complete' car produced in Australia on a large scale.[1] Reaching that stage, however, was a long, drawn-out and costly business for Australian taxpayers and car buyers.

This is a study of the emergence of car production in Australia in the twentieth century – to the Holden 48-215 and beyond.[2] Before the Holden, the model of development of the Australian car industry may be described as one of accretion, in which over time an expanding range of components was produced. The process began just after the birth of motoring with the production of motor bodies, and the range of products widened during the interwar period to the manufacture of 'peripheral' components, including radiators, lamps, sparkplugs, running boards and tyres. However, until the Holden was produced, the substance of the industry's activities remained motor bodybuilding and the assembly of imported chassis.

To provide a working definition of an 'automobile industry' and 'complete' manufacture, we have looked to the innovative study of the industry and its changing methods of production by Womack, Jones and Roos.[3] They chose the assembly process and plant as the appropriate units to compare across firms and across countries, and we have used their work as a guide. Though there have been important developments in automobile design which have changed aspects of the process (for example the introduction of the integrated chassis), a very large part of the industry has always involved the assembly of components or sub-assemblies and the process of their installation and final assembly, whether by batch or assembly-line methods. Many of the sub-assemblies (for example alternators/generators, seats and upholstery, etc.) are produced by outside suppliers, and these together with the components produced 'in house' are assembled to produce the final product – the automobile.

We define a 'complete' automobile industry to be the fabrication and assembly of body panels and engines, and the final assembly of these and other major sub-assemblies – including transmission, suspension and electrical equipment. By this definition Australia had a 'complete' industry only after the Second World War. Before this the industry was 'incomplete' consisting mainly of the process of final assembly, and the fabrication and assembly of body panels. Some components such as radiators, spark plugs, headlamps and tyres were also produced. The heart of the car, the chassis (which was then defined for Customs' purposes to include the engine) was imported, either assembled or unassembled.

In the process of establishing and maintaining 'complete' automobile manufacture in Australia, among the influences examined in this study are those of politics, trade barriers (especially tariffs) and foreign ownership. They have all played important and recurring roles in shaping the industry. In this process the production of the first Holden was only a part, though a very important one. In many respects Australian passenger motor vehicle manufacture may be viewed as a case study in protectionism, or even a laboratory for discerning the effects of differing barriers to trade.[4] Over nearly a century the production of vehicle components and, eventually, cars has been the subject of a greater variety of interventionist policies than the manufacture of virtually any other product in Australia. As policies have changed, so too has the structure of the industry – its productive processes and the types of components and vehicles it has produced. Ultimately, this is the story of some of the causes and effects of Australian government policies on the local development of an industry that is one of the most significant of the twentieth century.

Why did governments in Australia, as elsewhere, come to lavish so much attention on the development of complete automobile manufacture? Into the 1920s cars were viewed by many with little favour. They were considered to be a luxury, and therefore a legitimate target for raising government revenue. In particular the importation of cars, even stripped-down chassis, was considered to have an adverse effect on the balance of trade and payments, and there was a widespread view that tariffs were ideal taxes: there was a perception that the foreign exporter bore the burden.

Attitudes to local production, however, often proved to be a different matter. Apart from any feelings of national pride, car production came to signal that a country had reached a crucial stage of national development. The integrated domestic manufacture of automobiles requires the support of a wide range of industrial activities. Among them at a basic level is the manufacture of glass, certain types of steel and alloys, rubber and paint; at higher stages of fabrication, the production of a range of components and sub-assemblies, and ultimately their assembly into the final product, the car. With these processes comes the acquisition of valuable labour skills such as precision machining, sheet metal fabrication, engineering and design. Many of the skills developed for, and the products produced by the automobile industry (for example engine design and manufacture) were claimed to have applications in other, sometimes strategic industries such as aircraft and tank production.

The view that the industry was of strategic importance was far from universal, even in 1939. While labour skills were certainly a mobile resource, in evidence given to the Tariff Board in the late 1930s, the managing director of Ford Australia dismissed out of hand claims that car manufacture could easily be switched to tank manufacture.[5] As far as aircraft and car manufacture is concerned, any link between the two is tenuous. Modern aircraft of the late 1930s were of aluminium construction and many of the most popular types (particularly those of United States design) were powered by air-cooled engines, rather than liquid cooled as were almost all cars of the time. (The Volkswagen was a notable exception.) Similarly, aircraft components had little in common with those of cars.

Nevertheless, in acquiring the capacity to manufacture cars a country was presumed to derive the related benefits, and many governments have been willing to go to great lengths to foster a local industry and its underlying infra-structure. Moreover, in Australia there were additional influences at work. There was a long-standing concern regarding the country's heavy reliance on agriculture. Export prices for pastoral and farm products were volatile and generally depressed in the interwar era. As well, productivity growth in agri-culture had resulted in the sector becoming less and less capable of absorbing significant amounts of labour – at a time when the call to 'populate or perish' was becoming an increasingly important issue in Australia. Manufacturing, with its capacity to employ labour and its import-substitution effects, seemed to be an answer to the problem.

For much of the twentieth century in Australia the primary means of fostering the establishment and growth of manufacturing industries has been through the tariff, and automotive manufacturing has been no exception. Achieving the 'Australian' motor vehicle production capacity of the late 1940s required high levels of tariff protection on components, and still higher protection for the production of finished cars. Once 'complete' manufacture was established, high tariffs and other forms of protection were then required to maintain the capacity to produce motor vehicles. These have acted as substantial taxes on motorists and the public generally, as motor vehicles came to meet a growing share of public and commercial transport needs. Even in recent years while the tariff rates protecting most Australian manufacturing have fallen considerably as part of a continuing process of tariff reform, the motor vehicle manufacturing lobby has proven particularly effective in maintaining its privileged position. The Federal government's 1997 decision to implement a 'tariff pause' for the industry at 15 per cent for five years after 2000 (about three times the average rate protecting the remainder of manufacturing), rather than the Industry Commission's recommended continued phased reductions in tariff rates, is a good example of the industry's continuing political influence.[6]

## A century of auto industry policy

While a few cars were produced in Australia before 1914, a combination of circumstances inhibited the establishment of a local motor vehicle industry. The failure is attributable at least partly to a tariff structure influenced by an established carriage-building industry (for horse-drawn vehicles) that effectively precluded the establishment of chassis production.[7] Imported motor bodies were subject to protective tariffs, chassis to low revenue duties. The success of the carriage builders in influencing policy was assisted by the climate of contemporary opinion, especially the widely accepted belief that protective tariffs could eventually create an autonomous Australian motor vehicle manufacturing industry. However, the relatively specialized skills of carriage builders, and the structure of the tariff they helped shape, established a disincentive to broaden manufacture beyond motor bodies to the local manufacture and assembly of chassis.

Until 1908 when Henry Ford began manufacturing the Model T, the most profitable strategy in the car industry was the low-volume production of luxury vehicles.[8] This changed with the appearance of the Model T Ford. When imports of the Model T began in Australia in 1909, followed by those of other mass-produced vehicles from the US, such as Buick and later (from 1916) Dodge cars, they provided the *coup de grâce* to an embryonic motor vehicle industry in Australia. These relatively cheap and reliable vehicles quickly came to dominate the market. The most profitable response by Australian firms was to abandon any effort to produce cars and acquire dealerships from US manufacturers.

A shortage of shipping space towards the end of the First World War resulting in a temporary prohibition of motor body imports in 1917 brought the beginning of large-scale production of bodies in Australia.[9] Given this initial impetus the immediate post-war protective structure – low revenue duties on chassis and protective rates on bodies – provided the framework shaping local production for much of the interwar period.

This study contends that during the interwar period, as far as the automobile industry was concerned, government policy did not represent a thought-out plan for either 'national development' or later 'national defence', as has been intimated elsewhere.[10] Rather, such policy was characterized by '*ad hockery*', expediency and sheer greed. Compared with other forms of taxation, tariffs constituted an important and politically expedient means of servicing the national debt that had risen twentyfold as a result of the demands of the First

World War. Imported automobiles were an ideal target. Taxing them could be sold to an electorate on the popular grounds that import duties soaked both foreigners and the rich who indulged in the luxury of conspicuous consumption.

Moreover, the administration of tariffs and by-laws by Customs provided significant scope for effectively changing tariff rates without the approval of Parliament. The 'lobby' – representatives of special interest groups that endeavoured to influence government policy in their favour – came of age with the 'tariff touts' of the 1930s, and reciprocal favours (or at least the hope of them) became part of the lobbying process. It was exemplified by GM-H's participation in the Commonwealth Aircraft Corporation in the late 1930s, 'although it did not suit us too well', in the belief that it would bring preferential government treatment of the company in the future.[11]

What was the outcome of interwar tariff policy? The production of a greater range of products, certainly, but this was not without economic cost. The Australian automobile industry of the 1930s was characterized by technological stagnation, and the fragmentation of a market (many small firms producing many products with short production runs) already smaller than it would otherwise have been owing to the tariff-inflated price of cars. The scope for exploiting economies of scale in local production of components and of vehicles themselves was correspondingly limited. Many of the industry's products – motor bodies and other motor vehicle components – were of poor quality. The shelter of high, protective tariffs fostered all of these dubious attributes.

The Motor Vehicle Engine Bounty Bill of 1936 signalled a realization by the government that the manufacture of engines and chassis – complete manufacture – could not be accomplished by the 'traditional' means: increasing tariffs. The Bounty Bill took more than three years to enact despite pressure exerted in the Federal Parliament by its proponents on both sides of the House. Even after the measures were passed by Parliament, the bounty scheme was not enough to make local production of engines and chassis attractive. To make it so required the Motor Vehicles Agreement Act (1940) that relied on exercising the extraordinary wartime powers of the National Security Act to 'safeguard the interests of the Australian company [Australian Consolidated Industries] from foreign or foreign-controlled companies which might desire to manufacture motor cars in Australia'.[12]

Just seven months before the Agreement was passed the Defense Department had denied the direct defence significance of the manufacture of engines and chassis. Now it appeared the security of the nation depended on it. The measures of the initial Agreement conferring a monopoly of car production on Australian Consolidated Industries (ACI) were extraordinary, negotiated in secrecy and introduced with haste. They were, however, destined never to be implemented.[13]

At war's end, the Acts were repealed as a condition imposed by the major foreign producers (including Ford and General Motors-Holden (GM-H)) if they were to engage in complete manufacture in the post-war period. Their repeal effectively determined ACI would not be a part of the post-war industry. The foreign firms that had dominated the pre-war industry had won, but what was the foundation they had themselves laid down for the post-war industry? Had the nation received value for money for the pre-war assistance of the 'foreign' producers? According to an analysis of the potential for the post-war development of a motor vehicle industry in Australia undertaken by the Secondary Industries Commission during the Second World War, the nation had not. It was the Commission's evaluation that the industry had provided a poor return for the high prices consumers had had to pay for the industry's protection.[14]

Despite this the government went ahead with its plan for complete automobile production after the Second World War. It culminated in the production of the Holden 48-215 in 1948 and, over the next few years, the implementation of the more limited production proposals of Ford, Chrysler Dodge and Nuffield.[15] While British cars dominated Australian market sales in the immediate post-war years owing to the 'dollar shortage', once the capacity constraints which hampered GM-H's early production were overcome, by the early 1950s the Holden had become easily the best-selling car in the country. Import licensing which applied from 1952 limited imports of CKD (Completely Knocked Down) kits and provided significantly greater protection than the tariff alone for the production of a wide range of automotive components. In effect, for a period the tariff became largely redundant as a protective measure.[16]

Behind the higher import barriers local production and assembly expanded, and by the end of the 1950s the result of 15 years of post-war policy was there for all to see. Australia had acquired four vehicle manufacturers (British Motor Corporation, Chrysler, Ford and GM-H) and a number of assemblers all competing for a market the size of which could sustain just one producer operating at near optimum scale of output. When import licensing controls were lifted in 1960, the tariff once again became the predominant protective measure, but it was not enough to preserve the existing firms from unhealthy (for them) import competition.

The answer to their problem – local content 'plans' which provided tariff concessions for imported components as long as certain levels of local content were achieved – again largely overrode the protection provided by the tariff. The plans were announced in May 1964, and operated for more than five years (though there were numerous modifications along the way). By 1971 their effects were clear. Instead of the production of a small range of models with high local content, the plans had encouraged a proliferation of models and especially the fragmentation of the small car market, which was then the fastest-growing market segment.[17]

It was, however, these small cars which were providing the biggest headaches for Chrysler, Ford and GM-H.[18] Their threat in 1974 to retrench 7,000 employees as a result of loss of sales to mainly Japanese small-car imports was the trigger for implementing still another policy bypassing the protection of the tariff: market-sharing, in which imports were limited to 20 per cent of the local market. This in turn resulted in the entry of Nissan and Toyota as full producers. Had they not been 'invited' to participate by the government it would have resulted in the need for continuing import restrictions, contrary to GATT, and damage to Australia's trading relationship with Japan. By the second half of the 1970s there were five manufacturers in the Australian market in which the local share could only be maintained by stringent import controls.

It was obvious by then that controls on imports had failed to create an industry structure that was even remotely viable without continuing high levels of assistance. The measures which had been applied since the 1950s – at various times and in various combinations tariffs, import licensing restrictions, local content schemes and market-sharing were all tried – had produced an industrial nightmare. There were too many firms, too many models and too few sales.

The solution a new Labor government applied to the problems was even more prescriptive than past policies it supplanted. It was the 'Button' Plan, implemented in 1984, which was to take a restructured and efficient industry into the 1990s.[19] The means was to gradually increase the pressure from import competition on local producers with the aim of encouraging high-volume local production of a few models and the efficiencies that went with it. Over the period of its operation the plan saw the abolition of market-sharing and local content schemes; reductions in tariffs; and the introduction of the export facilitation scheme.[20] The target set for the industry at the beginning of the plan – three manufacturing groups, producing a total of six models – was, for a short time, achieved.[21] Over the Button and post-Button period the productivity of local producers and the quality of their vehicles improved markedly. These improvements have not been reflected in their profitability, however. Imports have taken an ever-increasing share of the market in recent years – from an import quota controlled 20 per cent of the local market in 1988, to nearly 55 per cent in 1998 – and it is difficult to foresee a reversal of the trend. With significant excess world production capacity, any prospect of long-run salvation of the local industry though exports is likely to be disappointed.

The takeover of Chrysler in the United States by Daimler-Benz is surely an indication of things to come. The consolidation of world production into five or six manufacturing groups appears certain within the next 10 years. It seems unlikely that the Australian industry and its current four producers – Ford,

GM-H, Mitsubishi and Toyota – will remain unaffected. The government, with its 1997 decision to implement a tariff pause to provide 'certainty' for the industry at the beginning of the new millennium, is most likely to find that its visions of certainty are an illusion.

## Notes

1. For some time manufacture of the 48-215 required the importation of key components. Despite its immediate success, the Holden failed to outsell the imported Austin A40 until the end of the Korean War boom in 1953, though this was due mainly to a shortage of production capacity.
2. Space is limited and as a consequence we have been selective in our approach. Our work concentrates on the participation of the two major 'local' producers, Ford and GM-H. Both of these firms have played central roles in the development of the automotive industry in Australia.
3. J.P. Womack, D.T. Jones and D. Roos, *The Machine That Changed the World* (New York, 1990), p. 76.
4. As it is difficult to obtain valid time-series of protection, most studies of the effects of trade barriers on industries are cross-sectional, examining their effects across a number of industries at a particular time.
5. See Chapter 4.
6. See Chapter 8.
7. In those days the chassis was defined for Customs' purposes to include virtually everything that went to make up a vehicle except for the car's body.
8. This was the approach adopted by the Packard Company in the US making it the most profitable firm in the industry in the mid-1900s.
9. It was replaced within months by less stringent import restrictions.
10. For example J. Laurent, '"Industry Policy" and the Australian Motor Vehicle Industry, 1920–1942', *Journal of the Royal Australian Historical Society*, LXXX (1994), pp. 91–115.
11. See Chapter 4.
12. J.N. Lawson, Minister for Trade and Customs, *Sydney Morning Herald*, 28 December 1939.
13. See Chapter 4.
14. See Chapter 6.
15. See Chapter 7.
16. The 'dollar shortage' referred to a shortage of foreign exchange, a result of maintaining a fixed and overvalued exchange rate. The exchange rate was maintained by direct quantitative import restrictions through a system of import licensing.
17. See Chapter 7.
18. The Australian operations of Chrysler were taken over by Mitsubishi in 1980.
19. See Chapter 8.
20. Under the export facilitation scheme, duty-free import entitlements of both vehicles and components are provided to local producers in return for their exports. See Chapter 8.
21. Nissan withdrew from full manufacture and a joint venture between GM-H and Toyota formed United Australian Automotive Industries. The arrangement was ended in 1996.

# 2   False Start: the Early Years of Motoring and Automotive Manufacturing

## The supply side

At the beginning of the motoring age, around the turn of the twentieth century, there were several engineers in Australia who devoted their efforts to what was then the novelty of producing horseless carriages. David Shearer, for example, a South Australian who manufactured agricultural machinery, built a steam-powered vehicle in 1896. In the same year Herbert Thompson of Melbourne produced the first of his nine 'Pioneer' steam cars, and a vehicle powered by an imported Benz internal combustion engine appeared on the roads of that city. These and a few motor tricycles and motorized bicycles were in operation in Melbourne and Sydney before 1900.[1]

At that time, and until the mid-1900s, the internal combustion engine as a source of power had yet to demonstrate convincingly its superiority over steam and electricity. Indeed, steam-powered cars continued to be produced in the United States into the 1930s.[2] As late as 1906, according to one source, 'steam seemed destined to become the motor power for future cars'.[3] All of the requirements were there for its widespread adoption. The technology involved was well established, developed from the railway locomotive and the later widespread adoption of steam traction engines for threshing grain crops. There was a pool of skilled labour available for maintenance. Water was also readily available in urban areas from the many public horse troughs. Until the late 1900s steam-powered vehicles had the potential for higher speeds (a desirable objective among early motoring enthusiasts) than those depending on electricity or internal combustion engines fuelled by oil derivatives. A steam car established the world land speed record in 1906. Above all, steam was a relatively reliable source of motive power and the engine was relatively uncomplicated. When a Stanley steam-driven car from the US was exhibited in Melbourne in 1922, the reported advantages stressed were that 'there are no gears, clutch, fly-wheel, timing gears, universals, noise, leaking radiator, overheating; no magneto troubles, ignition troubles, spark plugs, carbon

9

troubles; no stalling in traffic, or when in mud, sand, or on a steep hill'. Repairs as a consequence were 'almost unknown' and the rate of depreciation was estimated to be a third that of a car with an internal combustion engine.[4]

Moreover, the performance of early combustion engines was poor, especially with the oil derivatives then generally available. At the 1897 Australian Cycle Show in Melbourne the Australasian Horseless Carriage Syndicate, formed in that year, exhibited a 'motor car', 'built on the lines of a dog-cart, but of much larger proportions', which was powered by 'an oil engine on the spray system, utilizing ordinary kerosene as a fuel'. The vehicle – which turned out to be the one and only vehicle produced by the dentist-inventor – was driven from the company's factory in the suburb of Fitzroy to the exhibition venue and there made a few trial runs. However, 'the defects most noticeable were the overpowering smell of burning kerosene, the noise made by the engine, and the smoke which issued from the body of the vehicle when stationary'.[5] Presumably the vehicle was in other respects exemplary.

At the turn of the century petroleum was not readily available and some pioneer motorists met their own requirements by importing from Britain. Of the petroleum derivatives, apart from kerosene, low octane fuel used in stationary combustion engines, stove naphtha and even 'gas fluid' used in painters' blow lamps all fuelled vehicles at various times. The organized importation of petroleum for motor vehicles appears to have commenced in 1902. However, other than in the major cities, it took time to organize its distribution.[6]

The first four-wheeled car in Sydney was a De Dion imported from France in 1900. In the early 1900s several individuals and firms in Australia began to produce similar vehicles. The best known were those manufactured by the Tarrant Engineering Company of Melbourne. This firm, a manufacturer of oil-fired engines for agricultural purposes, produced its first car in 1901.[7] Indeed, the first 'petrol' brought into Australia was imported in 1899 by F.B. Roche who later became the managing director of Tarrant.[8] ('Petrol' was a trademark and the name was then not commonly used.) When the Tarrant Company built its first four-cylinder car in 1905 no more than six comparable vehicles had been imported into Australia. Except for the initial model, which was equipped with an imported engine, the remainder of the 10 to 12 cars produced to 1907 (the exact figure is not known) incorporated a local content of 90 per cent.[9] Tarrant and would-be car producers in Australia enjoyed considerable natural protection because of shipping and the many other costs associated with importing. In 1919, for example, it was estimated that the cost of freight, packing and landed charges amounted to £65 on an assembled chassis valued at the equivalent of £156 ex-factory in the US.[10] In 1923 the freight charged to ship a motor body to Australia was £17 10s. on one costing £12 10s. to produce in Britain.[11]

From the end of the nineteenth century the engineering skills needed for the development of the motive power for horseless carriages were readily available in Australia. In rural communities there was a considerable demand for stationary internal combustion engines, many of which were locally produced. Herbert Austin, a pioneer of the British motor industry during the 1900s, acquired what he later described as 'a thorough training as a mechanic' in Australia in the 1870s and 1880s, mainly with a firm manufacturing shearing equipment.[12] Access to new technology was rarely a problem. Until quite recently a feature of the automotive industry has been the widespread copying of innovations developed by other manufacturers. This rarely resulted in litigation over patent rights, because of the relative ease of engineering a design that performed substantially the same function but in a way that did not infringe a patent.[13] There was also the option of locally manufacturing motor vehicles under licence, an arrangement several German companies (including Opel) entered into before 1914 with French producers.[14] French firms entered into similar arrangements. Rochet-Schneider, for example, sold manufacturing rights to firms in Switzerland, Belgium, Italy and the US.[15]

In the very early years of motoring in the small Australian market, limited access to economies of scale was not a significant obstacle to local manufacture. With the obvious exception of the United States, in most countries where cars were manufactured, before 1914 the activity was undertaken in the main by comparatively small firms. During the pioneering era of motor vehicle manufacturing almost all firms in Europe and the US were very small-scale concerns, producing to individual order or by batch methods. Around the turn of the century a 'long series' was 20–25 vehicles, and production on such a scale could be quite profitable.[16] In the eight months following the 1906 opening of Austin's Longbridge plant in Birmingham, England, 50 workers produced 12 cars – making a profit of over 10 per cent on the capital invested – and the firm assembled only 120 vehicles during the following year.[17] At the time the most successful strategy was that adopted by the most profitable firm in the industry in the mid-1900s, the Packard Company in the US: the low-volume production of luxury vehicles.[18]

Scale economies only became of more widespread significance during the period between the two world wars. From the time Henry Ford launched the Model T in 1908, and adopted the moving assembly line in 1913, the motor vehicle industry has been associated with mass production methods. Outside the United States, however, these innovations were not widely adopted, even during the interwar era. Around 60,000 cars were produced in the UK in 1920; some two-thirds were Ford Model Ts and the remainder were the output of 88 firms, of which only a handful manufactured more than 1,000 units.[19] By 1929, when the number of car producers in the UK had fallen to 41, the average output per firm (including Ford) was only 4,367 vehicles, which was less than 5 per cent of Australian chassis imports in 1928–9.[20]

There is little evidence that difficulties of access to finance were a real inhibition on the early development of the motor vehicle industry in Australia – or elsewhere. Certainly the experience of Europe and the United States suggests that the growth of motor vehicle manufacturing was not held back by the reluctance of established financial institutions to provide capital. A number of firms that came to occupy leading positions in the industry overseas, including Ford, Morris and Renault, began as vehicle assemblers relying on credit extended by suppliers of components and the deposits of purchasers. In the early conditions of excess demand for cars, producers were able to extract spot cash from buyers, or from dealers who were keen to acquire exclusive franchises in exchange. Once established and making an increasing proportion of components in their own facilities, these producers relied for finance largely on earnings generated by sales.[21]

While a feature of very early motor vehicle development in Australia was the emergence of engine producers, such as David Shearer and Herbert Thomson, they played a limited role in pioneering car production. More important was learning to overcome the problems involved in transforming power, from whatever source, into motion. Here one significant reason for the few initial and short-lived efforts to produce motor vehicles in Australia was the almost complete absence of a bicycle manufacturing industry. It is notable that the Cycle Engineers' Association in Britain, formed in 1898, rapidly evolved through the Auto and Cycle Engineers' Association of 1904 to become the Institute of Automobile Engineers from 1906. A remarkably large number of early car manufacturers in Europe began as bicycle producers. The pioneer Rochet-Schneider of Lyons was one of 'many automobile concerns [originating] from the bicycle trade'. Other French bicycle firms that became outstanding pioneers in car production included Darraque and Clement-Talbot.[22] In Britain by the early 1900s the pioneers included a number of bicycle manufacturers, including Humber, Singer, Swift and Enfield, and Riley. The Rover, Hillman, Rudge-Whitworth and Armstrong-Siddeley companies later joined them.[23] Montagu Napier, the founder of the largest British car manufacturer by the mid-1900s, had a background in cycle racing.[24] The Opel brothers, in the mid-1890s, were Germany's largest cycle manufacturers.[25] In the US, bicycle manufacturers who were prominent among early motor vehicle producers included Albert A. Pope (by 1890 the Pope Manufacturing Company was the largest bicycle producer in the world), John and Horace Dodge, the Duryea brothers, George N. Pierce (Pierce-Arrow), Thomas B. Jeffery (Rambler) and Erwin R. Thomas (Thomas 'Flyer').[26] The Dodge brothers were bicycle manufacturers who eventually, in 1915, began motor vehicle production after earlier supplying gears to the industry.[27]

The large-scale manufacture of bicycles, which commenced in Europe and North America after the appearance in the mid-1880s of the 'safety model' (replacing the 'penny-farthing'), required machine tools capable of replicating parts with a high degree of accuracy. The bicycle initiated the use of chain-drive and spoked wheels – which were adopted for early motor vehicles – ball and roller bearings, gears, pneumatic tyres, steel tube frames, differential axles and variable-speed transmissions. The attention of European bicycle producers was drawn to car manufacture by falling prices and reduced profit margins caused by the collapse of the 'bicycle boom' of 1895–97.[28] This was, for example, what motivated the Opel brothers in Germany to explore motor vehicle production.[29] As well, at the time the technical development of the bicycle appeared to have reached its peak. At least some bicycle producers were attracted to motor vehicle manufacture by the novel mechanical problems involved in overcoming the difficulties of transmitting the power of an engine to drive what was then, in other essentials, a bicycle.

There was some limited bicycle manufacture in Australia, but commercial production of bicycles does not appear to have begun in Australia before the 1900s. This was at least in part the result of a general consumer preference for imported products and in most of the Australian colonies before Federation, the availability of cheap, mass-produced American bicycles.[30] Nevertheless in Australia as elsewhere, bicycle producers played a role in early motor car production. The first successful car in Australia powered by an internal com-bustion engine, the Tarrant, was made by the Tarrant Motor and Engineering Company formed by Harley Tarrant and a man who had spent a number of years making bicycles, Howard Lewis.[31] Other bicycle manufacturers who produced motor vehicles included Archibald M. Campbell of Hobart (he produced three cars between 1900 and 1912) and the Bullock Bicycle Works in Adelaide (one in 1901). Prominent among early importers and distributors of motor vehicles were bicycle dealers who maintained repair facilities.[32] Whether the bicycles were locally made or imported, their popularity provided a livelihood for the numerous bicycle repair shops that gradually emerged. Many of these became motor vehicle repair workshops, providing an important part of the basic infrastructure (if not the manufacturing expertise) required for the future 'motorization' of Australian society. Other effects of the bicycle on the development of the industry may not have been so favourable. When commercial bicycle manufacture made a belated appearance in Australia – stimulated by the 20 per cent duty imposed in the Federation tariff – it provided a more steady and secure market for talent that might otherwise have been devoted to the production of motorized transport. To the extent it did, it represents an early instance of the tariff acting to divert resources into an activity that was in a sense, rapidly becoming an outdated technology. It was a process that was to bedevil the Australian automotive industry for much of its history.

## The demand side

Real income was and has remained a fundamental determinant of demand for cars, and a sizeable proportion of the inhabitants of early twentieth-century Australia possessed the means to buy one. At an estimated $US 263 in 1914, per capita income in Australia was exceeded only by the $US 335 of the United States.[33] While the income distribution in the United States was more skewed in favour of the rich who could afford the luxury of car ownership, there was, however, a significant number of Australians with the means to purchase the typical custom-built car of the vintage era. Nevertheless, the pioneering efforts to create a motor vehicle manufacturing industry in Australia effectively ended in the mid-1900s.

That Australia was a colony of Britain was an important influence on the way Australians viewed the motor car. The initial reaction of the Australian public to the 'horseless carriage' was in general negative and in part, at least, this reflected contemporary attitudes in Britain. Many were recent immigrants from that country. Britain was the source of almost all information regarding the outside world that appeared in the local press, and a country that a sizeable proportion of the Australian population continued to call 'home' – even those who had never been there. Around the turn of the century Australian attitudes towards the car to a considerable extent reflected those held in Britain. Britain lagged behind Continental Europe, particularly France, in the acceptance and development of motor vehicles. The 'horse culture' of 'home' had an important place among the potential car buying classes in Australia, with their hunts and passion for horse-racing.

Public opinion was anti-motoring in Britain well into the 1900s and, though perhaps an overstatement of Australian attitudes, as late as 1909 it was claimed by one enthusiast that: 'The bulk of the public here, as in England, is anti-motorist in feeling.'[34] In Australia, as elsewhere, the mass of the population was at best indifferent to the new, and for most, unaffordable means of transportation. Others showed hostility to the noise and danger the motor vehicle posed (especially in frightening the horses) and envy of those able to afford what before 1914 and beyond was largely the prerogative of the well-to-do.

Perhaps of more influence was that Australians then saw themselves as British citizens and consequently they tended to adopt innovations that had been tried and proven in Britain. This was especially the case with mechanical devices that had more or less universal application. (It was less so where the technical challenge was unique to the Australian environment.) The tendency to adopt British innovations is illustrated by the delayed introduction of the motorized taxicab – a potential source of demand for standardized cars. By late 1908 when over 1,000 cabs were on the streets of London, a visiting group of Australian businessmen became sufficiently convinced of their profitability to form a syndicate to operate a service in Melbourne. They decided to import Renault vehicles from France, as these were the most common in use as taxis in London at the time. Even so, taxi services were slow to develop in Australian cities. In early 1910, Sydney, with a population of about 600,000 people, had only six registered motor-cabs operating – though the number had increased to 67 by October of that year and to 102 by July 1911.[35] Together with the particular concentration of vehicle sales in rural Australia by that time, it suggests a slower tempo of 'motorization' in the cities of Australia, where the overwhelming majority of the population resided.

Despite the negative influences, Australians were among the pioneers in adopting the motor car. In promoting the new form of transportation, sometimes trivial factors could be quite influential. A significant boost for the image of the car in Australia was provided by the 1907 return of the opera diva Nellie Melba, on this occasion with a six-cylinder Napier. On her previous visit she had brought out from England a horse-drawn 'very fine double brougham'.[36] The opera star, born in Australia, was something of a leader of local fashion and it is likely the car was provided by Napier to promote its product.

As in other societies where motorization was emerging, medical practitioners serving the relatively well-to-do provided an early source of demand for cars, once vehicles achieved a reasonable degree of reliability. The response time in emergency cases was far quicker than by horse and carriage. A doctor without a motor car perhaps conveyed the impression of being old fashioned; of not being abreast with the latest developments in medical knowledge. Once one general practitioner acquired a car the others in the area inevitably soon followed, fearing they would lose their patients. In Australia, with a particularly high proportion of the population concentrated in a few large urban centres, the rate of adoption was accelerated. By early 1909, for example, a feature of Adelaide was 'doctors almost universally adopting this modern means of locomotion'.[37] At the same time the many wealthy graziers living in rural Australia encouraged local medical practitioners to acquire a motor vehicle. By this time doctors had begun to acquire a degree of social status and were therefore emulated by those lower in the social order.

The support for motorization from the public sector was limited. State governments, as owners of the railway and tramway stems, came to see the motor vehicle as a threat to their revenues and thus a potential drain on their treasuries. (The workers they employed and their unions became vociferous opponents of motor transport in the 1920s.) The Commonwealth Postmaster-General's Department (PMG) began to investigate the possibilities of using motor vehicles in the early 1900s when it experimented with motor vehicles for the collection of mail from pillar-boxes. However, 'the constant stopping and starting at the short intervals for pillar-box clearance imposed so great a strain on the mechanism that they were in a continual state of breakdown and disrepair'. Further progress by the PMG in adopting motorized transport was slow, especially in New South Wales. A couple of two-ton trucks entered service in December 1912, to transport mail in Sydney between the wharves, the GPO, the Central Railway Station and suburban post offices. By the outbreak of war the only additions to the 'fleet' were two half-ton trucks, for pillar-box collections – and they were still at a coachbuilders. The early motorization of the Post Office in Sydney seems to have been sabotaged by the 'Horse-master' of the PMG, who was placed in charge of the project. The two-ton trucks, according to a 1913 report by a New Zealand official, 'were of a fifth-rate make and their original design so altered at the direction of the Horse-master ... that their design was further weakened, thus endangering the safety of the mails and the lives of the drivers'. The two 12 hp trucks selected for clearing pillar-boxes were 'of a make of pleasure car' that has 'proved totally inadequate for private use'. If this were not enough to ensure their unsuitability for mail collection, the vehicles were 'burdened with heavy box bodies and inadequately shod with tyres'. The 'Horse-master' – the name should have provided a clue – was apparently 'openly hostile to the introduction of motors'.[38]

By comparison the Post Office in Melbourne was quite progressive in adopting motor vehicles, though the experience there was hardly promising. The first vehicles were acquired in mid-1909. By mid-1913 the vehicle pool consisted of seven one-ton vans used for carrying bulk mail and eight tri-cars for emptying pillar-boxes. The latter were under-powered for the purpose, even on the flat terrain of Melbourne. However, at least the service there was supervised by a mechanical engineer who was keen to acquire more suitable vehicles.

The experience in Adelaide when the PMG introduced motor vehicles in 1907 had been even worse. In this case the vehicles were over-powered for their employment in pillar-box clearance, where the maximum weight was around 100 kilos. The wear and tear caused by these loads through vibration was so excessive that it was four years before another attempt at motorization was made. In the interim the lessons of the earlier effort were apparently ignored. In September 1912 four one-ton vans were acquired for pillar-box clearance, and suffered exactly the same problems from excessive vibration.[39]

In spite of the limited initiative shown by government agencies before the 1914–18 war, and the problems they suffered, Australia was characterized by a relatively high rate of motor vehicle adoption. In 1907 the ratio of motor vehicles to inhabitants was 1:608 in the US, 1:640 in the United Kingdom, 1:981 in France, 1:3,824 in Germany and 1:3,053 in Canada.[40] While comparable national data for Australia are unavailable, in 1911 the ratio was 1:414 for New South Wales, and 1:468 for Victoria, both higher than in North America.[41] By 1914 the number of motor vehicles had increased to what Theo Barker, Britain's pioneer historian of the industry, has described as 'the remarkable total' of 19,000 cars, 1,000 lorries and 14,000 motorcycles.[42]

### The Model T Ford in Australia

The arrival of the Ford Model T in Australia, and to a lesser extent earlier Ford and other US makes and models, had a profound effect upon the local car market. Their success was a major cause of the stillbirth of an embryonic local motor vehicle industry. On the one hand, the qualities of the Model T transformed the market for cars; it gave access to the new form of transport to new classes of buyers. On the other, selling and repairing the Model T became a far less risky business than attempting to produce a competitor, and there was no doubt motor vehicle manufacture in the first quarter of the century, and especially before 1914, was a particularly high-risk activity. Of 279 manufacturers who began manufacturing in Britain before 1905, 80 had failed by that year. Of 181 companies that produced cars in the US between 1903 and 1926, including 24 already in existence in 1903, 137 had left the industry by 1926. In Australia the risk for a prospective local producer was magnified by a general public preference for imported over local manufactures. As one car dealer observed in 1911: 'the people would not purchase colonial productions'.[43] In the circumstances, for those interested in motor transport, acquiring a dealership from an overseas producer was likely to be far more profitable (and far less risky) than the local manufacture of cars.

The Model T found a ready market particularly among well-to-do graziers and other affluent country dwellers.[44] In early 1908, more than a year before the arrival of the first Model T, an observer stated:

> the car that is going to do well out here will have to be something on the following lines: 8–10 h.p., light, but very strong, specially in the frame and axles, solid tyres, chain transmission, bodywork need not be too high class, price to come out at about £150 (landed Sydney), and last but not least (for back country work), a minimum clearance of a foot is desirable, perhaps, in fact, eighteen inches would not be superfluous on account of the obstacles encountered.[45]

The Model T fitted the bill easily.

Country people were less concerned about the rather undistinguished appearance of the car than the affluent few of urban Australia who had hitherto provided the main market for cars.[46] As an early Model T salesman and enthusiast described the Ford, it was 'not much to look at'.[47] However, the car had a high ground clearance, sturdy construction and with its use of tough vanadium steel alloys in components most subject to stress, a capacity to withstand the pounding from the dirt tracks that passed for roads in the Outback.[48] Australian motorists were quick to realize the Ford's other virtues. For the time, the vehicle was exceptionally reliable. 'In clumsy hands, with non-mechanical minds, it ran well. Its illnesses were few, and the average citizen could attend to them with dime store parts.'[49] Another attraction of the Model T was its relatively low purchase price, which over time continued to fall. The falling resale values that were a consequence did not particularly concern rural purchasers, who rarely 'updated'.

In a very large, sparsely populated country with relatively poor access to railways beyond the major urban centres, the Model T, for those who could afford one, considerably lessened the isolation of Bush life.[50] The vehicle provided easier transport to country towns, and by 1912 it could be said of Australia that: 'The farmer has found in the car his salvation, and the uplifting of the pall that once enveloped the life of those who live on the outskirts of civilization.'[51] The vehicle also found a use on farms in towing trailers. With its arrival in Australia there was a shift in the urban–rural ratio of car ownership, within a context of rapidly expanding sales. Previously cars had essentially replaced expensive carriages, such as landaus and broughams. They had had a limited impact on demand for the cheaper horse-drawn buggies and sulkies. After the Model T the situation changed radically. The car was known as a 'motor buggy' and its particular acceptance in rural Australia largely accounts for a rapid rise in car sales.[52] Of nearly 2,000 'motor buggies' registered in New South Wales in late 1910 – nearly half of all registrations – the owners of all but 70 lived outside Sydney.[53] In the state of New South Wales the number of registered motor vehicles increased nearly fourfold, from 4,477 in 1910 to 17,218 in 1914.[54]

It was not just Australian motorists who were quick to realize the virtues of the Ford. The Tarrant Engineering Company, the most important pioneer of car manufacturing in Australia, in 1907 decided to abandon production and acquire a Ford dealership (adding to those it held for De Dion and Argyll) shortly after vehicles from Ford Canada began to arrive in late 1906.[55] Others, including a number of bicycle repair shops, followed Tarrant's example. The success of the Model T in the Australian market effectively sounded the death knell of local vehicle manufacture. In what was in any case a risk averse society, selling Model Ts seemed virtually a 'licence to print money'. For such a reliable vehicle the cost and effort of providing service/repair facilities was minimal. However, with such a wide variety of makes imported into Australia, the many dealerships attracted talent that might otherwise have been engaged in promoting local production. Instead, a lobby emerged that was vehemently opposed to the idea.

### The tariff and the 'spoke-shave and hammer brigade'

By the 1890s there was a well-established carriage-building trade that met most local demand using local materials, though some key components such as springs were imported. Relatively small firms predominated in the industry, producing carriages and coaches by craft methods to the order of individual customers. Initially coachbuilders were opposed to the new means of transportation as inimical to their interests, and it was they who emerged as early and effective lobbyists against the local manufacture of motor vehicle chassis (which included the engine). During the second half of the 1890s there were frequently published examples of the inadequacies of motor vehicles by the mouthpiece of the industry, the *Coachbuilder and Saddler*. 'The news of a breakdown of a motor car was the signal for rejoicing [by those in the trade], and no opportunity was allowed to pass of bringing ridicule on the user of a motor car.' [56]

As late as 1905 the local coachbuilders' organization in Melbourne protested against the exhibition of motor vehicles in the 'carriage shed' at the Royal Agricultural Society Show in Melbourne. The organizers of the event responded with the decision 'that in future the carriage shed shall be reserved for carriage exhibits, and that motor-cars shall be shown westward of the sheep sheds, provided the exhibitors supply their own shelter'. In addition, it was resolved 'to prohibit motor-cars running about the ground, on account of the danger of frightening valuable stock'.[57]

Initially coachbuilders ' "pooh-poohed" the idea of motor cars ever affecting the trade'.[58] Subsequently – at least for a time – they viewed cars as a threat and as direct competitors for their own products. There were, however, rational reasons for the initial antagonism of coachbuilders to the 'horseless carriage' and their early reluctance to take up the manufacture of motor bodies. In 1903 the *Australasian Coachbuilder and Wheelwright* advised its readers against becoming involved in motor vehicle production, largely because of the high capital costs involved. 'Motor car building', the periodical emphasized, 'is essentially a capitalist business. If it is intended to manufacture them outright, an extensive and valuable plant is required, and even where the "making" proposed is merely mounting a body on running parts supplied by local engineers, or imported, the capital required is still considerable – much more than the majority of coachbuilders can afford to tie up in stock.'[59]

A major problem, both psychological and practical, for coachbuilders considering taking up motor-body construction concerned the use of steel. By the mid-1900s steel for panels and moulded seat bases had become standard in motor bodies. The coachbuilder was essentially a woodworker. 'Metal for panels had always been anathema for the coach body maker, and it was with extreme reluctance that he accepted it for motor work.'[60] Forming metal into shapes to form the basis for car seats was beyond his capability. According to the *Australasian Coachbuilder and Wheelwright* of 15 October 1907:

> To the Australian coachbuilder when asked to build an automobile body of modern design, the big problem is the difficulty regarding the seat panels. These he cannot make in his own shop, and there are no places in Australia where they could be made to his order; consequently many who would otherwise have taken up this class of work have been compelled to pass it.

The supply problem was solved by the late 1900s, by outside purchasing, but this reduced the potential profitability of body construction and the scope for exercising the coachbuilder's skills.

The perceived difficulties and high capital cost involved in building motor bodies certainly contributed to the reluctance of coachbuilders to enter the industry. Primarily, however, they lacked understanding of the workings of the mechanical components of a motor vehicle, and at least some in the trade recognized that. By 1903 it was claimed (with perhaps a little exaggeration) that: 'Every aspect of the problems connected with the advent of the motor car has been thrashed out in [the coachbuilder's] mind, bar one, and that is the motive power and its workings.' This problem was, as the contemporary term put it, the 'Clinker'. As an Adelaide coachbuilder remarked in 1909 about an activity he described as 'legitimately ours': 'had coachbuilders taken up the safety bicycle when it came in the eighties, they would have had a better grip of the motor trade'.[61] At the same time another commented that: 'Much profitable work in the shape of repairs at present goes past the coachbuilder, because of his want of familiarity with the mechanical side of the motor.'[62] Even when the coachbuilder got the business, there were problems. As a result of the poor state of most roads, especially in the countryside, and the generally poor standard of local body construction, the bodies of closed cars soon developed defects, such as loosened windows, and the noise of the body rattling on a rough road could soon become unbearable. These remained problems into the 1920s.

According to one contemporary observer, the typical coachbuilder, unlike 'bicycle dealers', lacked the personality needed for successful motor vehicle production.

> Coachbuilders are modest and always underrate themselves .... Not so the bicycle dealer. The mere fact that he has ridden over some thousands of miles of our roads is sufficient for him to be and [sic] authority of the relative strength of wheels, axles, springs, etc., etc., of a motor car. This question of wheel base, height of component parts from [the] ground, etc., are too insignificant to detail. Words flowing freely from his mouth is his 'practical' knowledge of some of the most particular parts of a motor Chassis. Yet, if he is called upon to take an order, he does so, and, what is more, makes a success of it. Say he wants a set of artillery wheels made, what does he do? Sends to the wheel builder. He wants a steering gear, send to the forge; he wants a body made, sends to the body shop; and so on with the trimming and painting; he SENDS. Now, when he comes to the engine, frame, accumulators, carburetors, radiators, coils, driving, steering, and change gears, etc., he imports these, and employs a man to assemble them.[63]

The 'bicycle dealer', as befitted the relatively recent innovation he sold, was a kind of 'modern man' of his era. The coachbuilder was the product of a traditional craft. He dealt mostly with domestic suppliers of inputs, or bought imports from long-established merchant houses. The bicycle producer was heavily dependent upon imported components, through connections developed in relatively recent times. Yet somehow the typical coachbuilder was 'emphatic in the belief that the motor-trade should by rights belong to him'.[64]

Given their conservative craft orientation, the notion of motor vehicles as but a fad tended to persist among many coachbuilders. In 1910 one declared that 'he had no fear that horses would be turned into German sausages'.[65] In 1912 another was willing to 'reluctantly admit that in the large cities the gasoline and the electric cars have in some measure temporarily displaced the horse-drawn vehicle'. However, he was convinced that the phenomenon 'will prove but temporary, as there is a close affinity between the trained family horse and its owner that is sure to bring back into use the handsome four-in-hand which but three or four years ago was the pride of our city boulevards'.[66] Even those prepared to invest the necessary capital to produce motor bodies on more than a customized, individual basis, like Duncan & Fraser in Adelaide, were convinced that there would always be a demand for horse-drawn vehicles.[67]

At the turn of the century the Sydney-based journal the *Australasian Coachbuilder and Wheelwright*, was an ardent advocate of free trade, fearing 'the blighting effects of Protection', embodied in the Federation tariff of 1901. This sentiment was not so evident among the readership of the journal, especially those in the protectionist-orientated colony of Victoria. Even readers in Sydney, in 'free trade' New South Wales, while concerned about duties on inputs such as springs and axles, feared 'the cheap Yankee buggy' and therefore welcomed the 25 per cent *ad valorem* duty imposed on the hoods of such vehicles. The duty imposed on motor vehicles under the same Federation tariff was 20 per cent, and there was then no differentiation between complete vehicles and chassis.[68]

As late as 1908, and the advent of 'New Protection', the *Australasian Coachbuilder and Wheelwright* questioned the overall benefits the increased protection provided, and in particular the increased tariffs on carriage components such as axles and springs.[69] Not surprisingly the coachbuilders welcomed a combination of a 35 per cent *ad valorem* duty on complete vehicles, and a tariff on chassis of only 5 per cent (general rate) and duty-free if they qualified for the Imperial Preference introduced in the new tariff. The duty on bodies when added to the cost of shipping what was a bulky and fragile item provided considerable protection for local motor body construction. For Customs' purposes, the chassis was more or less defined as being any component the local coachbuilding trade was incapable of producing. In effect, the low revenue duty on the chassis (including the engine) meant it was treated as an input – a 'raw material' – to local body manufacture. However, any dream of a local monopoly of this major component of the motor vehicle was not to be realized, even though at the time it was considered that the 'duties on finished cars is practical prohibition for [the import of] motor car bodies'.[70]

The structure of the 1908 tariff, with its increased duties on motor bodies, while retaining revenue rates on chassis, seems to have resulted mainly from pressure by those who held agencies for the distribution of foreign cars.[71] Coachbuilders appear to have played only a limited role in the lobbying process. The lobbyists acted from a variety of motives. One head of a firm providing vehement support for the increase 'practically admitted that they manufactured [bodies for] cars principally to keep the hands in their repair shop fully employed in slack time'.[72] Some simply desired to expand their businesses by adding the manufacture of motor bodies to their existing activities. Others saw an opportunity to exercise market power over the many small-scale coachbuilders. The situation became such that: 'A good deal of the [motor-body] work in coachbuilders' shops is being done for the city garages, which, by getting one man to tender against another, often get bodies built at prices below their proper value.' It was possible because of the absence of anywhere near perfect market knowledge: 'there seems to be no standard of value or quality, and prices vary considerably for the same class of work'.[73] In any event, with the many makes and models on the market, distributors by standardizing bodies sought to lower costs and thus enhance sales, whether by establishing their own production facilities or negotiating with coachbuilders.

Despite these influences which acted to stimulate coachbuilding, a noticeable feature of the urban motoring scene before 1914 was 'the small proportion of locally made bodies'.[74] In the Australian countryside local motor bodies were even rarer than in the cities. Within a year of implementing the 1908 tariff, the Model T complete with body began to arrive in increasing numbers. Local producers were unable to compete with the low invoice price placed on the imported body, which had to be more or less accepted as value-for-duty by Customs in the absence of knowledge of the home consumption price.[75] In the context of this widespread practice, Ford also avoided paying the general rate duty on chassis by sourcing them from Ford Canada, enabling the company to take advantage of Imperial Preference.[76] (See Table 2.1 for a summary of the origins of chassis and body imports.) Another important influence on local motor bodybuilding was the Tariff Act of 1911, known as the Tudor tariff after the then Minister of Customs. It made ineffective the practice of 'loading' the value of the chassis on invoices by introducing a specific duty on bodies. The rate set was an alternative duty of £70 or 35 per cent *ad valorem*. The rate applying was that which yielded the greater revenue. At the time the body on the imported Model T was invoiced at £15.[77]

The specific duty, although it was substantially higher than the *ad valorem* rate that for most imports it effectively replaced, did little to divert demand for Model T bodies to domestic producers. As a Brisbane motor bodybuilder commented in 1914: 'we cannot touch the Ford car-body in price, as they turn out in such quantities'.[78] Aside from this, local motor bodybuilders had other reasons for their reluctance to compete in this low-priced end of the market. It was perceived as tantamount to 'deskilling'; to the elimination of pride in craftsmanship. In any case, for local bodybuilders who were protected by the 35 per cent *ad valorem* rate that applied to bodies valued at £200 or more, meeting the demand for bodies for luxury vehicles was a far more profitable line of business. Perhaps typical, therefore, was the response to a Sydney dealer when he approached local producers about making bodies for imported Buick chassis. It was: 'We will not disgrace ourselves by making such rubbish.'[79] They were probably afraid of the effect of manufacturing 'cheap' bodies on their image with the affluent 'carriage trade' among their clientele.

When the large-scale manufacture of bodies for lower-priced vehicles eventually developed, it stemmed from a wartime decision of the Commonwealth Government. In August 1917, in response to the Allied shipping shortage caused by the German U-Boat campaign, an embargo was placed upon the importation of complete motor vehicles. (It was thought when taking the decision that for utilitarian purposes farmers at least would be content to sit on a box and eschew all-weather protection.) While the measure was soon modified to permit the entry of a completed motor vehicle for every two chassis imported, the embargo marks the real birth of an Australian motor body-building industry.[80] Reflecting the anticipations generated by the government decisions of August/September 1917, in October that year the coachbuilders' trade journal changed its name from the *Australasian Coachbuilder and Wheelwright* to the *Coach and Motor Builder*. By 1918 dealers had a definite

**Table 2.1**  Motor chassis and body imports by country of origin, 1911–1914 (%)

| Year | Canada | USA | UK | Other[a] | Total |
|------|--------|-----|-----|----------|-------|
| Chassis |  |  |  |  |  |
| 1911 | 4.8 | 19.6 | 41.9 | 33.7 | 100 |
| 1912 | 9.3 | 22.5 | 39.0 | 29.2 | 100 |
| 1913 | 11.9 | 25.3 | 36.5 | 26.3 | 100 |
| 1914 | 17.1 | 34.6 | 34.6 | 13.7 | 100 |
| Motor Bodies |  |  |  |  |  |
| 1911 | 7.6 | 37.3 | 45.0 | 10.1 | 100 |
| 1912 | 12.3 | 43.0 | 38.0 | 6.7 | 100 |
| 1913 | 17.4 | 43.0 | 32.3 | 7.3 | 100 |
| 1914 | 20.1 | 48.6 | 29.7 | 1.6 | 100 |

*Source*: Customs data published in the *Australian Motorist*, March 1912, April 1913, April 1914 and May 1916.
*Notes*:
[a]   Until 1911 France was the second largest exporter of motor chassis and complete bodies to Australia after the United Kingdom.
The data are for chassis and imports separately *assessed*, not separately *imported*.

interest in promoting chassis-only imports that they wanted to equip with relatively low-cost, standardized bodies. The outcome was the development of a market providing scope for the large-scale production of bodies. One of the first to take advantage of the new situation was the firm of Holden and Frost (which shortly afterwards became Holden's Motor Body Builders Ltd) of Adelaide, which was to figure prominently in the subsequent history of the automotive industry in Australia.

In Europe and North America early chassis producers were at least partly motivated to take up motor body construction because of difficulties in finding carriage builders who could consistently achieve high standards of accuracy in measurement and construction. Having entered the field they began to experiment with alternative materials, particularly steel and the new steel alloys that began to become available from the 1890s. They were more familiar with these materials than timber, and the new materials had the added advantages of giving the body strength and durability without increasing weight. By 1914, at least in countries other than Australia, it was clear that body manufacture was 'becoming more a metal-maker's industry than a body-makers'.[81] In Australia, by contrast, as a result of tariffs dating from the 1900s, the activity was dominated by hands of what one interested observer described in 1919 as 'the old spoke-shave and hammer brigade'. Some of the 'brigade' survived the war as motor-bodybuilders, to enjoy enhanced protection thereafter. At the same time the handful of comparatively large-scale producers that emerged in the early 1920s were hampered in their efforts to standardize their product by the even greater diversity of chassis makes and models that arrived after 1918.

## Notes

1. J. Goode, *Smoke, Smell and Clatter* (Melbourne, 1969), pp. 7, 10ff.: P. Davis, *Wheels Across Australia* (Sydney, 1987), pp. 2ff.; K. Winser (ed.) *The Story of Australian Motoring* (n.d.), pp. 15–6, 29–30, 88. For detailed information on the pioneering cars in Australia, see T. and M. Giltrap, *Australian Cars from 1879* (Sydney, 1981).
2. E.D. Kennedy, *The Automobile Industry* (New York, 1934), p. 13.
3. L.A. Everett, *The Shape of the Motor Car* (London, n.d.), p. 77.
4. *Coach and Motor Builder*, November 1922.
5. *Australasian Coachbuilder and Saddler*, March 1897. See also J. Goode, 'Australian Early Car Manufacturers', *Bulletin of the Business Archives Council of Australia*, I, 6 (1961), pp. 1–3.
6. See D.F. Dixon, 'Origins of the Australian Petrol Distribution System', *Australian Economic History Review*, XII, 1 (1972), pp. 36–51.
7. *Australian Motorist*, June 1925 and December 1926.
8. P. Davis, 'This Motoring Century', *Sydney Morning Herald*, 1 October 1999.
9. See P. Stubbs, *The Australian Motor Industry* (Sydney, 1972), pp. 1–3; D. Holmes, 'Australia's Early Car Manufacturers: A Note on the Tarrant Engineering

Company', *Business Archives and History*, III, 2 (1963), pp. 240–42; Goode, 'Australian Early Car Manufacturers', pp. 55ff.; Goode, *Smoke, Smell and Clatter*, p. 17ff.; Giltrap, *Australian Cars from 1879*, p. 55; *Australian Motorist*, October 1917.

10. *Australian Motorist*, July 1919.

11. *Australian Motorist*, September 1923.

12. Z.E. Lambert and R.J. Wyatt, *Lord Austin: The Man* (London, 1968). See also, 'Sir Herbert Austin KBE, His Life Story', *Autocar*, 23 August 1929, pp. 369–72; R. Church, *Herbert Austin* (London, 1979), pp. 1–2.

13. G. Maxcy and A. Silberston, *The Motor Industry* (London, 1959), pp. 126–7.

14. V. Kohler, 'Deutsche Personenwagen Fabrikate zwischen 1886 und 1965', *Zeitschrift für Unternehmensgeschichte* (1996), 12, pp. 129–30; G. Horras, *Die Entwicklung des deutschen Automobilmarktes bis 1914* (Munich, 1982), pp. 128–30.

15. J.M. Laux, 'Rochet-Schneider and the French Motor Industry to 1914', *Business History*, VIII, 2 (1966), p. 80.

16. W. Bade, *Das Auto Erobert der Welt* (Berlin, 1938), p. 91.

17. Church, *Herbert Austin*, pp. 23–4.

18. Kennedy, *The Automobile Industry*, pp. 37–8.

19. R.J. Overy, *William Morris: Lord Nuffield* (London, 1959), pp. 15–16.

20. See Table 5.7.

21. See L.H. Seltzer, *A Financial History of the American Automobile Industry* (Boston, 1928), pp. 19ff.; Horras, *Die Entwicklung des deutschen Automobilmarktes*, pp. 155ff.; J.P. Bardou et al., *The Automobile Revolution* (Chapel Hill, NC, 1982), p. 75; Kennedy, *The Automobile Industry*, pp. 60–64 Cf.; A. Pound, *The Turning Wheel* (New York, 1934), pp. 44–5. Pound argued that the turn of the century success of R.E. Old with the 'Oldsmobile' produced in Detroit (and considered the first 'mass-produced' car) explains the subsequent concentration of the US industry in that area because 'pioneer manufacturers could find capital support there easier than elsewhere'. In the opinion of J.B. Rae: 'Upon close analysis it becomes clear that the location of the [US] automobile industry was to a considerable degree determined by factors of personality and business leadership' (J.B. Rae, *American Automobile Manufacturers: The First Forty Years* (Philadelphia, 1959), p. 48).

22. Laux , 'Rochet-Schneider and the French Motor Industry' pp. 77, 80.

23. A.E. Harrison, 'The Competitiveness of the British Cycle Industry, 1890–1914', *Economic History Review*, 2ⁿᵈ Series, XXII, 2 (1969), p. 103; H.G. Castle, *Britain's Motor Industry* (London, 1950), pp. 22, 49, 130; J. Wood, *Wheels of Misfortune: The Rise and Fall of the British Motor Industry* (London, 1988), p. 3; S.B. Saul, 'The Motor Industry in Britain to 1914', *Business History*, V (1962), pp. 23, 26. British car producers with origins in bicycle manufacture also figured prominently among the survivors to 1913 and the major producers of that year (See Saul, 'The Motor Industry in Britain', p. 25 (Table 3)).

24. C. Wilson and W. Reader, *Men and Machines: A History of D. Napier & Son, Engineers Ltd 1808–1958* (London, 1958), pp. 67–8.

25. Horras, *Die Entwicklung des deutschen Automobilmarktes*, p. 129.

26. See C.E. Pratt, 'A Sketch of American Bicycling and Its Founder', *Outing*, XVIII, 4 (1891), pp. 342–9.

27. Everett, *The Shape of the Motor Car*, p. 31; Rae, *American Automobile Manufacturers*, pp. 8–9.

28. Harrison, 'The Competitiveness of the British Cycle Industry', pp. 298, 301;

B. Beaven, 'The Growth and Significance of the Coventry Car Component Industry', *Midland History*, XVIII (1993), p. 105.

29. Horras, *Die Entwicklung des deutschen Automobilmarktes*, p. 129.
30. A 20 per cent duty was imposed in the Federation Tariff of 1901 (*Coach and Motor Builder*, November 1922).
31. See Holmes, 'Australia's Early Car Manufacturers', pp. 240–42.
32. Ibid., p. 240; Giltrap, *Australian Cars*, pp. 19–20; S.A. Cheney, *From Horse to Horse Power* (Adelaide, 1965), pp. 36, 53.
33. Seltzer, *A Financial History*, p. 71.
34. *Australian Motorist*, April 1909.
35. *Australian Motorist*, September 1908, February 1910; *Australasian Coach-builder and Wheelwright*, October 1910 and July 1911. The number of unregistered taxis is an unknown quantity. In Melbourne in 1911 there were no registered cabs, as the companies objected to the rates fixed by the city council and instead operated from garages (*Australasian Coachbuilder and Wheelwright*, July 1911).
36. *Australasian Coachbuilder and Wheelwright*, October 1907.
37. *Australasian Coachbuilder and Wheelwright*, April 1909.
38. Australian Archives (hereafter AA) Vic. MP273/1 G1914/13096.
39. AA Vic. MP273/1 G1914/13096.
40. Bardou *et al.*, *The Automobile Revolution*, p. 20.
41. Stubbs, *The Australian Motor Industry*, p. 5.
42. T.C. Barker, 'The Spread of Motor Vehicles before 1914', in C.P. Kindleberger and G. di Tella (eds) *Economics in the Long View* (3 vols, London, 1928), II, Part 1, p. 159.
43. *Australian Motorist*, January 1912.
44. In Canada the arrival of the Model T largely explains a marked rise in the proportion of cars owned by residents of rural areas, from 41.3 per cent in 1907 to 53.8 per cent in 1911 (G.T. Bloomfield, 'Motorisation on the New Frontier: The Case of Saskatchewan, Canada, 1906–1934', in T.C. Barker (ed.) *The Economic and Social Effects of the Spread of Motor Vehicles* (London, 1982), pp. 172–3).
45. Cited in *Australasian Coachbuilder and Wheelwright*, January 1908.
46. M.L. Berger, *The Devil Wagon in God's Country: The Automobile and Social Change in Rural America, 1893–1929* (Hamden, CT, 1979), p. 48.
47. Cheney, *From Horse to Horse Power*, p. 99.
48. Alloy steels were not produced in Australia until well into the Second World War and this may also have been an inhibiting influence on the early emergence of complete manufacture of motor vehicles in Australia.
49. S. Longstreet, *The Boy in the Model T: A Journey in the Just Gone Past* (New York, 1956), p. 105.
50. There were around 2.8 million square miles of land in Australia over four miles from a railway (*Australian Motorist*, June 1921).
51. *Australian Motorist*, January 1912.
52. *Australasian Coachbuilder and Wheelwright*, August, September 1908 and April 1910.
53. *Australasian Coachbuilder and Wheelwright*, October 1910.
54. J.W. Knott, 'Speed, Modernity and the Motor Car. The Making of the 1909 *Motor Traffic Act* in New South Wales', *Australian Historical Studies*, XXIV, 103 (1994), p. 224.
55. Goode, 'Australian Early Car Manufacturers', p. 24.
56. *Australian Motorist*, June 1926.

57. *Australasian Coachbuilder and Wheelwright*, June 1926.
58. *Australasian Coachbuilder and Wheelwright*, October 1903.
59. *Australasian Coachbuilder and Wheelwright*, June 1903.
60. *Australasian Coachbuilder and Wheelwright*, September 1912.
61. *Australasian Coachbuilder and Wheelwright*, November 1903 and April 1909.
62. *Australasian Coachbuilder and Wheelwright*, April 1909.
63. *Australasian Coachbuilder and Wheelwright*, November 1903.
64. Ibid.
65. *Australasian Coachbuilder and Wheelwright*, June 1910.
66. *Australasian Coachbuilder and Wheelwright*, February 1912.
67. *Australasian Coachbuilder and Wheelwright*, April 1909.
68. *Australasian Coachbuilder and Wheelwright*, October 1901.
69. Alleged dumping of American products on the Australian market was a significant issue in the 1906 election. Following this was the first general revision of the Federation Tariff. The term 'New Protection' was coined by the then protectionist Prime Minister Alfred Deakin to denote a tariff policy that compensated workers for resulting higher prices by higher money wages. The revised tariff received assent in June 1908. It provided for general increases in rates of duty and preferential rates for goods from the United Kingdom (R.M. Conlon, *Distance and Duties* (Ottawa, 1986) p. 12). For a general economic history of Australia since the 1890s, see B. Dyster and D. Meredith, *Australia in the International Economy in the Twentieth Century* (Cambridge, 1990).
70. *Australasian Coachbuilder and Wheelwright*, December 1907.
71. *Australasian Coachbuilder and Wheelwright*, October 1907.
72. Ibid.
73. *Australasian Coachbuilder and Wheelwright*, June 1911.
74. *Australasian Coachbuilder and Wheelwright*, October 1912. In 1916 local motor body makers accounted for about 10 per cent of total body supplies (*Australasian Coachbuilder and Wheelwright*, September 1917).
75. The Model T was not available in North America as chassis only. There was in any case an obvious incentive to reduce the invoice price of components subject to a high duty and balance the factory price on the invoice by inflating the prices of components on which lower duties were levied.
76. In the years immediately prior to the First World War Australia became the best export market for Ford Canada, a company that effectively acted as exporter for the Ford Motor Company in the United States. The initial Ford decision to manufacture in Canada was taken in response to the 35 per cent *ad valorem* duty on car imports inherited from carriage manufacturing. The decision by Henry Ford to grant Ford Canada – a company in which he held a minority shareholding – the sole right to supply the British Empire market (excluding Britain itself) was a result of Imperial Preference, especially that provided by Australia. It quickly emerged as the major destination of Ford Canada's exports, and Canada as a major source of Australia's imports. See Chapter 5 for an outline of Canada's role in the development of the Australian industry.
77. *Australian Motorist*, April 1921.
78. *Commonwealth Parliamentary Papers*, Vol. VII, 1914–17, p. 524.
79. *Commonwealth Parliamentary Papers*, Vol. VII, 1914–17, p. 513.
80. Cars ordered before 10 August and shipped from the overseas factory before 31 December 1917 were exempted from the import restrictions (*Australasian Coachbuilder and Wheelwright*, October 1917).
81. The eventual outcome, by the 1930s, was the integrated chassis and body.

# 3 Acceleration: the Accretion Model of Automotive Industry Development in Australia, 1919–1939

Concern for the development of industrial strength provided a widely supported and nationalistic rationale for protectionism in Australia. It was a rationale effectively summarized by S. Butlin when he wrote,

> The doctrine of 'development' is an old story in Australia. Part of the general thinking of all Australians on economic affairs is a not very coherent prejudice in favor of an increase in total 'production', especially the introduction of new industries, coupled with the assumption that the natural way to promote such new industries [was] government aid.[1]

'Complete' manufacture of automobiles was just such a case.

Motor vehicle industry policy for the greater part of the period between the world wars was essentially an outcome of the interplay of two influences. First, the often pressing needs of governments for revenue (particularly in the early years after the First World War) and, second, the influence that relevant interest groups, often themselves the product of earlier tariff measures, could exercise upon the political process.[2] Indeed, Winder and MacPherson in 1931 aptly noted the major element of the tariff-making process of the day: 'the lobbies of Canberra resound with the cries of the tariff touts'.[3] By the mid-1930s, while policy towards the motor industry may have furthered some aspects of national development – at high cost – it had very little to do with promoting the defence capacity of the nation as some have argued.[4] It was only in the few months before the Second World War that defence became an important determinant of policy, and even after the outbreak of war the defence significance of the industry was disputed. (The issue is discussed in more detail in Chapter 4.)

Here, the term 'policy' is used in two senses. A 'passive' policy – essentially one of non-interference by government – is a policy nevertheless. 'Active' policy may be considered as planned and coordinated measures, actively pursued, and designed to have a specific outcome. The Greene tariff, which was introduced in Parliament in 1920, was such a policy.[5] For much of the interwar period it provided the basic protective framework for the manufacturing sector, of which the motor industry was part. From the early 1920s until 1936, government policy towards the industry was essentially passive. It was controlled by the bureaucracy that, mainly by administrative means, extended, *ad hoc*, the range of components subject to protective tariffs. In the view of the Australian Automobile Manufacturers' Association, complete local manufacture would eventually follow inevitably from the establishment of components manufacture. The secretary of the Association saw the sequence of development as, 'First the parts, then the units, and ultimately the completed car.'[6] Experience demonstrated this view to be fallacious. Rather than the manufacture of a complete motor car, providing high levels of protection for an increasing range of automobile components resulted in a proliferation of small-scale producers of a wide range of parts, often of poor quality, encouraged by the diversity of makes and models available in the 1920s and 1930s. It inhibited the adoption of mass production methods for the manufacture of both spare parts and original equipment, but was insufficient to encourage any large-scale manufacture of the motive force of the vehicle: its engine.

The Greene tariff of the 1920s provided an environment that encouraged the three major North American producers to enter local assembly and limited manufacture. Ford was the first of the dominant manufacturers to do so. In 1925 the Ford Manufacturing Company of Australia Pty Ltd was formed to manufacture and build motor bodies and parts, while the Ford Motor Company of Australia was responsible for assembly and distribution of vehicles. (For simplicity we will refer to these two companies as Ford Australia or just Ford.) The manufacturing operations associated with the Chrysler Corporation in Australia also had its origins in 1926 when T.J. Richards & Sons were contracted to build bodies for chassis imported by the South Australian distributors of Dodge cars. The first bodies were built under the arrangement in 1928.[7] General Motors (Australia) Pty Ltd (GMA) was registered in 1926, having earlier contracted with Holden Motor Body Builders Ltd (Holden's) for the exclusive use of its new plant at Woodville, South Australia. In 1931 GMA took over Holden's which was facing insolvency as a result of the Depression. The firm then became known as General Motors-Holden's Limited (GM-H).[8] By the mid-1930s the three largest car producers in the United States were therefore firmly established in Australia. The local bodybuilding industry also accommodated major British interests. The Melbourne Motor Body Company, (later Ruskin Motor Bodies Proprietary Limited) was linked with Austin and Morris, though the firm produced bodies for a number of other makes.[9] None of these firms was a 'complete' manufacturer, however.

A policy of complete automobile manufacture was part of the trade diversion measures introduced in May 1936, and an additional duty was then imposed to finance proposed bounty payments for the local manufacture of engines.[10] This *was* an active policy of promoting the Australian automobile industry, and an 'indirect' contribution to defence was seen as one of its benefits. However, the 'active' policy then remained inactive for more than three years (no bounties were ever paid). It was only in the months immediately before the outbreak of war in September 1939, that the Australian government began to implement the 1936 bounty measures to promote complete motor car manufacture, with a view to meeting the perceived threat to the nation's security. It was indeed a policy *of the government*, as neither representatives of the major firms in the industry, nor the bureaucracy which advised the government were persuaded that the industry was of direct significance to the country's defence. The events of the intervening three years provide a model of self-interest. They were characterized by conflict within the government; between the government and the major producers; and among the major producers (despite unanimity in their opposition to the bounty proposals). Supporters of the proposal saw the period not as one where the government was striving to implement its plans for the development of the industry and the nation, but as one characterized by government procrastination and back-sliding, of bad faith and conspiracy. This period and these events are examined in more detail in the following chapter.

### Tariffs as a source of revenue

Since Federation import duties had provided the major source of Common-wealth government revenues. During the course of the First World War these revenues virtually dried up. With Australia's expenditures as a belligerent, a 'national debt' of around £20 million in 1914 had grown to about £400 million by the time of the Armistice, and extra revenue was needed to service it.[11] Prime Minister Hughes was unsuccessful in his effort at the Versailles negotiations to force Germany to redeem the war bonds his government had encouraged Australians to buy, and the money had to be found elsewhere.[12]

At the time, the Commonwealth government did not have the power to impose income tax, and tariffs, which seemingly punished 'foreigners', were politically more acceptable than other forms of taxation then available to the central government. In these circumstances the motor vehicle was an ideal target for raising revenue.[13] The chassis, the major part of a car, was imported – after the Armistice, in increasing numbers – and there was a widespread perception that the foreign exporter bore the burden of the tax. A people who had endured several years of sacrifice to support the 'war effort' viewed the motor car as a luxury. It was in fact a perfect example of conspicuous consumption, and therefore a legitimate object for the imposition of increased duties. As Senator Greene observed in 1921 when justifying the increase in duties on automobile components: 'Although serving many utilitarian purposes, motor transport was still more or less a luxury, and the government was entitled to get what revenue it could out of it.'[14] Even the Country Party leader in the conservative coalition, Earle Page, who was of the view that cars were 'an absolute necessity throughout Australia', supported increased duties on vehicle components as necessary for revenue purposes.[15]

Politicians were not the only ones who saw car imports as popular targets in the 1920s and early 1930s. In the economic downturn of 1921 a deputation from the Associated Chamber of Manufactures presented the Minister for Customs with a list of 'luxury' imports it urged be prohibited. Motor cars and motor cycles headed the litany. An organization was formed in 1924 to lobby for a ban on the import of automotive products, as an expression of what was then apparently the 'popular idea that investments in property, and absorption of factory production is adversely affected through people buying motor cars'; while in 1927 the Secretary of the Preservation of Australian Industries League publicly expressed the view that motor cars, oil, gramophones and pianos were unnecessary imports.[16] In response to the Great Depression demands for the prohibition of imports of automotive products were frequently presented as at least a partial solution to the economic crisis.[17] Indeed, 'prohibition' of a sort was almost achieved through a combination of increased duties on motor vehicle chassis; a devastating decline in per-capita income; and rapidly increasing unemployment which made potential purchasers understandably wary of buying at a time when the great majority of sales were made on hire purchase. By the first half of 1931 motor car registrations were only 14 per cent of the figure for the same period in 1927 and proportionately even lower in the case of commercial vehicles.[18]

The general perception of the motor car as a luxury persisted throughout the interwar era. The actions of the state governments in imposing vehicle registration fees and state taxes on petroleum reflected that view, though they were justified politically as necessary for increased expenditure on road-building. For Labor governments, taxes on motor vehicles were a means of accommodating the interests of the unions representing railway and tram workers, whose livelihoods were perceived to be threatened by motor transport.[19] All of this was supported by the rhetoric of 'taxing the rich'. In these circumstances, understandably those who profited from motor vehicles acquired a common interest in defending the trade as a whole through such organizations as the state-based Chambers of Automotive Industries.[20]

## The lobby

Apart from the revenue it raised, the development of the tariff created a role for the Commonwealth government in dispensing patronage to interest groups and was instrumental in the formation of 'the lobby' that continues to thrive. By the early 1930s when the lobbies of Canberra 'resounded to the cries of the tariff touts', the automobile industry was there with all the rest.[21]

In a practical sense, reasserting control over the tariff – the revenue and protective effects of which had been limited by the curtailment of imports during the 1914–1918 war – was an important means by which the Commonwealth government of the interwar era could show its authority and power to the manufacturing lobby, its prospective 'client'. It was apparent that successful lobbyists could realize relatively easy and more or less guaranteed rents by means of tariff protection. By granting protection virtually on demand, the Commonwealth government was able not only to satisfy the various manufacturing interests, but to convey the impression to the electorate that it was acting to promote 'national development'.[22]

The beginning of the lobbying process in the motor industry was discernible even before the First World War. From about the turn of the century, low, revenue duties were applied to imported chassis, and local motor body production was sheltered by high tariffs. These measures were in response to lobbying by the extensive coachbuilding trade, which would otherwise have faced extinction. For duty purposes the chassis was very widely defined to incorporate almost anything local coachbuilders were then incapable of producing, including the sub-frame, engine and transmission, pneumatic tyres, bonnet, dashboard, scuttles and running boards.[23] For tariff purposes the chassis was therefore treated as an input, and taxed at minimum rates so as not to disadvantage the protected motor bodybuilding activity.

The framework of assistance to the industry after the First World War was provided in the Greene tariff revisions of 1920, and involved the redefinition of the 'chassis' to extend the range of components subject to protective rates of duty. This was at least the partial result of lobbying by the numerous small workshops that had emerged to provide replacement parts while supplies from North America and Europe were interrupted during the war. Under the new tariff, the chassis was broken down into 14 component elements, many of which corresponded with the products or potential products of particular interest groups. The engine was classified as 'motive power machinery' and thereby subjected to a 40 per cent *ad valorem* duty (17.5 per cent British preferential), on the ground that a motor vehicle engine was 'commercially useable for more than one purpose'.[24] Of course, the measure was not designed to stimulate the manufacturers to produce engines capable of powering a motor vehicle and nor did it. While it was imposed to protect the extensive manufacture of stationary and marine combustion engines in Australia,[25] the fact that a tariff of this magnitude was insufficient to encourage local production of automobile engines was an indication of the significance of Australia's disadvantage in their manufacture.[26]

A 55 per cent *ad valorem* tariff on the lamps that by 1920 had become standard on motor vehicles served the interests of manufacturers of electrical lighting equipment. A local capacity to produce tyres and other rubber components that developed during the war was similarly protected, often to an extraordinary extent. In 1923, for instance, a mechanic had to remove two rubber buffers valued at about 6d. from caps on the front axle of an imported chassis, so they could be weighed and assessed for the duty of 2s. 6d. per lb. on imported rubber goods. To serve the interests of local toolmakers, the components of the kit supplied with imported chassis were individually assessed for duty at the relevant highly protective rates. Australian textile producers' interests were even protected to the extent that the cloth in which the tools were wrapped became separately liable to a 45 per cent duty. In one case, on such a cloth valued at 7d. on the chassis supplier's invoice, and at 9d. for duty purposes, a duty of 4d. was levied.[27]

The success of the lobby and its effects did not go unnoticed by those who were adversely affected by the system. In 1930, the *Australian Motorist* reported that, 'Dr. Earle Page [the Country Party leader] a few years ago told a meeting of motor traders that until they were stronger numerically, they would continue to be victimized in the process of taxation.' The journal then went on to complain that, 'Only those groups that have political significance seem to be immune from additional taxation, or reduced earning capacity.'[28]

How did a group acquire 'political significance'? The claim was made that 'A gift to party funds has never been resorted to by the motor industry because the industry does not consider legislation should be influenced by gifts to party funds.'[29] But money supposedly isn't everything, and a good example of the lobby's evolving methods is illustrated in a letter dated October 1937, in which H. Rickards, the Managing Director of Rickards Bros Pty Ltd, distributors of Nash cars, wrote to T.W. White, Minister for Trade and Customs.

> We have received a request from your committee rooms ... to supply them with two cars to assist you in your electioneering tomorrow, and we have replied expressing our willingness to do this for you. ... Your party can be assured of the members of this company's wholehearted support, and our managing director, who is in your electorate, has already used his influence on your behalf. He has instructed me to inform you that at least four members of his household with be voting for you.

At a time when components from the dollar area were subject to import controls, then comes the *quid pro quo*: 'We would appreciate if you could use your influence regarding our request to bring in 50 sets of body panels to tide us over.'[30]

Another example of the nascent lobbying process involved R.G. (later Lord) Casey – Commonwealth Treasurer 1935–39 – whose seat of Corio included Geelong where the Ford Company's works were located. According to the Managing Director of Ford, H.C. French, Ford had him 'in the bag'.[31] This widely held perception seems to have reduced Casey's effectiveness in Cabinet

on matters concerning the motor industry, with his opinions arousing the
suspicions of his ministerial colleagues. L.J. Hartnett, the head of GM-H at the
time did not envy the 'particular relationship with the government' of his Ford
equivalent at the Ford Company. As Hartnett observed:

> I consider it a *faux pas* on the part of the Ford Co. too heavily mesmerizing or
> overselling a particular Minister believing he can fight a cause for them where as he
> is suspect on the subject in Cabinet discussions. We learnt from this experience, and
> although I'm particularly friendly with two Ministers, I have endeavored to spread
> my contacts throughout the Cabinet.[32]

The 1936 proposal to impose a specific duty on imported chassis to fund a
bounty promoting local manufacture saw a falling-out between the representatives of the two major local producers, Ford and GM-H. (The proposal was
incorporated in the Motor Vehicle Engine Bounty Act, which, with the Motor
Vehicle Agreement Act is discussed in Chapter 4.) Hartnett of GM-H was
convinced that his counterpart at Ford had 'played his cards rather badly by
becoming extremely excited about it and filling Casey, the Federal Treasurer,
with a great deal of detailed data and a certain amount of invective against the
government'.[33]

The motor bounty and the issue of bringing about the complete local
manufacture of motor vehicles were referred to the Tariff Board. The Board
had been formed by the Commonwealth government in 1921 to provide an
'independent' body that would give the impression of authority, neutrality and
expertise in the tariff-making process. It was a ploy on the part of the
politicians, creating a safety valve to ease the pressure of competing interests in
providing assistance to industry. Like the government, for its inquiries the
Tariff Board (comprised of government appointees) effectively depended on
information provided by vested interests in determining its recommendations.
The significance (and likely bias) of results emerging from such a procedure
was publicly recognized in 1937 by Sir Henry Gullett, who had been Minister
of Trade Treaties when the motor engine bounty was first proposed. A strong
proponent of support for local manufacturing and of the bounty proposal in
particular, he informed the House of Representatives 'that the only relevant
testimony available [to the Tariff Board] ... was from those interested in the
importation of motor chassis into the Commonwealth or their exportation to
this country from overseas'.[34]

In the evolution of the lobby reciprocal favours were required. GM-H
reluctantly agreed in 1936, the year of the engine bounty proposal, to
participate in the government's formation of the Commonwealth Aircraft
Corporation. As Hartnett of GM-H observed, R.G. Menzies (the rising star of
the United Australia Party) and Earle Page (still leading the Country Party in
the coalition government) were in this regard 'highly appreciative of GM-H
activities and undertakings'. From the GM-H perspective, 'perhaps it did not

suit us too well'. However, in Hartnett's opinion the resulting 'goodwill which we have with the government ... is of considerable value right now, and will be more so in the future because they will endeavor to treat us *fairly and on as preferential grounds as is possible* for them'.[35]

The lobby representing pecuniary interests was not the only influence on governments during the interwar period, however. The interests and rivalries of the states had to be taken into account, particularly the possible electoral consequences of seeming to favour one or other of the more populated states of southeastern Australia. Attempting to reconcile these rivalries could produce quite bizarre outcomes. For example, the fact that by the mid-1930s most civil aviation maintenance and repair work was concentrated in Melbourne was apparently 'the main reason for the selection of the University of Sydney for the government endowed Chair in Aeronautics'.[36]

With the tariff we see the origins in Australia of the phenomenon of 'corporatism' which involves a community of interest between government, employees and organized labour. The conservative governments that predominated in the interwar era were almost obsessive in their views that the considerable labour unrest of the time constituted a threat of 'Communism'. The tariff served to promote the very useful sense of common interest between employers and employees.[37] For employers the tariff underwrote their profits. For workers, protection provided jobs and relatively high wages by international standards. Indeed, the tariff provided something for everyone – provided they were a 'producer'. To that end the interests of the consumer were sacrificed.

## The role of the bureaucracy

Between the world wars, as high levels of protection were extended to the manufacture of a wider range of parts, the range of motor vehicle components produced locally also gradually expanded. There was no government 'plan' involved, no legislation; the changes to the duties imposed were achieved by administrative means. From the early 1920s the administration of the tariff on chassis by Customs became a significant issue with those who were allied with the interests of motor traders. There were allegations of manipulation of values-for-duty, and tariff classifications of components.[38] Of the former, in 1923 it was alleged that Customs used overvalued foreign exchange rates to effectively shut out imports of chassis from France, Italy and Belgium, and to disadvantage American imports.[39] Of the latter, the Secretary of the Federal Council of Motor Traders, H.W. Harrison, pointed to 'administrative' protection by which, 'the duties have been more than doubled by the departmental regulations.'[40]

By late 1923, according to the Secretary of the Federal Council of Motor

Traders, the general tariff of 12.5 per cent on non-British chassis agreed to by Parliament in 1920 had come to range between 30 and 55 per cent (and 10 to 35 per cent instead of 7.5 per cent in the case of imports under the imperial preference arrangement) as a result of administrative decisions applying protective rates to various additional components.[41] Some of these duties were extraordinarily high. From 1931, for example, a duty of £93 was levied on sets of imported brake drums with a value-for-duty of £23, an *ad valorem* equivalent rate of nearly 450 per cent.[42]

Enabling the range of motor vehicle components subject to protective tariff to be progressively and significantly broadened by *ad hoc* administrative decisions stemmed from a legislative omission. Nowhere was the 'chassis' or the 'body' defined for Customs purposes in the relevant legislation. According to the Melbourne *Argus*, 'The weakness at present is that the Minister has power to determine what constitutes a chassis.'[43] Changes in Customs regulations and administration over time stripped the chassis of its components (which were then usually subject to high protective rates) so that the 'chassis' of the 1930s was far less complete than the 'chassis' of a decade earlier.[44] The administration of the tariff by Customs was a source of contention throughout the 1920s, and with the introduction of the Scullin tariff during the Depression it was noted that:

> The idea that the British chassis is duty free is merely one of those statements, which are accepted without inquiry by the general public. The British chassis, which the public believes is tariff free, pays duty on the parts [listed]. The reader [having examined the list] will realize that there is not much of the 'free of duty chassis' left.[45]

The components listed included fenders, bonnets, running boards, bumper bars, radiator shells, springs and other suspension components, shock absorbers and steering components. Most were subject to rates of duty of at least 60 per cent, general rate, with 'British chassis pay[ing] a slightly lower duty on the[se] parts, which shows that in practice the alleged duty-free import from the United Kingdom barely exists'.[46] The procedure of 'stripping' the chassis was explicitly recognized by the Tariff Board in its report on the motor industry released in 1938.[47] Just how the range of components produced locally depended on extending the reach of protective tariffs was also highlighted in the report when the Board noted, 'there has been no appreciable progress [in] extending into the manufacture of additional chassis parts since 1931, since which date there has been no extension of protection to further chassis parts for [original] equipment'.[48]

The administration of the tariff was not the only problem. The related 'by-law' system that evolved from the Greene tariff of 1920 was particularly open to what was in effect abuse by officers of the Customs Department. Under this arrangement goods (most often machinery) otherwise subject to a protective duty could be imported at a concessional rate through the issue of a by-law if there was no 'reasonably available' local equivalent. Such by-laws could be terminated where a domestic supplier was deemed to produce an adequate alternative. Individual officers of the Customs Department more or less arbitrarily made the decisions. As an illustration of the problems that could be caused by the system, the Demco Machinery Company of Sydney which imported machine tools and precision equipment from Germany, complained to its supplier in 1933:

> whenever we propose to import a highly useful machine tool into Australia, the Customs Authorities contact [a possible manufacturer] and ask if they can make the machine in question. They almost always say yes, and in response a tariff is imposed that makes it impossible to import the German machine. It is a fact that most of the machines cannot be made in Australia, at least not to anything like the quality of the German machines.[49]

## Industry structure and performance

The 1920 tariff revision and subsequent extensions of protection to other motor vehicle components which widened the range of automotive parts produced in Australia contributed to the impression that producing complete motor vehicles in Australia was simply a matter of accretion – by extending protective duties to more and more components. It seemed as if the Secretary of the Automotive Manufacturers' Association was right when he said in 1929: 'First the parts, then the units, and ultimately the completed car.'[50]

The development of the manufacture of motor vehicles in other countries to that point was quite different. Cars were mainly produced by enterprises that marketed the finished product, often by 'out-sourcing' the supply of components, and in the interwar period economies of scale emerged as the main source of minimizing production costs in the industry, including the manufacture of components. However, in Australia, for those components where manufacture had become established, the tariff, the major instrument of government policy, did nothing to facilitate the exploitation of such economies. In fact the contrary was true. There were at least two important influences at work. First, influenced by high tariffs (and transport costs), retail prices of cars in Australia were considerably higher – in some cases at least twice as high as those of the same models in North America and Europe.[51] As a consequence of these relatively high consumer prices, market demand for motor cars in Australia was lower than it would otherwise have been, and the scope to exploit scale economies correspondingly restricted in the manufacture of most components.[52]

Second, prices inflated by high tariffs and transport costs also provided scope for higher profits than otherwise, and tended to attract the entry of new firms to a market which was already smaller that it would otherwise have been. The result was a structure of manufacturing consisting of a large number of firms and plants, many of which were very small indeed.[53] By 1928–29, there were 22,841 persons employed in 2,199 factories engaged in 'motor vehicles and accessories production', an average of just 10.4 per factory. By comparison, in Canada – a country with a higher population and lower levels of protection[54] – there were at that time 16,749 persons employed in 14 factories engaged in 'motor vehicle manufacture', an average of 1,196; while for 'automobile parts and accessories' there were 3,509 persons employed in 77 plants, an average of 46 persons per plant.[55] Differences between the industries of the two countries of the same magnitude may be observed throughout the interwar period.[56] In terms of overall productivity, output per person in the industry was about twice as high in Canada as in Australia.[57] (The link between the industry in Australia and in Canada is examined in Chapter 5.)

The very small-scale establishments involved in the production of replacement parts in Australia were characterized by the use of very little capital equipment (rarely anything more sophisticated than lathes was used) to produce a variety of vehicle components to individual order for a diversity of makes and models. The industry structure and methods of production in local replacement components production were partly the results of this extraordinary diversity. The 9,793 chassis imported from Britain in 1935–36 comprised 20 makes and over 40 models.[58] According to a list compiled around the same time, 59 makes of cars, 30 of trucks, 14 of motorcycles and 16 of buses were imported into Australia.[59] Apart from the high cost of locally produced parts, their quality was often very poor. As the Victorian Chamber of Automotive Industries conceded in the late 1930s: 'gears made in small quantities with tolerances and contours produced without the aid of copies of the original blue prints are usually very troublesome to fit and generally noisy'.[60] Moreover, in an era of swift technological change, the products of the motor vehicle components industry in Australia quickly became outmoded, shielded as they were by protection. In an opinion expressed in the September 1923 issue of the *Australian Motorist*, 'due to the stultifying effect of monopoly, the master craftsmen, who lay out and design, have fallen behind'. In shutting out import competition, the tariff effectively provided a captive market for local producers.

Despite the tariff preferences provided for imports from Britain, over the course of the interwar period the Australian market for motor cars – mostly made up of locally built bodies and imported, but locally assembled chassis – became dominated by the major US producers. By 1935 GM-H accounted for almost 40 per cent of car sales, Ford Australia, for just over 20 per cent, and Chrysler Dodge for 15 per cent. They each operated a large number of assembly plants, limiting the exploitation of potential scale economies in vehicle assembly. Ford had plants in Victoria, New South Wales, Queensland and Western Australia; GM-H in every state but Tasmania; and Chrysler Dodge, a total of 14 plants with locations in all states.[61] The problem was mainly a function of Australia's geography and producers' attempts to minimize delivery costs (including transport charges) of vehicles to the various regional markets, though presumably they had balanced any savings in transport costs with the loss of scale economies in diversifying production.

The diversity of models produced further inhibited the abilities of even the largest enterprises to exploit economies of scale in the manufacture of motor bodies which was the core of the industry that emerged between the world wars. Despite their dominance of the Australian market, the relatively large-scale motor bodybuilding enterprises – Ford, Holden's/GM-H, and Richards/Chrysler Dodge – still faced the problem of model diversity.[62] Each of the major overseas automobile manufacturers marketed a range of models catering for different consumer demands, and the makes themselves had distinctive brand 'images'. Firms such as Ford, Oldsmobile (R.E. Old), Buick and Dodge (from 1915) created trademarks that became associated with a particular image in the minds of potential buyers. The reputation of Ford, its image of ruggedness and reliability for example, came to be largely based on the performance of the Model T and its ability to negotiate the dirt roads of the rural areas of the period.[63]

Moreover, models were subject to frequent styling changes as a result of the shift of orientation in US automobile manufacturers' marketing strategies after the First World War. While the early emphasis had been on standardization and efforts to lower product prices, after the First World War, with the emergence of a rapidly expanding used-car market in the United States, frequent style changes acquired increasing importance in the promotion of new car sales; and 'style' was expressed in the bodywork of the vehicle.[64]

Poor product quality was a significant problem in Australian motor body-building, as it was for motor parts. In one extreme case in the early 1930s, an attempt was made to exploit the economies of a longer production run by using bodies built by Holden's originally for GM Australia, bent and twisted into shape to fit the Nash chassis. The result was 'a threat to the safety of owners and other road users'.[65] The problems were usually far less serious, but they had persisted for some time. According to a report on the second annual show of the Motor Traders' Association of NSW, held at Moore Park, Sydney, in January 1921:

> In painting, the greater proportion was finished in dark shades … . This tendency deserves encouragement, if only because it makes the prevailing weakness in motor bodywork less conspicuous. Almost every job finished in light shades showed faulty workmanship.[66]

During 1923 numerous adverse comments on locally produced bodies appeared in the Melbourne and Sydney press. They included complaints concerning 'rattling doors, "drumming panels", [and] badly-mortised woodwork that produces squeaks and squirms'.[67] To a large extent these early problems were caused by the rapid expansion of the labour force in motor bodybuilding, which necessitated the employment of unskilled workers who were trained on the job.[68]

In North America, by the middle of the 1920s the closed car giving all-weather protection was fast superseding the open car. With the increasing dominance of the closed car, changes in body styling became of increasing importance in the marketing of what had become a symbol of status for the rapidly increasing numbers of urban car buyers.[69] Having a new Chevrolet, the bottom of the range of cars manufactured by General Motors, became preferable to a Model T Ford (where the basic styling had not changed since 1908) or a Dodge (a company that from 1915 boasted that the styling of their product would never change – presumably to assure potential purchasers of high resale values).[70]

By the mid-1920s in the United States, hydraulic presses were being used for the task of forming the curves of the roof panels of the increasingly popular closed bodywork.[71] In Australia, this type of vehicle was extremely costly to produce, in part because the roof panels were hand-formed. Despite this, the closed body (local production of which was highly protected) became the standard type produced in Australia by the end of the 1920s – by which time, overseas closed-body construction was in the process of further technological development. In North America and Europe, automobile manufacturers were adopting the all-steel body employing the Budd pressed steel principle.[72] By contrast, in Australia in the 1930s almost all closed bodies were produced by attaching steel panels to a wooden frame. The process was really just an extension of the carriage-builder's craft and the quality of the bodies it produced was to some observers still clearly inadequate.[73] When interviewed during a visit to Sydney in 1936, Sir Albert Atkey, a former Lord Mayor of Nottingham 'who is engaged in the motor trade in England', said that

> the attitude of Australia towards imported motor cars was wrong. ... our great motor car manufacturers Lord Austin and Lord Nuffield, make cars, and take as much interest in the bodywork as in the mechanical side .... What we object to is the taking to pieces in Australia of essential parts of cars from abroad, and clothing them with materials which may reflect on the reputation of the manufacturer.[74]

### Tariffs and the 'motorization' of society

By inflating the prices of motor vehicles, government policy towards automotive manufacturing between the world wars effectively inhibited the 'motorization' of Australian society. At the beginning of the 1920s the price of an automobile selling for the equivalent of A£290 in the United States was A£680 in Australia.[75] International freight costs also made an important, but lesser contribution to the price differential. In 1928, for example, the freight charge for a six-cylinder sedan imported from the USA fully assembled was A£62, compared with a duty of A£93.[76] In 1939 the popular General Motors Chevrolet, priced at the equivalent of A£160 in the US, retailed for A£360 in Australia.[77] The high cost of cars in Australia was reflected in a low ratio of cars to commercial vehicles. In late 1938 the ratio was 2.2:1 in Australia, compared with 5.3:1 in Canada and 6.1:1 in the USA. At 3.0:1 the ratio in Argentina, a country then in the process of acquiring 'Third World' status, was higher than in Australia.[78]

The adverse effect of the tariff on the motorization of Australian society was only partially offset from the early 1920s by the rapid development of hire purchase as a stimulus to motor vehicle sales. By 1925 an estimated 50 per cent of all motorists 'paid as they rode'[79] and four years later an estimated 70 per cent of sales of General Motors' vehicles were sold on instalment terms.[80]

In the mid-1920s in New Zealand a Ford Model T was about 20 per cent cheaper than in Australia. There a low revenue duty applied to chassis that had not been 'stripped' of parts for tariff purposes as they had been in Australia. At least a partial consequence of lower prices was that in the interwar period New Zealand became a far more motorized society than Australia.[81] From roughly the same per capita vehicle registrations in the mid-1920s, by 1930 and for the remainder of that decade, New Zealand outstripped Australia by a considerable margin.[82]

The demand in Australia for motor cycles, described at the time as 'the wage-earner's motor car', and also a common first step towards owning a car, was particularly inhibited by the tariff. It was said that 'the motor cycle stands between the bicycle and the cheap motor car', but high tariffs on motor cycles and sidecars severely limited their purchase. In the mid-1920s imported motor cycles were dutiable at 40 per cent (30 per cent British Preferential) while the corresponding duties on motor car chassis were 20 per cent and 10 per cent. The cost of a locally built sidecar (which were then fitted to about 80 per cent of imported motor cycles) was about A£50, just A£10 less than a locally built body for a small, single-seat car. The result was to remove much of the differential between prices of motor cycles and 'cheap' motor cars, making it 'apparent that a gross injustice is being done to that section of the public who need motor cycles'.[83] The high duty levied on imported motor cycles in part arose from a mistaken belief that their manufacture could be quickly established in Australia through the tariff.[84]

The price differential between British cars in Australia and in the United Kingdom, where the basic chassis could be imported duty-free and components at the imperial preference rate, was also considerable. In the mid-1930s a 7 hp Morris saloon available in Britain for the equivalent of A£163 was priced at A£298 in Australia. With a 25 hp Morris the respective prices were A£331 as against A£442. In general the relative price disparity was greater for small cars than for large, an arrangement – as with motor cycles – hardly serving to encourage the emergence of mass motoring.[85] Moreover, with high import duties on oil and state taxes such as registration fees, the cost of running a car in Australia was also comparatively high. By one estimate, in the late 1930s the annual cost of running a car in the United States was 40 per cent of that in Australia.[86]

One of the results of the comparatively high cost of cars in Australia was the relatively high average age of vehicles on the country's roads. In 1934 the average life of cars in Australia was 10.7 years compared with about 7.5 years in both the United States and the United Kingdom.[87] By 1939 more than one-half of the vehicles registered in Australia were over eight years old, a proportion that was significantly in excess of that in North America and Europe.[88] While this generated a high level of demand for replacement parts and repair facilities, its influence was counteracted by the impact of the tariff in retarding the 'motorization' of Australian society.

### The outcome of interwar 'policy'

As a result of high and increasing levels of tariff protection Australia did acquire the capacity to produce a range of motor vehicle components between the world wars. However, the outcome did not extend to the local manufacture of motor vehicle engines nor to other key components. The industry structure that emerged – many small firms producing a wide range of products – contrasted with its evolution in the countries of North America and Europe where the industry became concentrated to exploit economies of scale.

By 1938 there were 36,530 workers engaged in automotive manufacturing. They were employed in 3,369 companies: an average of 11 per enterprise. Under the shelter of the tariff, the great majority of small-scale enterprises manufactured replacement parts such as gears and pistons for a very wide range of makes and models of motor vehicles. Although many basic chassis components were identical across a particular firm's models, the diversity of makes sold in Australia – encouraged by the tariff – created a niche market for replacement parts made by small-scale producers with relatively basic equipment. The quality of their products generally left much to be desired.

The tariff also inhibited the transfer of automobile technology to Australia. This was most clearly the case in the early 1920s, when a rapid shift to 'closed cars' occurred in North America and Europe, and by the mid-1930s when the integrated body/chassis structure became the technological standard. In the former case, the transition in Australia from 'roadsters' and 'tourers' (that is cars equipped with only a retractable hood for weather protection) to 'sedans' was considerably delayed by the duty on motor bodies, imposed to protect numerous companies that had emerged as constructors of horse-drawn carriages.[89] This was recognized by the members of the Motor Vehicle Importers' Association – another lobby group created by the tariff – and the major firms that had emerged in the motor body industry immediately after the First World War, notably Holden's and T.J. Richards and Sons.[90] They lobbied unsuccessfully for a relaxation of the high duties on 'closed' car imports to establish a local market for a product with more value added, and with greater potential for profit. Once volume sales were achieved, the idea was to have protective duties reimposed to cover the large firms' outlay on the necessary capital equipment.[91] They were, in effect, prepared to face a temporary reduction of market share for the prospect of a larger one later, with the elimination of most imports and many local small-scale producers.

With the maintenance of the high duties on motor bodies, closed cars only gradually came to predominate among vehicle sales in Australia during the second half of the 1920s. This lagged by several years the same development in the United States.[92] By the time the 'closed' car body was widely produced in Australia (consisting of metal panels with windows attached to a wooden frame), it had already been superseded overseas by the 'all-steel body' produced by the Budd company's presses.[93] The innovation was introduced by GM-H in Australia in 1936, almost a decade later than overseas.

Providing protective duties also inhibited technological progress in the local manufacture of a range of automotive components. Improvements in manufacturing technology overseas that lowered production costs often necessitated further tariff increases for the activity to survive in Australia. As an illustration, in 1924 the duty on gear wheels was raised from 10 to 55 per cent which was sufficient to stimulate local manufacture. However, by the late 1920s US prices had been halved and production only survived in Australia through the further duty increases of the Scullin government.[94]

For even the larger motor bodybuilders (the core of the automotive industry in Australia), the diversity of chassis types imported limited their access to economies of scale in manufacturing. By the early 1920s three relatively large body producers had emerged: Holden's and Richards in South Australia and the Melbourne Motor Body Company (later Ruskins). They were compelled to produce an extensive range of motor body styles for the diversity of imported chassis makes. Output diversity not only affected the ability of local firms to exploit scale economies. The wide range of motor bodies produced by the large manufacturers (who were most concerned about first satisfying the demands of their most important clients) occasionally caused production bottlenecks, creating shortages of bodies for small assemblers. In at least one instance, Nash automobiles which relied on Holden's for its bodies, was left without supplies as General Motors' requirements had priority.[95]

By the mid-1930s Australia had still not achieved the manufacture of complete vehicles. Since the Greene tariff of 1921, what had been a passive policy on the part of government (if not the bureaucracy) towards the industry was coming to an end. One of the reasons was technological. The integrated chassis and body was taking over from the simple 'put-a-body-on-a-chassis' process. Decisions had to be made about the direction the industry would take in the future, and if greater local manufacture were to be the aim, what means of assistance would be needed to achieve it. A second reason was political: quite simply the Lyons government explicitly decided that it would encourage the manufacture of complete motor cars and particularly engines, and it chose a new means of going about it. Tariff policy as it had been pursued in the 15 years since the First World War had failed and moreover tariffs had reached the stage where further increases would 'materially reduce demand'.[96] The means chosen was direct subsidy for engine manufacture as part of the government's trade diversion policy designed to boost economic recovery from the Depression and assist national development. These issues are dealt with in the following chapter.

## Notes

1. S. Butlin, *War Economy, 1939–1942* (Canberra, 1955), p. 9.
2. This is not to deny the tariff was used at times as a counter to unemployment. Similarly, a typical response to pressures on the balance of trade and payments was to increase the level of tariffs, as did the Scullin government with the onset of the Great Depression in the late 1920s.
3. G.H. Winder and C. MacPherson, *The Delusion of Protection* (Sydney, 1931), p. 129.
4. J. Laurent, ' "Industrial Policy" and the Australian Motor Vehicle Industry, 1920–1942', *Journal of the Royal Australian History Society*, LXXX (1994), pp. 91–115.
5. Named after Senator Walter Massey Greene, then Minister for Trade and Customs.
6. Frank Edwards, Secretary, Automotive Manufacturers' Association, 17 January, 1929 (AA ACT A461/1 D418/1/6, Part 1).
7. Chrysler cars first came to Australia during the early 1920s. They were initially sold by Maxwell dealers who later formed the basis for the Chrysler dealer network. Later, many dealers acquired Dodge and de Soto franchises and in 1935 18 of these dealers formed Chrysler Dodge de Soto Distributors (Australia) Pty Ltd (hereafter Chrysler Dodge). The company bought out T.J. Richards & Sons to build their bodies. Chrysler-Dodge and Chrysler Corporation in the United States were quite separate firms with the US firm having no share of the Australian operations.
8. Holden's origins as a large-scale producer of bodies date from the shipping embargo on motor bodies. S.A. Cheney, the South Australian distributor of Dodge cars approached H.J. Holden of Holden and Frost (later Holden's), an Adelaide saddlery firm which had undertaken some motor bodybuilding in the past, to undertake large-scale manufacture of a standard body for Dodge and Buick vehicles which were of similar size.

9. *Australian Motorist*, February 1938.
10. Trade diversion was designed to stifle Japanese and United States imports in the interests of British, and to a lesser extent, Australian producers; to divert trade towards 'good' customers for Australian exports and away from 'poor' customers. 'The measures boomeranged. Australian producers lost Japanese and American markets to a greater degree than supply from those countries was staunched' (B. Dyster and D. Meredith, *Australia in the International Economy in the Twentieth Century* (Cambridge, 1990), pp. 150–51).
11. R.C. Mills, 'The Tariff Board of Australia', *Economic Record*, III, 4 (1927), p. 53. Regarding 'revenue considerations', the contemporary Australian economist R.C. Mills was of the view that 'Since the [1914–18] war this aspect of the tariff has been considerably emphasized' (ibid.).
12. Hughes even wanted Germany to pay in cases where Australians had gone into debt to buy war bonds and had in consequence become bankrupt and 'lost their homes'. (See B. Baruch, *The Making of the Reparations and the Economic Sections of the Treaty* (New York, 1920), p. 6; T.W. Lamont, 'Reparations', in E.M. House and C. Seymour (eds) *What Really Happened At Paris* (New York, 1921), p. 269; C. Bergmann, *The History of Reparations* (London, 1927), p. 5.)
13. The states did not cede the power to impose income tax to the Commonwealth until the uniform Taxation Act, 1942. The states levied income tax until June 1942.
14. Cited in *Coach and Motor Builder*, June 1921.
15. At the time rural Australia was significantly more 'motorized' than the cities. In 1921 it was estimated that nearly 75 per cent of vehicle sales were to country residents (*Australian Motorist*, May 1921).
16. *Australian Motorist*, July 1921, September 1924 and June 1927.
17. See, for example, *Sydney Morning Herald*, 5 February and 10 July 1930.
18. *Sydney Morning Herald*, 25 September 1931.
19. In the late 1920s and early 1930s the Victorian Labor government introduced a series of measures which sought to protect the interests of rail- and tramways employees by limiting competition from private lorry and bus operators. Amendments to the Highways and Vehicles Act, and provisions of the Country and Urban Motor Omnibus Act and the Ministry of Transport Act had the practical effect of prohibiting the use of commercial passenger and freight carrying motor vehicles (of capacities specified to exclude taxis) where there was a rail or tram service in operation. (See *Australian Motorist*, especially March 1928; May 1928; September 1930; and April 1933.)
20. The State chambers were reconstituted to form a single Federal Chamber of Automotive Industries in 1939.
21. Winder and MacPherson, *The Delusion of Protection*, p. 129.
22. Butlin, *War Economy*, p. 9.
23. AA ACT A425/1 38/4030.
24. *Coach and Motor Builder*, November 1923.
25. By the late 1930s of the local market for stationary internal combustion engines of more than 7,000 units a year, local manufacturers held about 80 per cent (AA Vic. MP730/19 IT20). (See also AA ACT A425/1 39/9503, Ronaldson Bros. & Tippett to Minister of Trade and Customs, 4 July 1934. The letterhead of this firm, located in Ballarat, claimed it to be the 'Largest Manufacturers of Engines ... in the Southern Hemisphere'.)
26. That stationary engine producers did not move on to automobile engine manufacture was at least partly due to an apparently unbridgeable 'technological gap'

between the locally produced stationary engines, almost all with a power output of less than five hp operating under even loads at low revolutions, and the varying power output (usually more than 10 hp) and high piston speeds required of an automobile engine.

27. *Coach and Motor Builder*, November 1923; *Australian Motorist*, November 1923.
28. Reported in *Australian Motorist*, 1 August 1930, p. 649.
29. Ibid.
30. AA ACT A461/1 D418/1/6 Part 2.
31. L.J. Hartnett to E. Riley (General Manager of General Motors, New York) 10 December 1936 (GM-H Deposit, Mortlock Library, Adelaide (hereafter 'Mortlock'), BRG 213/65/9). See also Hansard, 16 November and 11 December 1938, for the suspicions in this matter of Frank Forde, the Deputy Leader of the Australian Labor Party Opposition at the time.
32. Hartnett to Riley, 10 December 1936.
33. Ibid.
34. Hansard, 7 December 1937.
35. Hartnett to Riley, 10 December 1936 (emphasis added). GM-H's original partners in the Commonwealth Aircraft Corporation were the Broken Hill Proprietary Company (BHP) and Broken Hill Smelters Pty Ltd. Imperial Chemical Industries (ICI) and the Orient Steamship Company soon joined them.
36. H.V.C. Thorby to J. Lyons, 15 July 1938 (AA ACT A6006/1).
37. The economist J.B. Brigden, a 'moderate' supporter of protection, identified this function of the tariff in the mid-1920s. (See J.B. Brigden, 'The Australian Tariff and the Standard of Living', *Economic Record*, I (1925), p. 29.)
38. Of these alleged malpractices, the *Australian Motorist* commented, 'Even Ned Kelly [a well known Australian highwayman] had loftier ideas of honor among thieves, and the National Government, which permits of pernicious methods in the Customs House, might study the history of the Kelly Gang' (*Australian Motorist*, September 1920, p. 35).
39. For example, Customs assessed duty on Italian goods 'on a conversion of 25 lira to the £ irrespective of the current value of the lira [about 65 lira to the £]' (*Australian Motorist*, November 1923, pp. 147–8). Thus, if an Australian purchased an Italian car for 32,500 lira it would cost £500 at 65 lira to the £. Customs would then assess the car's value-for-duty at the exchange rate of 25 lira to the £ (32,000l/25 = £1,300). For the importer of the Italian car, the artificial exchange rate and the 20 per cent *ad valorem* rate applying to the chassis bought for £500 would therefore have resulted in the payment of £260 in Customs duty. The same £500 chassis imported from Britain, which was subject to a (preferential) 10 per cent *ad valorem* tariff and a 'true' exchange rate, by Customs would pay £50 in duty.
40. 'A former Minister of Customs drew up ... what he considered to be the definition of a chassis. He decided to dissect and distribute the motor car chassis under numerous sections of the tariff; the result is that instead of the duty being what Parliament agreed to [12.5 per cent, general; and 7.5 per cent, preferential], we find that the tariff taxes collected by departmental regulations vary [from 30 per cent to 55 per cent, general; and 10 per cent to 35 per cent, preferential]' (quoted in *Australian Motorist*, November 1923, pp. 147–8).
41. *Australian Motorist*, November 1923.
42. *Australian Motorist*, May 1931.
43. Quoted in *Australian Motorist*, April 1926, p. 13.

44. In the mid-1920s, the *Australian Motorist* commented, 'Parliament fixed the duty on "chassis" and on "motor bodies" but omitted to say what is a chassis and what is a motor body ... Customs Ministers have so reduced the chassis that few parts are so classified. We find parts of a chassis classified as manufactured metals not elsewhere included, and duties of up to 55 per cent are collected, and not 12½ per cent as fixed by Parliament' (*Australian Motorist*, 1 July 1925, p. 585). The major components of motor cars were defined for tariff purposes by Customs General Order (G.O.) 577 for much of the 1920s. This was replaced by G.O.B 112 in September 1928.
45. *Australian Motorist*, May 1931, p. 389.
46. Ibid.
47. Tariff Board, *Engines and Chassis for Motor Vehicles* (Canberra, 1938), p. 11.
48. Ibid., pp. 9, 15.
49. Zentrales Staats Archiv Potsdam, Auswärtiges Amt, Abt. II, Bd. I, Krogmann to Foreign Office, 6 May 1933.
50. AA ACT A461/1 D418/1/6 Part 1.
51. See 'Tariffs and the "motorization" of society' later in this chapter.
52. To our knowledge no formal estimates of demand elasticities for automobiles are available for this period in Australia. However, the following statement from the Tariff Board's report on the industry suggests that at the ruling prices it is likely to have been relatively high: 'Evidence submitted to the board was strong enough to convince it that any appreciable increase in the price of popular cars would *materially* reduce the demand' (Tariff Board, *Engines and Chassis*, p. 20, emphasis added).
53. That high levels of protection encourage entry of firms and provide an environment leading to markets characterized by many sub-optimally sized plants and enterprises is well known in the economics literature. See for example R. Caves, I. Ward and P. Wright, *Australian Industry: Structure, Conduct and Performance*, 2nd edn (Sydney, 1987).
54. While Canada shares with Australia a protectionist development of manufacturing, the levels of protection available to manufacturing were generally lower than in Australia, and this was true for automobile production. An outline of the development of protection in the two countries may be found in R.M. Conlon, *Distance and Duties* (Ottawa, 1986), Ch. 2.
55. Motor Vehicle Manufacturers Association, *Facts and Figures of the Automotive Industry* (Toronto, various years); Dominion Bureau of Statistics, *Automobile Statistics for Canada* (Ottawa, various years); Commonwealth Bureau of Census and Statistics, *Production Bulletin* (Canberra, 1919–20 to 1938); AA ACT A461/1 D418/1/6 Parts 1 and 3.
   While in some parts of the Australian industry there was some degree of rationalization, this often involved merely a change of ownership of assets, such as the formation of GM-H, caused by the takeover of Holden's by General Motors in 1931. There was also some rationalization of the tyre industry in the late 1920s, with the merger of Dunlop and Perdriau and the combined firm's acquisition of a majority shareholding in Barnet Glass, the third largest producer. However, this did not involve a rationalization of plants to exploit economies of scale (J. Stanton, 'Protection, Market Structure and Firm Behavior: Inefficiency in the Early Australian Tyre Industry', *Australian Economic History Review*, XXIV, 2 (1984), p. 102).
56. For example in 1936–37 in Australia 'motor body construction and repair' employed 12,267 persons in 201 factories, an average of 61; 4,626 persons in 85

factories were engaged in 'motor vehicles and cycles construction and assembly', an average of 54 persons per factory. In Canada in 1936, 12,933 persons were employed in 16 factories engaged in 'motor vehicle manufacturing', an average of 808 persons per factory; and 6,842 persons in 85 factories engaged in producing 'automobile parts and accessories', an average of 80 persons per factory.

57.  It is difficult to compare outputs of the motor car manufacturing industry in the two countries in the interwar period, owing to differences in the Canadian and Australian statisticians' definitions of the activities covered by the published data. As an illustration, for Canada in 1936 there were 162,200 motor vehicles produced (of which 128,400 were automobiles). Total employment in motor vehicle manufacturing was 12,933 persons (separate figures for employment in automobile manufacturing are not available), an average output of 12.5 motor vehicles per person. For Australia in 1935–36 there were 67,300 motor bodies produced and 12,008 'hands' employed in motor body construction and repair (no separate data are available for those employed in repair) – an average of 5.6 motor bodies per hand. In the same year 74,100 unassembled chassis were imported and 4,007 hands employed in motor vehicle construction and assembly – an average of 18.5 chassis per hand. Both bodybuilding and chassis assembly was required to produce a finished car. Taking the number of completed cars to be about 71,000 and the total number of employees to be between 10,000 and 14,000, the average number of cars produced per employee was between 7.1 and 5.1 cars per employee during the year. See R.M. Conlon and J.A. Perkins, *The Origins and Interwar Development of the Automobile Industry in Australia and Canada*, School of Economics Discussion Paper (University of New South Wales, 1996), for a comprehensive list of statistical sources.

58.  AA ACT A461/1 B418/1/6 Part 2.

59.  AA ACT A425/1 36/10700.

60.  AA ACT A461/1 D418/1/6 Part 1.

61.  About 100 importers who assembled vehicles throughout the Commonwealth supplied the remainder of the market (Tariff Board, *Engines and Chassis*, p. 12).

62.  As an illustration of the diversity of models produced, the Melbourne Motor Body Company was making 41 different types of bodies when visited on a day in late 1926 (*Australian Motorist*, December 1926). A further illustration was provided by L.J. Hartnett who became managing director of GM-H during the 1930s: 'In one year the Woodville plant of Holden's produced 78 models of body, in volumes ranging from 18 to 4,000' (L.J. Hartnett, *Big Wheels and Little Wheels* (Melbourne, 1963), p. 63).

63.  See E.D. Kennedy, *The Automobile Industry* (New York, 1934), p. 74; S.A. Cheney, *From Horse to Horse Power* (Adelaide, 1965), pp. 63, 98ff.

64.  See R.P. Thomas, 'Style Changes and the Automobile Industry During the Roaring Twenties', in L.P. Cain and P.J. Uselding (eds) *Business Enterprise and Economic Change* (Kent, Ohio, 1973).

65.  AA ACT A425/1 45/3666.

66.  *Coach and Motor Builder*, February 1921.

67.  *Coach and Motor Builder*, October 1923.

68.  'There is still a serious dearth of skilled body-builders in Australia, and, due to our apprentice laws, any man who can hack a piece of wood has been earning big money, due to the necessity of turning out orders for coachwork – somehow' (*Australian Motorist*, September 1923).

69.  General Motors especially developed 'Styling' as a challenge to the market dominance the Ford Model T had achieved by the early 1920s.

70. See R.P. Thomas, 'Style Changes and the Automobile Industry During the Roaring Twenties', in L.P. Cain and P.J. Uselding (eds) *Business Enterprise and Economic Change* (Kent, Ohio, 1973).

71. Ibid., p. 129.

72. D.G. Rhys, 'Concentration in the Inter-War Motor Industry', *Journal of Transport History*, New Series, III, 4 (1976), p. 253.

73. The first all-steel bodies were produced in Australia in 1935/36, nearly a decade after their first appearance overseas, and then they were for a coupé model. The first for a sedan was not made until 1937 (Ibid.).

74. *Sydney Morning Herald*, 3 November 1936.

75. *Australian Motorist*, May 1921.

76. C.F. Baldwin, 'The Automotive Market in Australia', [US] *Trade Information Bulletin*, 611 (1929), p. 26.

77. AA ACT A461/1 D418/1/65 Part 3.

78. AA Vic. MP394/1 5/81/15.

79. *Coach and Motor Builder*, June 1925.

80. C. Forster, *Industrial Development in Australia, 1920–1930* (Canberra, 1964) p. 34.

81. *Australian Motorist*, July 1919, May 1921 and October 1925.

82. For Australia in 1926 the ratio of motor vehicles to population was 52 per thousand inhabitants; for New Zealand in 1924 the ratio was 54/1000; in 1931 for Australia 81/1000, and New Zealand 130/1000; in 1937 for Australia 102/1000, and New Zealand 163/1000. (Sources: Populations: Australian Bureau of Census and Statistics, *Yearbook of Australia* (various years) and Department of Statistics, *Official Yearbook of New Zealand* (1991). Motor Vehicle registrations: *Australian Motorist*, March 1926 and November 1938; Australian Bureau of Census and Statistics, *Australian Yearbook* (1930); Tariff Board, *Engines and Chassis*, App. C.)

83. *Australian Motorist*, March 1925

84. *Australian Motorist*, February 1921 and March 1925.

85. Tariff Board, *Engines and Chassis*, App. E.

86. G. Maxcy and A. Silberston, *The Motor Industry* (London, 1959), p. 48. The estimate is based on a car with a 1,500 cc engine travelling 8,000 miles in a year.

87. *Australian Motorist*, March 1935.

88. AA ACT A461/1 D418/1/8 Part 3.

89. In the USA the proportion of 'closed cars' in total sales increased from 10 to 22 per cent between 1919 and 1922, came to predominate in the mid-1920s and effectively eliminated the 'roadster' (Thomas, 'Style Changes and the Automobile Industry', p. 128).

90. The last company became Richards Industries in 1941 and was eventually to become part of Chrysler Australia after the Second World War.

91. *Coach and Motor Builder*, February 1925. The major Australian motor body producers were responding to increasing imports of completed 'closed' cars, in spite of the heavy import duty involved.

92. By 1925 around 75 per cent of the bodies produced by the Fisher company for General Motors were of the 'closed' type (*Coach and Motor Builder*, May 1925).

93. Rhys, 'Concentration in the Inter-War Motor Industry', p. 253.

94. AA ACT A461/1 D418/1/6 Part 1.

95. To deal with the problem, Chevrolet panels were hammered into shape to 'fit' the Nash chassis (AA ACT A425/1 45/3666).

96. Tariff Board, *Engines and Chassis*, p. 12.

# 4 Stalled: Politics and Government Policies of the Later 1930s

## Trade diversion and the motor vehicle engine bounty proposal

By the mid-1930s the tariff that had evolved since the First World War had encouraged the development of an automotive industry that was essentially composed of two elements. One comprised the many local producers of mainly replacement parts who were sheltered by high, protective tariffs. Over much of the period protective rates had been progressively applied to more and more components. In the view of the Australian Automobile Manufacturers' Association 'full' local manufacture would eventually follow inevitably from the establishment of components manufacture. By 1936, experience had demonstrated this view to be fallacious. Providing high levels of protection for an increasing range of automobile components had created a fragmented components industry with many small producers, short production runs, poor product quality and outmoded technology.[1] Rather than the manufacture of a 'completed' motor car, the tariff inhibited the adoption of mass production methods for the manufacture of either spare parts or original equipment, but was unable to encourage any commercial manufacture of the motive force of the vehicle: its engine.

Dominating the Australian market for motor cars was the second element of the industry – the leading North American-based producers. Their products were made up of locally built bodies (protected by high tariffs and international transport costs), and imported, locally assembled chassis (the components of which as original equipment were subject to low revenue duties). By 1935 GM-H accounted for almost 40 per cent of sales, Ford for just over 20 per cent, and Chrysler-Dodge for 15 per cent.[2] The manufacturing/assembly arrangements were highly profitable, and not surprisingly, the major producers did not want them to change.

By the mid-1930s, however, the automotive industry had reached a turning point. Of likely future importance was newly emerging technology: the development of the integrated body/chassis, first introduced by Opel, General Motors' German subsidiary in the mid-1930s.[3] The implications of this for local production were realized by L.J. Hartnett, then managing director of GM-H when he informed Prime Minister Joseph Lyons in 1935:

> in the course of the next two or three years ... the Australian Government and the Australian body industry will be faced with a major issue as to whether to move on, and deeper into the manufacturing of a car, or whether to go backwards and allow more of the car to be imported.[4]

Of more immediate importance was that if a complete car were to be produced in Australia, and particularly if engines were to be manufactured, it had become apparent that further broadening and heightening of the protective tariff structure which sheltered the industry in the 1920s and early 1930s would, by increasing consumer prices, 'materially reduce demand'.[5] An alternative means of stimulating local manufacture had to be found.

All of these influences on the industry were superimposed on an international trading environment that in 1936 was only beginning to recover from the worst of the Depression. While Australia's trading position had been assisted by the 1932 Ottawa Agreement,[6] four years later full recovery was still far off. In order to provide a further boost to economic recovery and national development, Sir Henry Gullett, the minister directing negotiations for trade treaties, announced to Parliament the Lyons government's intention of implementing a policy of 'trade diversion'. According to Gullett,

> We have decided that circumstance compels us, however reluctantly, to follow the policy adopted by a large number of countries throughout the world, and divert a certain amount of our import trade from countries which are very indifferent purchasers of Australian exports, ... to countries which are, or recently have been heavy purchasers of our exports.

The government confidently expected that they would 'become greater customers if we increase our purchases from them'.[7]

A central part of the policy was halting some imports of commodities with a view to their manufacture in the Commonwealth.[8] 'The chief of these is the motor chassis, which we hope will be manufactured in Australia on a large scale in a very few years.'[9] Without reference to the Tariff Board, he announced the government's intention to pay bounties for the production of engines and chassis with the aim of 'encouraging the manufacture of motor engines and chassis in order to permit the manufacture of complete motor cars in this country'.[10] The bounty payments were to be financed by a fund created by the imposition of an additional duty of 7d. per lb. on all motor vehicle engines and chassis imported into Australia (the equivalent of about £5 per car).[11] As a result, the government anticipated that 'satisfactory engine production can be commenced within two years, and within five or six years, Australia should be producing 80 per cent of its engine requirements'.[12]

### National interest or self interest? Conflict and cooperation among the leading firms

The bounty proposal was highly controversial, and the over the next four years there was bitter conflict among the various interests. Opponents of the scheme representing the retail motor trade, particularly its mouthpiece the *Australian Motorist*, were especially vocal. 'The offer of a bounty for locally produced engines to displace imported unassembled chassis is viewed as a step to create a monopoly with consequent destruction of the motor industry as it exists.'[13] It had no doubt with whom (or rather where) the blame lay: 'Canberra is instructing the motor industry amongst others, how to conduct its business, and business is being ruined'; its results were a 'travesty of Government interference'.[14] The Chamber of Automotive Industries of New South Wales expressed its view that the government had considerably underestimated the task involved in full manufacture. 'Contrary to some opinions it [is] considered by the motor trade that the building of a complete motor vehicle in Australia presented colossal difficulties.'[15]

The reaction was strong and widespread, and in late 1936 the government finally gave in to pressure for an inquiry by the Tariff Board, though it loaded the terms of reference. When the Minister for Trade and Customs, T.W. White, referred the matter to the Tariff Board for inquiry and report, the Board was to investigate 'The best means of giving effect to the Government's policy of establishing in Australia the manufacture of engines and chassis of motor vehicles, with consideration given to the general national and economic aspect.'[16] It was, therefore, not a matter of *if* the industry should be established, but how. Indeed, the last phrase referring to 'consideration' of the economics of the scheme was an afterthought, included only after pressure by the Country Party.[17]

Despite the apparently strong and obvious support of the government for the proposal for almost immediate, full manufacture, the Board ignored the instructions in its rider. It found that 'it would be unwise at present to encourage or enforce the manufacture of the complete motor vehicle in Australia [development in one step]', but Board members were 'unable to agree on the best means of giving effect to the Government's policy'.[18] Such a result was hardly welcome to proponents of the project, and in a memorandum to the Board published in its report, White, as the Minister for Trade and Customs, expressed dissent from many of its conclusions. He claimed that the Board's objections to the government's policy could have been equally applied to every secondary industry in Australia that had been created and had flourished under protective measures. To this the Board retorted, 'The expansion of local industries referred to by the minister has taken place gradually. The dramatic and sweeping changes visualized in "development in one step" would create a position for which there is no precedent.'[19] To White, the reason for the Board's opposition was obviously that 'the preponderance of evidence tendered to the Board related to the disadvantages associated with domestic production'.[20] By accepting this evidence, in his view the Board's conclusions lacked balance and the value of the report as a guide to the government was lessened as a consequence.

For proponents of the scheme the problem was that the potential producers – at least the serious ones – were those who had provided the evidence on which the Board had relied for its adverse conclusion. They saw the proposal as contrary to their interests. It had even been a struggle to get GM-H to participate in the Board's inquiry at all. Hartnett 'endeavored to sidestep giving any testimony ... but finally did appear after a third request, when he was told he might be subpoenaed if he refused'.[21] The terms of reference were the reason for Hartnett's reluctance. He, as the representative of GM-H,

> received a request from the Secretary of the Tariff Board asking that we give evidence, but I replied to the effect that we could not fulfill this obligation as long as the terms of the inquiry were on the basis that the manufacture of the car had to be accomplished. By this means I hoped to have the terms of reference altered.[22]

In this, however, he was unsuccessful.

There was no doubt that Chrysler, Ford and General Motors, and their local representatives were united in their opposition to the government's proposal. When eventually Hartnett did appear before the Board, he presented the views of GM-H succinctly: 'Definitely we do not favor the manufacture of cars in Australia; we prefer the nice conditions that now exist.'[23] Chrysler simply informed the Board that it would definitely not enter into a manufacturing programme. Ford was openly hostile to the government's plans.[24] According to H.C. French, Managing Director of Ford, 'The proposition [is] at heart, uneconomic, and the efforts of the Government to create a local industry with the intention of diverting imports could be better directed into channels other than the motor car industry.'[25] However, in the face of the threat the plan posed to them, the three firms were also attempting to protect their individual interests should the proposal go ahead.

Throughout the period of the currency of the plan – from the time of Gullett's original proposal in 1936 to its effective end in mid-1940 – each of the three major producers or their local representatives were busy insuring their own positions, often to the detriment of their 'allies'. Chrysler's attempted insurance was indirect. It was the US Chrysler Corporation's policy not to invest abroad, however a major Chrysler distributor was exerting pressure (unsuccessfully) on the Victorian Premier and Cabinet to purchase 30 acres of land at Fishermen's Bend, next to GM-H, on the same favourable terms the land had been sold to GM-H. Of these efforts Hartnett noted in early 1937:

> [The] disturbing element is the fact that one indirectly interested party told me Nathan [the distributor concerned] and the Chrysler group are convinced [the]

government will succeed in its endeavors to have a car entirely manufactured in Australia, and they are taking this action as an insurance against losing their distribution business so they will be in a position to participate as manufacturers of the entire vehicle.[26]

From GM-H's point of view, Ford had also been up to no good. According to Hartnett, H.C. French, a Canadian, saw his loyalty as being to Ford Canada which wholly owned Ford's operations in Australia. 'What is uppermost in Mr French's mind is to preserve his company as an outlet for Ford Canada and if it means treading roughly on Ford US, I do not think he would hesitate.' The means of preserving the Canadian interest (and disadvantaging GM-H) was by lobbying 'to have a much lower preferential tariff established on Canadian raw materials as well as having the [local] "content" [of cars assembled in Australia] raised to 65%–70% at the same time making it impossible to import Pontiac, Oldsmobile, Buick and other makes'.[27]

Meanwhile, for the other US producers, GM-H was the problem. In a report of a meeting in New York of the Export Committee of the Auto Manufacturers' Association R.A. May noted,

our American competitors generally feel that GM has failed in Australia to declare itself with any definiteness as to the present Australian government proposal for complete auto manufacture – both Messrs Vaniman [Chrysler Corporation Export Division] and Budd [Packard Motors Export Corporation] very positively state that reports which they have from Australia are to the effect that due to an apparent inability to make up our minds in Australia as to what course of action to follow in regard to this official Australian government attitude and program, we have not only failed to make our viewpoint clear, but we have also made the situation considerably more difficult – by leading on the Australian government to believe we support its proposal.[28]

That the position of GM was perceived by others to be ambiguous is not surprising in view of correspondence within the firm at the time. On the one hand, the Board of General Motors wished to convey its attitude in the tariff inquiry as: 'Definitely we do not favor the manufacture of cars in Australia;'[29] on the other, it adopted tactics of pursuing 'a neutral course of neither subscribing to, nor drastically opposing government policies and desires re automobile manufacture in Australia'.[30]

In any event, GM-H thought it had already taken out sufficient insurance to preserve its future interests by assisting the Lyons government's aspiration to build aircraft in Australia. In 1935 the government was concerned about the likely inability to procure defence aircraft from overseas in time of need, and invited GM-H, the Broken Hill Proprietary Company, and Broken Hill Associated Smelters Pty Ltd to participate in the project. The three companies eventually formed the Commonwealth Aircraft Corporation in October 1936.[31] At the time, GM-H saw few immediate benefits from its participation, which had been vigorously supported by R.G. Menzies (then Attorney General) and

Earle Page (leader of the Country Party in coalition government With the United Australia Party (UAP)). Hartnett observed that both politicians were in this regard 'highly appreciative of GM-H activities and undertakings'. Participation did not 'suit' GM-H, but Hartnett was strongly aware of the value of goodwill with the government then and in the future. He was confident that the government's expression of its goodwill would be its 'endeavour to treat us fairly and on as preferential grounds as is possible for them'.[32]

In view of the clear opposition to the bounty plan expressed in evidence by the major producer/assemblers in the Tariff Board hearings, Sir Henry Gullett had come to believe that he was mistaken in agreeing with the decision to refer the proposal for motor car production to the Tariff Board. He later told Parliament,

> I recognize now that that was a grave blunder. I doubt very much whether anything but a negative result [could have been] obtained from the board ... for the simple reason that the only relevant testimony obtainable ... was from those interested in the importation of motor chassis into the Commonwealth or their exportation to this country from overseas.[33]

Gullett was quite right in his assessment. The attitude of GM-H was governed by a very fundamental objective: 'Protect [the] Corporation Investment in terms of Capital and Earning Power'. Among the means of accomplishing this was: 'Avoidance at any cost of being drawn into a venture which may be justifiable in terms of Australia's net object, but may not be commercially sound from [the Corporation's] viewpoint.'[34] The way the firm went about this was described three years later, in private correspondence to Hartnett from H.B. Phillips, General Motors' Regional Director. He referred to the company's policy of the time as 'one of passive resistance to natural aspirations and the trend of secondary industry, particularly as applied to auto manufacture'.[35] Ford's attitude of opposition was evident throughout its evidence to the Board, but its accompanying lobbying tactics, according to Hartnett, undermined its position.

> Mr French, the Managing Director of Ford adopted the old method – briefed several lobbyists and agitators and personally went to Canberra with these men, approached each member of the House and was able to prevail on half a dozen to take up his cause. The results were disastrous ... practically every newspaper throughout Australia came out with the headline 'Dirty lobbying accusations by Minister against Canadian car company.[36]

While Hartnett was critical of Ford's tactics in dealing with the government, his own, to some, ambiguous tactics, were hardly a success.

### Political conflict and the bounty scheme

During the two years following Gullett's announcement it became apparent that support for the scheme within the government parties was far from universal. The period saw two of the major proponents of the project, Gullett and White, leave the Ministry. Gullett who left shortly after tabling the bounty proposal, soon expressed doubts about the government's good faith regarding the bounty fund, and its commitment to the aims of the project. The funds collected for the bounty were an early source of controversy. According to Gullett,

> money has not been earmarked, but has been spent in other directions, or allocated for other purposes. ... I submit that the Government by its action, or rather inaction, in having failed to set aside for the specific purpose which was intended, and for which the House very emphatically asserted it should be used, has not kept faith with this proposed new industry.[37]

Indeed, the original proposal conveyed the clear impression that a separate trust account would be set up for the bounty fund, and the Labor Opposition was quick to support Gullett.

> The motor manufacturing interests were told that a bounty would be paid and that as a guarantee of good faith a special tax on imported chassis would be imposed in order to provide the necessary fund. What do we find? No such fund has been provided by the Treasurer; on the contrary, he has collected a special duty under false pretences.[38]

The delay between the reference to the Tariff Board (16 November 1936), and the release of the report (28 September 1938) was also a cause of suspicion. By November 1938, with still no discernable action by the government, there were allegations of undue influence being brought to bear to delay and frustrate the whole scheme: 'There can be no doubt that because of underground engineering, of the pressure, that has been brought to bear upon the Government from outside sources, the whole proposal has been sidetracked.'[39] Gullett went further: 'If [the Government] will not establish this industry, then there is some sinister and mysterious influence stopping it, and it is well for one to speak plainly on the subject.'[40]

So who was responsible? By the time Gullett had made this accusation White had resigned, allegedly as a protest against industry and trade policy being put in the hands of an 'inner Cabinet coterie' of free traders hostile to the project.[41] Behind all of this, the influence of the Ford Company was seen: 'almost the whole of the opposition, indeed hostility, to the manufacture of motor car engines in Australia was brought about by the activities of certain big importing companies, the chief ... being the Ford Company of Canada [sic].'[42] Who in government was behind the delay, and most receptive to Ford's alleged hostile activities? The Deputy Leader of the Opposition, Frank Forde, had a likely candidate: 'I greatly suspect the influence of the Treasurer [Casey] who represents the electorate of Corio, in which is situated the Ford assembly works. I also suspect the influence of the Minister for Commerce [Earle Page].'[43]

Forde's suspicion of Casey's interest in the matter was well founded if Hartnett of GM-H was correct in his assessment: '[Casey] is the member for Geelong [sic] where the Ford factory is situated, and as Mr French of the Ford Company often states, Ford has him in the bag.' However, on balance, Hartnett doubted this worked in Ford's interests. 'The result is that Cabinet generally discount Mr Casey and it looks as though possibly as a result he might become the Australian Government representative in London replacing Stanley Bruce.' Hartnett was of the view that French had

> played his cards rather badly by becoming extremely excited about it and of filling Casey, the Federal Treasurer, with a great deal of detailed data and a certain amount of invective against the government. In the main I have supported Mr French although I do not go hand in hand with him as I do not envy his particular relationship with the government.

Hartnett believed in a broader approach to lobbying:

> I consider it a *faux pas* on the part of the Ford Co. too heavily mesmerizing or overselling a particular Minister believing he can fight a cause for them where as actually he is suspect on the subject in Cabinet discussions. We learnt from this experience, and although I am particularly friendly with two Ministers, I have endeavored to spread my contacts throughout the Cabinet.[44]

When in October 1938 the government formally called for proposals from potential manufacturers to enter into an arrangement to produce engines under the bounty by 31 March 1939, 'preliminary inquiries' were received from Ford, GM-H, Chrysler and Nash but their responses were certainly not encouraging, Ford's least of all.[45] The company replied on 29 March 1939, stating that it was able 'to definitely indicate that the local manufacture of engines, even when supported by the suggested bounty, is unattractive'. In fact for the period of its existence, the bounty proposal failed to attract a single, serious bidder from within the industry.[46]

Gullett was scathing about the whole process.

> The moment the Government lifts its hand it can have this industry on extraordinarily good terms. ... That the Government knows. It has known it for two years, but it does nothing. Why this mysterious inactivity? ... When the proposal was sent to the Tariff Board by the Government its only purpose was to stifle it. When this invitation [to potential manufacturers was made] it was with the intention of killing the scheme or of delaying it as long as possible. ... The Minister for Trade and Customs said today that the Government would not extend its offer beyond the 31st March. I welcome that statement, because it is at last an honest declaration by the Government that it is not going on with the industry.[47]

When no proposals of substance had been elicited by the 31 March deadline, as far as Parliament was concerned, the matter then lapsed. The apparent inaction brought protests deploring the uncertainty and disorganization caused by the government's delay, and to deal with the problem, 'a statement on the subject became necessary so that the general principles in the Government's mind could be plainly set out'.[48] The new Prime Minister, R.G. Menzies, made the statement in the House of Representatives on 17 May 1939.[49] He announced that the Ministry had definitely decided that the motor vehicle industry should be established.

> Consideration of defense preparedness, industrial expansion, conservation of overseas funds, immigration, employment and the utilization of raw materials are among the principal reasons why the Commonwealth Government has decided that motor vehicle engines and chassis, are to be manufactured in Australia, and that there be no undue delay in establishing the industry.[50]

## War and the Motor Vehicles Agreement Act

With war imminent, defence was now the first in the list of considerations for the government's policy towards the industry. An 'indirect contribution to defense' had been a consideration when Gullett introduced the Government's plan to Parliament in 1936, though then its priority had been much lower. That the industry could make a contribution to the nation's defence was a view shared by others in the government at the time, apparently including Menzies, then the Attorney-General, and Sir Archdale Parkhill, then Minister for Defense. In December 1936, Hartnett described his interpretation of the government's view of the industry's defence potential following detailed private conversations with them and other members of the Federal Cabinet during the 1936 Premiers' Conference in Adelaide.

> Defense partly prompts [the] conviction [that motor vehicles should be fully manufactured in Australia], not so much on the score of the ability of such a factory to produce cars and trucks for defense purposes, but that the factory could be adapted – small tanks and ammo generally. Also these factories would be developing a training [of] mechanics who would be well versed in operating machinery to produce munitions.[51]

At the Tariff Board hearings in 1937, however, those who believed in defence benefits from the industry received little support in evidence. When it was claimed that a fully developed motor industry in Australia could be swung over to the production of tanks, armoured cars and other mechanized units, essential for war, it was strongly disputed by Ford, in keeping with its opposition to the whole project.[52] More important (in view of Ford's obvious interest), the defence rationale had been provided with little support from the government's own defence advisors. The Secretary of the Department of Defense, Mr L. Shepherd, while welcoming 'the establishment of the motor engine industry in Australia', gave his department's view that manufacture of engines would be of limited defence use, and that from the defence standpoint it 'cannot be said that the industry of itself, is gravely necessary'.[53]

While at the time of Menzies' announcement in May 1939 two years had passed since this evidence had been given, and there were now strong indications that Australia would very soon be at war, the Department of Defense was still apparently sceptical of the potential importance of complete manufacture of automobiles to Australia's defence. Indeed, only a week before Menzies' statement, the Minister for Defense had told the House of Representatives – in the midst of the crisis over Danzig and in the context of Britain's guarantee of Poland's western frontier in March of that year – 'My department has not at any time recommended the manufacture of motor car chassis [that is including engines] in Australia as a vital defense need.'[54]

The bounty proposal was finally enacted in December (Motor Vehicle Engine Bounty Act 1939 (No. 69 of 1939)), by which time, of course, the country was at war with Germany.[55] The government's view of the necessity of the industry was made clear. 'There are probably few industries in a nation's industrial make-up that rank higher than the motor car engine and chassis manufacturing industry. ... Today one of the standards of a nation's wartime strength is measured in terms of motor car production.'[56] The Act had the Opposition's full support. 'The Opposition rejoices to see that the government is making this move.'[57] Indeed 'This is one of the most popular pieces of legislation ever to be introduced to this Parliament.'[58] It was not popular with at least some members of the Country Party, however, and certainly the defence rationale was for them quite unconvincing.[59] In debate, H.L. Anthony disparaged the defence significance of the industry project, referring to Shepherd's evidence to the Board two years earlier. His colleague J. McEwen went further.

> Notwithstanding the most consistent and persistent efforts, the board was quite unable to secure evidence from any senior defense officer, either civil or military, to the effect that the establishment of this industry was at all concerned with the defense security of Australia. ... Notwithstanding the fact that the Tariff Board pointed out unanimously that the whole of the evidence which was placed before it by the defense authorities was contrary to the view that the development of this industry is necessary for defense purposes, we find the present government has stressed that aspect in giving its reasons for the introduction of this bill.[60]

It is ironic in the light of his post-war protectionist record as Minister for Trade and Industry that McEwen then expressed the view that, 'We should surely at a time like this pay some regard to the circumstances in which certain major secondary industries were established in this country years ago. We should not be willing to establish uneconomic industries merely at the whim of Government and regardless of economic considerations.'[61]

Even the Labor Party, supporters of the Bill, conceded the Country Party's fundamental point. Consider the following (almost Gilbertian) exchange;

| Mr Curtin [Lab] | Nobody will dispute the relevancy of the industry to defense preparedness. |
| Mr McEwan [C.P.] | No defense official will confirm the honorable gentleman's point of view. |
| Mr Beasley [Lab] | Not today? |
| Mr McEwan | No. |
| Mr Curtin | All right, not today; but defense experts frequently wake up tomorrow to the fact the country is in peril.[62] |

McEwan's point regarding the economics of the plan was well made, however. The funds that had accumulated since 1936 when the additional duty was imposed, to December 1939 when the bounty proposal was eventually enacted, exceeded £1 million, but even this was not enough to encourage an entrant. The reluctance of GM-H was not only a product of the economics of the scheme. The company had always been wary of the politics of the bounty proposal. In July 1937, Phillips and Hartnett had briefed the General Motors Board that a foreign-controlled firm, 'receiving a specific amount of bounty collected in turn from the taxpayer and that company earning substantial profits which are remitted abroad would be in an untenable position both from a political and national point of view'.[63] Following the passing of the Act, Phillips was more specific in where he thought the potential damage would occur. 'For a foreign-controlled enterprise to receive direct government bounty or subsidy would be political dynamite from the government's point of view, and would also lay the recipient open to rigid government control interference and public criticism.'[64]

In view of the lack of response by the major firms to the scheme, the Menzies' government then apparently dragooned Mr W.J. Smith, managing director, on behalf of his firm, Australian Consolidated Industries Ltd (ACI), into undertaking the project. According to Smith,

> Mr Menzies, then Prime Minister, and his Ministers approached me and pressed upon me a patriotic duty. I told them frankly that I could not entertain their project. But they were insistent, and after frequent interviews, they finally broke down my resistance. At this stage, the so-called monopoly was offered for five years, the maximum manufacture to be 25,000 cars a year in a field of 80,000 cars. When at last I agreed to meet the situation, I told Menzies that I would tear up the contract if any USA or British manufacturers would see Australia through.[65]

### A patriotic duty: Australian Consolidated Industries and the so-called monopoly

The first public mention of ACI's participation was on 22 December 1939, though rumours had been circulating at least since early December.[66] Their substance turned out to be right when the Minister for Trade and Customs, J.N. Lawson, announced that a company with a nominal capital of £1 million (initially subscribed to £250,000) would soon be formed to manufacture engines and chassis.[67] In May, Menzies had stated among the principles upon which the government would insist were that 'no single company would be granted a manufacturing monopoly'.[68] Now, in December, and in a complete reversal of 'principle', to 'protect the investment of Australian money ... the Commonwealth government has undertaken to use its powers under the National Security Act to safeguard the interests of the Australian company from foreign or foreign-controlled companies which might desire to manufacture motor cars in Australia'.[69] While defence was cited as the major reason for the extraordinary measures, the government also suggested it had an eye for the future: it was 'anxious to see the new industry established now, so that when the war ends, it may be available as a nucleus for expansion, to help to deal with the problem of employment that must inevitably arise'.[70]

Neither this nor the defence rationale was sufficient to offset the resulting uproar produced by the new proposals. If the Labor Opposition, led by John Curtin, favoured the bounty, it certainly did not favour the establishment of a monopoly. It was incensed about the secrecy surrounding the agreement[71] and of the proposal in which 'The new monopoly feeds certain groups of shareholders as a direct outcome of Government policy.'[72] The newspapers condemned it, particularly the *Adelaide Advertiser*, in a state, South Australia, which had special interests in building motor bodies and other motor parts. It referred to the 'indecent and inexplicable haste' with which the agreement was concluded, and declared that 'even if such a gift [the bounty] had been authorized by Parliament, it should have been announced and not unostentatiously handed over'. It further declared that 'the government, its responsibilities enormously heightened by the War ... ventured to announce that it will use its tremendous emergency powers for the unheard-of purpose of making a strictly commercial monopoly unassailable'.[73]

In the coming months the Opposition pursued the matter relentlessly, and gradually the story behind the agreement began to surface. It turned out that an arrangement of some kind had been in the works for some time. According to Curtin, Menzies consulted with 'certain representatives' in Canberra on 4 May 1939, making it clear that the government was not prepared to grant a monopoly.[74] As a result of the meeting, on 20 May Hartnett wrote to Menzies expressing the opinion that there was room for only one undertaking: 'to provide the necessary degree of protection for two manufacturers ... would mean that the existing importing and manufacturing interests would be severely restricted in their activities even to a disastrous extent'. However Hartnett was not interested in a GM-H monopoly. He saw potential political problems

> If one organization were to fill the role of sole manufacturer and was ... a foreign owned concern, we anticipate major difficulty in sustaining its position if there were a level of profit commensurate with the hazards of such an undertaking and operating as a virtual monopoly with government protection and assistance.[75]

Clearly Menzies accepted Hartnett's opinion regarding the need for only a single manufacturer for the project to be viable, for he then called the premiers together, suggesting that the states transfer their powers to the Commonwealth to enable it to confine manufacture to a single unit. 'The meeting produced no results, but nevertheless, it was clear that Customs officials regarded the Prime Minister's outlook as settled.'[76]

Having accepted the economic imperative of a single producer, Menzies then had to deal with the politics of the plan: the need for a local candidate if a monopoly were to be granted. By the middle of July ACI was the government's (or at least Menzies') choice. At that time according to Curtin,

> W.J. Smith was in Canberra [dealing with another matter] and the suggestion was made to him that his company might consider the manufacture of motor cars. It would appear that the negotiations had reached a stage about the end of October when the Prime Minister directed the Minister for Customs Mr Lawson to take the matter in hand.[77]

On 22 November, Smith wrote a letter making a proposal to the government which was substantially the one put to him earlier by Customs officials reflecting what they took, rightly, to be Menzies' acceptance of the view regarding the need for only a single producer. It suggested that ACI would manufacture cars if it were given privileges including monopoly rights and additional protection. The Cabinet, after considering Smith's proposition 'made one or two alterations of it', and on 2 December, Lawson discussed the revived proposal with Smith, asking him for a revised submission.[78] ACI rejected Lawson's overtures and in at letter dated 4 December, effectively withdrew from the project. Two days later Lawson introduced the Bill for the bounty on motor vehicle engines, but gave no indication to Parliament that the government had had negotiations with any particular company, nor that it would use its powers under the National Security Act.

It now appears that the government had secretly come to the arrangement with ACI on terms consistent with ACI's letter of 22 November. It then belatedly and clumsily attempted to head off the inevitable – and justifiable – criticism when it became public that the whole deal was a set-up in ACI's favour. The bill was passed on 8 December, and late on 15 December – a Friday – urgent telegrams were sent to companies asking if they were interested in the proposals and asking for a reply within 48 hours. According to Curtin

> No suggestion was made in those telegrams that in addition to the proposals made in the Act, proposals could be made which, if acceptable to the Government would involve the use of the National Security Act. It is extraordinary that this telegram was not sent to ACI. Certain of the companies replied that the provisions of the Bounty Act excluded them from eligibility to come within its provisions.[79]

What happened between ACI and the government between the passage of the Act and the dispatch of the telegrams to the other companies is not known, but on 19 December, when the Cabinet was meeting in Sydney, the Prime Minister wrote a letter to ACI in which he referred only to the letter of 22 November in which the company stated it would undertake the project provided it was the only manufacturer. Menzies made no mention of the discussions between Smith and the Minister for Customs on 2 December, nor to Smith's letter to the Minister on 4 December, rejecting the Government's invitation to submit a revised offer of participation without a production monopoly. In his letter, 'The Prime Minister quoted the salient parts of Mr Smith's letter of 22 November, stated that the Motor Vehicles Bounty Act was law and, on behalf of the government, gave ACI six specific assurances.'[80] The letter that was made public, in effect, constituted the agreement between ACI and the government.

> The assurances, plus the Act, involved the exercise of the National Security Act, which had rendered unnecessary for the duration of the war, and for one year thereafter, any action by the States to give effect to the Prime Minister's proposal that the States should transfer their powers to the Commonwealth, which was made in June, 1939.

That other firms were not given equal treatment after the passage of the Bill was clear, and the Opposition was outraged at what it perceived to be an obvious impropriety.

> The dispatch of telegrams on December 15 to certain companies giving them only 48 hours notice before the Cabinet meeting in Sydney can only be construed as a belated afterthought, following undisclosed and unrecorded renewal of negotiations on behalf of the Government with Australian Consolidated Industries. ... Outside of [ACI], no company or group that was interested knew that the Government would consider any agreement to manufacture engines, which in addition to providing a bounty on manufacture, would also ensure to it a monopoly for a period of years by invoking the powers conferred by the National Security Act.

According to Curtin, 'This was grossly improper. It means that the government treated ACI on a different basis from that on which it dealt with any other enterprise.'[81]

Despite the controversy (or perhaps because of it) plans quickly progressed. By the end of December 1939, several sites in Sydney were under consideration for the plant, the favoured one being one of about 100 acres on the Parramatta River. The Managing Director of ACI, W.J. Smith, was to leave Australia for the United States early in January 1940 to purchase plant for building engines and assembling vehicles, and to engage a number of experts who were to be brought to Sydney to install the plant and organize early production. His brother, Arthur E. Smith, also a director of ACI, had already been in the United States for some months (we are unable to verify if the car plan was the reason for his visit) and had indicated that suitable plant was available there, including a quantity of machine tools, which were then almost impossible to purchase in England. It was estimated that the plant would reach Australia within eight months, would be fully operational by July 1941, and that the new industry would employ 6,000 men directly and 4,000 to 7,000 indirectly. Licences to make standard overseas chassis and engine parts would also be purchased from the United States.[82]

By year's end the plan was coming under increasingly widespread attack. The Leader of the Opposition in South Australia, a Mr Richards, suggested that legal proceedings be taken against the Commonwealth challenging its power to make the agreement, and that a Royal Commission should inquire into the circumstances in which the agreement was entered into. The Premier, Thomas Playford, strongly opposed the agreement, fearing for the future of the South Australian motor bodybuilding industry.[83] Noting that the government had disregarded previous pledges, that 'no single company will be granted a manufacturing monopoly', Mr H.C. Jones, secretary of the Chamber of Automotive Industries of New South Wales, described it as a

> surprising procedure which the public must contemplate with the gravest misgivings. ... In effect, the government has given one company *carte blanche* to proceed on the basis of a government subsidy and with the highest possible degree of protection, both as regards import duties and restrictions on imports, without that privileged company being required to accept any responsibility with regard to the prices it charges or the profit it makes.[84]

In the proposed legislation there were to be no restrictions on prices or profits, though the principle was that 'prices of cars manufactured in Australia must be reasonable'.[85] The question was whether ACI was the company to deliver to the public 'reasonable prices', when just six months earlier the Minister for Trade and Customs had directed the Tariff Board to investigate a number of companies, including ACI, for taking undue advantage of tariff protection in making high profits while enjoying substantial tariff protection.[86]

Through all of this Menzies strongly defended the scheme, though he was selective in the facts he presented to support the government's decision.

> The proposal made by Australian Consolidated Industries was, in the opinion of the Commonwealth Government, the only worthwhile proposal it received for the manufacture of motor vehicles. ... The element of monopoly or of special rights contained in the agreement was in the opinion both of the Government and of the company, essential to any Australian organization undertaking car manufacture if real protection were to be given to the Australian capital and labour involved, and to the public interest in the early establishment of the new industry on an economic basis.[87]

By now it was apparent to even the most casual observer, that the government – or at least Menzies and Lawson – was firmly committed to the project. Hartnett of GM-H commented privately,

> There is no shadow of a doubt that Menzies is in deadly earnest and will go to great lengths to bring this thing about. Also Mr Lawson, Minister for Customs has his teeth firmly into this question and tends to believe at times that we and even perhaps I have

been scotching the government movement. The Federal Government has a number of nasty skeletons in the cupboard or bones to pick with ACI and Mr Smith and by one means or another they have made him the willing or unwilling victim. Anyhow Smith has an agreement from them and I have no doubt he will handle it with the shrewdness for which he is famous.[88]

Of Smith himself, and of ACI's ability to carry out the project, Hartnett was considerably less charitable. He described Smith as

thoroughly incapable and incompetent but armed with this agreement [with] the government Mr Smith will play both ends against the middle to obtain the best kind of bargain he can get. I am quite sure he will put the Chrysler group against us and vice versa. He will put Roots against Standard and he will create rumours, hearsay and develop all kinds of circumstantial aspects so that he can make the best kind of deal he can; himself his Company and the agreement versus someone who can do the job. There is no gainsaying the fact that he has the agreement and he has worked himself into a very strong position.

Moreover, Hartnett was convinced ACI and Chrysler were in cahoots.

In some subterranean manner Chrysler want to be in on this – to what extent I am not yet certain. ... In dealing with Smith and any other discussions with New York, I would be very wary of Chrysler and their funny little moves as they have been playing all the games under every known heading either as Chrysler Corp of America, Chrysler Export, Chrysler Dodge Distributors of Australia, Richards or as individual importers. ... I have not forgotten the fact that Chrysler and his distributors gave us a good double crossing on body contracts some four years ago when they played a particularly cagey game.[89]

In the face of the controversy Smith was outwardly showing his public spirit. When at the height of the public criticism Menzies had his only conversation with him, Smith 'offered to withdraw from the manufacturing project if any other Australian company which, in the opinion of the government, was adequately equipped, both financially and technically to undertake the mass production of motor vehicles without such assurances as had been given to Australian Consolidated Industries'. However, the offer to withdraw, according to Menzies was open only, 'until Mr Smith, who leaves for the United States tomorrow, arrives in there and enters into certain negotiations in that country'.[90] Shortly after, Menzies announced, 'The Commonwealth Government has decided that, having regard to the issues raised in relation to the agreement ... the whole transaction will be submitted to the Commonwealth Parliament for ratification. ...This will mean that, pending ratification, the operation of the contract will be suspended.' When Smith was informed of this 'suggestion', according to Menzies 'he promptly agreed'.[91] The suspension took effect on 31 January 1940.[92]

In suspending the agreement the government hoped the heat would be taken out of issue, and it had two pressing motives. Casey, the Treasurer, had been appointed High Commissioner to London, and a by-election was needed in his seat of Corio which had (and has) as its centre Geelong in Victoria, the location of Ford's main manufacturing facility. The second was to remove one of the chief obstacles to negotiation of an understanding between the UAP and the Country Party for a composite Ministry.[93]

The by-election was also crucial for ACI. With W.J. Smith in the United States his brother and fellow director of ACI, F.J. Smith, phoned W.J. advising him that the firm's voluntary retirement from the agreement would help the Government in Corio: 'the loss of this election means that Cameron [leader of the Country Party] can dictate a composite Government on his own terms, in which case our contract would certainly not be ratified'.[94] In spite of the advice W.J. refused to withdraw, citing in a telegram to Menzies his 'fiduciary obligation to shareholders' and moreover that he was 'compelled on behalf of the Company to intimate that if the contract is repudiated by the Commonwealth, it must be held liable for all consequential damages'.[95] In view of subsequent events, not to withdraw was a decision he is likely to have regretted.

The by-election resulted in a significant loss for the government (the seat was won by Labor's John Dedman), and a sidelight to the ACI deal played a part and precipitated Smith's return from the United States. It came in the course of the campaign as one of those interesting (and for the Menzies government) embarrassing incidents which seem to dog governments in decline. It concerned an arrangement by J.N. Lawson, the Customs Minister, to lease a racehorse from W.J. Smith. In a speech made in Geelong Town Hall supporting the Labor candidate, Curtin alleged that

> Soon after the agreement over the motor car industry was entered into between Mr Lawson as Minister, and Mr Smith as general manager, Mr Lawson under a 'nom de course' leased from Mr Smith a racehorse. The horse won a race at Randwick worth £300 and a few days later the lease was cancelled. I regard it as grossly improper … Among the obligations of a Minister is to have complete separation between his private affairs and his public business.[96]

Menzies admitted that the racehorse affair was a 'foolish blunder' but an 'honest blunder', and initially resisted calls for the Minister's resignation. Nevertheless, soon after it cost Lawson his job.

Lawson resigned on 23 February, prompting Smith's immediate return from the United States, after which he publicly expressed his lack of concern about the whole deal. It was, he said, 'a matter of small consequence [to ACI] whether we make motor cars or not. We had never contemplated doing so until approached by the Commonwealth Government last year.'[97] While the latter statement is almost certainly true, the former is almost certainly not. While outwardly professing willingness to relinquish ACI's apparent rights, privately Smith seems to have had other views. A confidential memo, dated 22 February 1940, reported a conversation between F.J. and W.J. Smith in which W.J. Smith was dead against withdrawing or cancelling the car contract. ... He considers it is time to fight it out. ... If Parliament decides to throw out the agreement, let them do it. ... Why should we say ... 'We will retire' ... he says. The contract was entered into at the Government's request. It would be a terrible thing now for us to withdraw.[98]

However the 'contract' was now essentially out of ACI's and the government's control. The Opposition opposed the ratification of the agreement in its original form, alleging the government had favoured ACI and acted 'with prejudice to fair dealing'. In redress, Curtin proposed an amendment that would eliminate the element of absolute monopoly.[99] When finally the Bill ratifying the agreement came before Parliament and Curtin's amendment was put forward, all of the antagonisms on the issue within the coalition surfaced, with open conflict between the two leaders, Menzies (UAP) and Cameron (Country Party). For the government, the problem came to a head when Curtin unexpectedly put Labor's proposal at the second reading, rather than the committee stage of the Bill. Had the amendment been passed at the second reading, the Bill would have been defeated and have passed from the notice paper. A Cabinet meeting to resolve the disagreement between the governing parties broke up with Cameron abruptly leaving the meeting to call a meeting of his party – which resolved to shelve the project indefinitely. A simultaneous meeting of the UAP decided that the project should go ahead, provided no firm was given a manufacturing monopoly. Menzies then told Curtin he would accept Labor's amendment in committee, but when Curtin sought leave to withdraw the amendment at the second reading, Cameron objected. The result, according to a contemporary account, was 'instant uproar'.[100]

After acrimonious debate the Motor Vehicles Agreement Act 1940 was passed in the early hours of 31 May – Labor (but not Dedman, the new Member for Corio) joining with the UAP to support it. The leadership of the Country Party opposed it to the last.[101] The Act incorporated Labor's amendments withdrawing the provisions giving exclusive manufacturing rights for engines and chassis to ACI – the offer was now open to other 'Australian' firms[102] – but authorized the execution of an agreement between the Commonwealth government and the company.[103]

Now the agreement was law, others were viewing ACI's position with envy. While under the amended legislation ACI had lost its exclusive right to manufacture, it was still in a strong position as there were no other obvious 'Australian' candidates. The established – 'foreign' – manufacturers did not qualify, and GM-H at least was regretting its previous stance.

In some respects it can be said that we overdid the passive resistance to the government's desires and intentions by reason of the fact that they were able to bring to light a large Australian enterprise of considerable financial resources and strength in the country – ACI who undertook by special agreement with the government to carry out the work of making a complete car in Australia.[104]

Now Hartnett was strongly advocating to the GM Board a change of mind. He wished to 'make it known in all quarters, both in writing officially, and in any other way that GM-H want to manufacture a complete car in Australia directly the war tempo enables the project to be satisfactorily handled'.[105] The stumbling blocks for GM-H (or any other 'foreign' producer) were the two Acts; they had to go.


### The end of the affair

At ACI's annual general meeting on 26 June 1940, E.N. Grimwade, the company's chairman, announced that plans for the production of cars had been deferred, probably until after the war.[106] The cause was the declaration of the Government's policy of an 'all in' war and the passing of amendments to the National Security Act which provided for powers to control, commandeer and utilize all of the country's resources for the defence of the Commonwealth and the efficient prosecution of the war.[107] According to GM-H, this and the amendments to the Agreement Act

> have combined firstly, to remove the subject of complete auto manufacture from the political arena as an issue of major political significance and controversy, and second, to relegate the subject ... to a position of relative unimportance, compared with the all in war effort for maximum concentration and production of essential and urgently required war materials for defense of Australia.

All of this had caused government, at least for the present, to go cold on the idea of executing the agreement.[108]

Nevertheless, GM-H was planning for the future, seeking legal opinion on whether it was indeed likely to be excluded from complete manufacture by the Bounty and Agreement Acts. While the advice was encouraging overall, throwing doubt on the constitutional basis of Commonwealth legislation seeking to limit the company's freedom to manufacture, ACI was still considered to be in a strong position.[109] Aside from the constitutional issue, whether there was in fact a 'contract' between ACI and the government was in doubt even at the time of the debate on the Agreement bill. As John Dedman the new member for Corio pointed out,

> A contract is an agreement enforceable by law. I understand that it must consist in an offer and an acceptance. We have an offer by [ACI], but the letter of the Prime Minister to [ACI] does not, in any sense of the term, constitute an acceptance of the original offer. It does, in fact, make a counter offer. That counter offer has not been accepted by [ACI], and consequently, no agreement or contract exists for this Parliament to ratify.[110]

As far as the government was concerned, essentially the issue lay dormant until 1943 by which time the prospects for victory were improving by the day. The potential problems of the post-war period were on the minds of Curtin and his colleagues who were now in government, and the automobile industry – and 'complete' manufacture – was seen as an important contributor to post-war reconstruction and employment.[111] The two major producers had seen the error of their previous attitudes to full manufacture and were busy trying to establish their place in the post-war environment.[112] Both were making every effort to see the two motor vehicle Acts repealed. Moreover ACI's champion, Menzies, was no longer in power, but even he had apparently cooled towards the whole arrangement. In discussions with a representative of a major British producer, Rootes, Menzies agreed with the proposition that the monopolistic elements of the Agreement Act were not in accordance with the Atlantic Charter, implied that he saw no reason why the Act should not be repealed, and agreed that the government should be free of any such commitments when planning post-war reconstruction. 'His attitude was such as to give the impression that he regarded the ACI Agreement as being in effect, obsolete, and that he saw no reason why the government should not take the necessary steps to free itself from this entanglement.'[113]

With Menzies no longer on side; Curtin and the Labor Party, both in opposition and in government, never keen on ACI's privileged position; opposition from the 'foreign' producers, and the motor trade; and the legal position unclear – ACI clearly faced a difficult time in having the government fulfil its 'obligations'. By the beginning of 1943, lawyers for the various interests were hard at work on the case.

There were three areas of legal doubt, each in its own right being potentially fatal to the arrangement. Two of the problems had been flagged back in 1940: its constitutional validity, and whether a contract had been entered into in the first place. To those were added apparent problems in the looseness and ambiguity in the wording of the schedule to the Act. In April 1943 the Chairman of the Tariff Board, H.F. Morris, had written to Sir George Knowles, the Solicitor-General, noting that pre-war importers were likely to test the validity of the Act, but that 'apart from the question of [constitutional] validity … it appears to us that the schedule to the Act is somewhat loosely worded in some respects'. Morris listed what the Board took to be eight cases of ambiguity and sloppy drafting and then sought the Solicitor's opinion. Knowles concurred with the Board's comments and, moreover, disavowed any role of his Department in drafting the legislation, giving the Department of Trade and Customs the 'credit'.[114]

As to how strong was ACI's position, the major producers had received conflicting legal advice. According to Rootes' representative, GM-H 'stress[ed] the legal strength of ACI's position; Ford on the other hand assured me they have legal advice to the effect that the Government could annul the Agreement Act without serious difficulty'.[115] The government was in the process of doing just that, although the difficulty turned out to be a little more serious, and the effort more protracted than Ford's advisors may have thought.

The major issue was whether there was a binding agreement between ACI and the Commonwealth. If one did not exist, the potential constitutional and drafting problems would not arise. As far as the 'agreement' was concerned, according to Smith the exchange of correspondence between Menzies and himself as Managing Director of ACI committed the Commonwealth to the agreement with his company, and ACI fully intended to proceed with complete manufacture as soon as conditions permitted. However, when in mid-1943 the government submitted the correspondence to the Solicitor General for opinion, his advice was that the letters did not constitute an agreement.[116] Despite this, even in January 1944, the government was still not certain where it stood. 'As far as is known no Agreement of the kind contemplated by the Act has ever been executed, but as things stand at present, there is considerable uncertainty as to just how far the Commonwealth is committed to Australian Consolidated Industries.'[117]

Whether the government was committed or not, pressure was increasing from the industry and the bureaucracy to scrap the agreement. In March 1944, the Secondary Industries Commission, through J.B. Chifley, then Minister For Post-War Reconstruction, recommended the repeal of the Agreement Act,[118] while in April the Federal Council of the Chambers of Automotive Industries informed the Tariff Board that 'certain concerns with overseas connections' were not prepared to plan local manufacture unless both Acts were withdrawn. In July the Chambers were advising that the post-war rehabilitation of the industry required their repeal.[119]

By early August the issue had come to a head, with both ACI and the government arguing their cases through the press. According to the *Sydney Morning Herald*, the Commonwealth, with the Curtin government contending that there was no binding contract between the Commonwealth and Smith, would investigate the dealings between the Menzies government and ACI. In reply, Smith said that there was 'a binding agreement beyond question, an opinion supported by the highest legal authority', however he would not state who had signed the contract on behalf of the Commonwealth.[120] On 31 July Prime Minister Curtin had written to Smith asking for a copy of the agreement but without success. Smith's reply merely stated *inter alia* 'That a contract exists is beyond question' and went on to ask 'Is my Company to understand from your letter that it is the desire of your Government to repudiate the contract of 19 December 1939? and if such be the case on what grounds?'[121] The dispute then aired in the press again with Curtin stating that if an agreement did exist,

the Commonwealth should honor it or pay compensation for not honoring it. I have asked Mr Smith to give me a copy of the agreement, but so far it has not been sent to me, and the advice given to me by my officers is that they do not know of an agreement. Any agreement must have been executed. Who executed the agreement on behalf of the Commonwealth? These are questions to which I cannot get answers. Mr Smith can readily supply these answers if he has the agreement.[122]

For Smith and ACI, that the writing was on the wall should have been obvious. Curtin's statement was made the day after the first meeting of a Cabinet sub-committee that had been appointed to inquire into the possibilities of motor car manufacture after the war, and investigate the alleged agreement, together with any claims that ACI might have against the government. On 7 September it recommended to Cabinet the repeal of both Acts; that interested parties submit proposals for post-war manufacture to the government for consideration; and if no satisfactory proposals were received, the government should set up a corporation to manufacture a complete car.[123] Following the committee's recommendation Curtin went further on the offensive.

The issue is simple. It is a legal matter. If the General Manager of Australian Consolidated Industries ... has an agreement with the Commonwealth, I would like him to supply me with a copy. I am unable to find one. The Motor Vehicles Agreement Act authorizes the making of an agreement. What agreement was made after the passage of the Act? Surely if there was an agreement, Mr Smith could supply me with a copy of it.[124]

Smith replied through the press,

The agreement for manufacture was conveyed to me as a unanimous decision of [the Menzies] Cabinet. ... [T]he possibility of repudiation in any circumstances never occurred to me. ... It is now said that no contract exists. If there was, as Mr Curtin says, no contract, I must be the only person in Australia who didn't know it. When the Motor Vehicles Bill [sic] came before Parliament, and was duly passed, Mr Curtin and all other Labor members voted for it.[125]

Following the recommendation of the Cabinet sub-committee, in October the government invited persons interested in the manufacture of motor vehicles in Australia, including chassis and engines to submit proposals. There was no mention of any limitation on the origin of the capital required.[126] By then as far as ACI was concerned, the battle, and in fact the war, was lost. In reply to GM-H's expression of interest, Curtin wrote to Hartnett giving approval to foreign producers in establishing full manufacture after the war.

I can say authoritatively that it is the intention of the Government to ask Parliament to repeal [both Acts]. With reference to the question of the ownership and origin of capital ... you may be assured ... that the Government would not discriminate in any way against General Motors–Holden's in the enterprise under discussion because of the origin of capital and the nationality of ownership.[127]

Smith was not impressed by any of this.

According to Mr Curtin, we are back again to pre-war invitations to manufacture motor cars. With, of course this difference. It is now proposed to rescind the Motor

Vehicles Act [*sic*] and schedule for which he himself voted. Why it should be necessary to repeal an Act of Parliament if it is of no consequence to his government or to me, he has not explained.[128]

In Parliament, the formal process of repeal began in March with the introduction of a Bill for an Act to repeal the two motor vehicle Acts. In explaining the Bill to the House the Minister for Post-war Reconstruction, Mr Dedman, noted the government had, by that time, received one specific proposal from GM-H and a second was on its way. Others had been notified as being nearly ready for submission. If the Acts were not repealed, the government could not expect the parties to implement their proposals.[129]

Even then Smith had not given up. In letters to Curtin, he made his views on the government's actions clear: 'It is surely incumbent upon a government to discover what undertakings were given by its predecessor and strictly to honor them in all circumstances. The facts in this particular agreement speak for themselves.' With the provisions of the Bill including a clause to the effect that any claims ACI may have against the Commonwealth would not be affected by its passing, Smith then wrote, accusing the government of casuistry, and noting, 'It does appear to me to be unfortunate to ask a member of the Royal Family, as Governor General, to attach his signature to a Bill which bears on the face of it all the indications of an uneasy conscience. For my part, I would prefer His Royal Highness to be spared an Act so inherently un-British.'[130]

It was all too late, however. By May, with the passing of the Motor Vehicles Manufacture Legislation Repeal Act, 1945, the deal was undone. The only loose end to tie up was the matter of the compensation that ACI duly claimed. Negotiations between ACI and the Commonwealth resulted in a mutual decision to appoint an arbitrator – Mr Justice Roper of the New South Wales Supreme Court. The final words on the issue came more than two years after the repeal of the Acts from J.B. Chifley, now Prime Minister. In answer to a question without notice, he reported Roper's finding that 'The Commonwealth was under a moral obligation to pay compensation, and [he] decided that a sum of £55,000 should reasonably be paid.'[131] For ACI it was the end of the affair.


**Evaluation**

By the mid-1930s the result of automotive policy was a fragmented and inefficient industry, with many of its products – motor bodies and other motor vehicle components – of poor quality. These dubious attributes were fostered by the shelter of high, protective tariffs. The Bounty Bill of 1936 signalled a realization that the manufacture of engines and chassis could not be accomplished by the 'traditional' means in Australia: increasing tariffs.

The Bounty Bill took more than three years to enact despite pressure exerted in the Federal Parliament by proponents on both sides of the House. There were, however, significant opponents of the scheme in Parliament, including Casey, Treasurer in the Lyons UAP government, and Country Party members, especially Page, McEwen and Anthony. Ford had apparently captured Casey; the Country Party saw the scheme as being inimical to the interests of its constituents (an irony considering its post-war record on protection). The main assembler/producers – Chrysler and its distributors, Ford and GM-H – were all opposed to the scheme. While opposing it, they each then proceeded to insure against any detriment they would suffer should the scheme go ahead: Chrysler distributors by laying the groundwork for local manufacture, and later seeking an arrangement with ACI; Ford by lobbying for lower tariffs on its Canadian imports, and local content rules which would have excluded the importation of some of the most popular GM makes; and GM-H with its participation in the Commonwealth Aircraft Corporation (though 'it did not suit us too well'), and taking a 'neutral course' in its dealings with the government (while passively resisting full manufacture), which its competitors viewed as undermining their 'united' opposition.

The government, having unwillingly placed the proposal for manufacture before the Tariff Board in November 1936, then apparently delayed releasing the Board's report with its (to some) unwelcome findings until September 1938. Its seeming procrastination brought accusations of 'some sinister and mysterious influence stopping [establishment of the industry]'.[132]

Even when enacted, the bounty scheme was not enough to make local production of engines and chassis attractive. To make it so required the Motor Vehicles Agreement that relied on exercising the extraordinary powers of the National Security Act. Seven months after the Defense Department denied the direct defence significance of the manufacture of engines and chassis, now it appeared the security of the nation depended on it. The measures of the initial agreement conferring a monopoly on ACI were extraordinary, negotiated in secrecy, and introduced with haste. In pursuing the package of measures, the significant defence benefits anticipated and pursued by the Menzies government (the Opposition supporting the aim if not all the means of bringing about production) were at odds with the views of its defence advisors in the bureaucracy, and representatives of the existing producer/assemblers (who, of course, had their own interests to pursue). Members of Country Party most of whom had consistently opposed the Bounty and Agreement Acts, and the use of the National Security Act remained unconvinced of claims of the defence significance of the industry well after the outbreak of war with Germany, and with the Opposition, and finally with Menzies' grudging support, removed ACI's position of monopoly from the Act.

That the Menzies government, following the announcement in mid-1940 of a policy of 'all in' war, effectively let the Agreement lapse is evidence enough that the Country Party was right in its assessment. Nevertheless it appeared ACI was left in a strong position, despite constitutional uncertainty and doubt whether the Agreement was in fact a contract. That for the next three years the 'foreign' producers attempted to clarify ACI's and their own legal positions (obtaining sometimes conflicting advice) and energetically lobbied the Curtin government for the repeal of the Acts is evidence of their concern for their post-war future and the strength of ACI's position. Smith's extreme reluctance to withdraw from the 'contract' and his bitter opposition to the Curtin government repealing the two Acts is an indication of his assessment of the potential advantage which would accrue from the exercise of the Agreement in favour of ACI.

At war's end, with the repeal of the Acts, ACI would not be a part of the post-war industry. The pre-war producers had won. What was the foundation they themselves laid down for the post-war industry? Had the nation received value for money for the pre-war assistance of the 'foreign' producers? According to an analysis of the potential for the post-war development of a motor vehicle industry in Australia undertaken by the Secondary Industries Commission during the Second World War, an estimated 38.4 per cent, less than two-fifths, of original equipment for complete motor cars was manufactured in Australia by the time hostilities commenced in September 1939. Of this local content, two-thirds (24.6 per cent of the total) comprised body assembly. Excluding the body which had been subjected to very high rates of duty from Federation and more or less irrelevant for any military purpose, over the course of the interwar era Australia had acquired through protective measures the capacity to manufacture 13.8 per cent of the 'content' of a motor vehicle (about half of which consisted of tyres and inner tubes). The remainder of local manufacture included such components as radiators, sparkplugs, windscreen wipers, the batteries, bumper bars and rear-vision mirrors.[133] It did not extend to the core of a motor vehicle: the subframe, engine and transmission. The outcome was, as the analyst concluded, 'a poor return for the high price the consumer has had to pay for the tariff protection afforded the industry'.[134]

## Notes

1. The very small-scale establishments involved in the production of replacement parts in Australia were characterized by the production of an extraordinary variety of vehicle components to individual order for a diversity of makes and models which was fostered by the tariff structure. The diversity of models they produced, and the number of plants they operated hampered even the large producers. Ford had assembly plants in Victoria, New South Wales, Queensland and Western Australia; GM-H in every state but Tasmania; and Chrysler Dodge, a total of 14 plants with locations in all states. About 100 importers who assembled vehicles

throughout the Commonwealth supplied the remainder of the market (Tariff Board, *Engines and Chassis for Motor Vehicles* (Canberra, 1938), p. 12).

2. Ibid.

3. As it turned out, the Holden cars of the post-war years still comprised bodies manufactured in Woodville, South Australia, which were placed on chassis produced at Fishermen's Bend, Victoria.

4. AA ACT A461/1 F418/1/6.

5. In this respect the Tariff Board recognized that this would 'increas[e] the cost per unit of Australian manufacturers supplying that demand' (Tariff Board, *Engines and Chassis*, p. 20).

6. Under the agreement, in return for providing a secure market for their wheat and other foodstuffs, Empire countries (mainly Australia and Canada) offered tariff reductions on Britain's exports of manufactures

7. Hansard, 22 May 1936, p. 2211.

8. The government decided to proceed in two ways: first it adopted an import licensing system over a limited range of imports; and second it imposed higher duties 'where this course appears more desirable'. Except for motor chassis, all goods of British Empire origin were to be exempted from the licensing proposals. The licensing restriction was not to apply to motor chassis from the United Kingdom. Here the main target was chassis imports from Canada. 'Under the licensing scheme ... the importation of specified commodities will be prohibited except with the consent of the Minister for Trade and Customs' (H. Gullett, Hansard, 22 May 1936, p. 2211).

9. The trade diversion measures were an economic and diplomatic disaster. Most were abandoned in 1936, though not the major measures applying to the automotive industry. See B. Dyster and D. Meredith, *Australia in the International Economy in the Twentieth Century* (Cambridge, 1990), pp. 150–53.

10. Hansard, 22 May 1936, pp. 2211–19; *Sydney Morning Herald*, 23 May 1936.

11. The proposed bounty payments per engine were £30 in 1938 (or 1st year of production); £26 in 1939 (or 2nd year of production); £8 in 1940 (or 3rd year of production); and £3 15s. in 1941 (or 4th year of production) (Hansard, 22 May 1936, p. 2217). To put this in perspective, in 1935–36 the average value of the total of 74,118 unassembled imported chassis was £71; the average value of the 30,809 chassis imported from Canada, the major source, was £54 (Tariff Board, *Engines and Chassis*, Appendix B).

12. Hansard, 22 May 1936, p. 2217.

Among the anticipated effects of the trade diversion measures (of which the engine bounty was just one) was giving a 'great impetus to engineering and to the iron and steel industries; [making] a significant indirect contribution to defense' (Hansard, 22 May 1936, p. 2217). Indeed, the idea of the payment of a bounty to encourage local production is likely to have originated in the defence establishment. In a memo dated 3 March 1935, to G.K. Howard of General Motors Export Division in New York, L.J. Hartnett stated, 'The Defense Department headed by Air Vice Marshall Williams who is a personal friend of mine have quite made up their minds to influence the Australian government to make it possible by subsidy or any other means to develop the manufacturing of cars, trucks and aircraft in Australia' (Mortlock, BRG 213/65/9).

Claims before the Tariff Board of the 'defense significance' of the industry go back to the 1920s. In 1925 the *Australian Motorist* reported that in evidence given in Sydney, 'Mr Olding wanted also heavier duties. He is a body builder, and can see certain advantages in increased tariffs from a national defense point of view.'

The journal commented, 'We do not see how the motor body industry is likely to help in big gun manufacture, and we do not remember reading during the war that any battles were fought with mudguards and valances' (*Australian Motorist*, July 1925, p. 602).

13. *Australian Motorist*, August 1936, p. 373.
14. *Australian Motorist*, December 1936, p. 175 and March 1937, p. 356.
15. *Sydney Morning Herald*, 30 July 1936.
16. Hansard, 7 December 1937, p. 303. The reference was so amended on 1 December 1936 (AA Vic. IC 44/106).
17. See page 59 of this chapter for more detail on this point.
18. The Board's report concluded that it 'would not at present advise the encouragement or enforcement of the manufacture of the complete motor vehicle in Australia. The best approach to this end would be "step by step" development [of engine and chassis manufacture]' (Tariff Board, *Engines and Chassis*, p. 28).
19. Quoted in *Sydney Morning Herald*, 5 July 1939.
20. Tariff Board, *Engines and Chassis*, p. 30.
21. Memorandum dated 6 May 1937, from R.A. May, assistant to General Manager, General Motors, New York, to E.C. Riley, General Manager, General Motors Export Division (Mortlock, BRG 213/65/9).
22. Hartnett to Riley, 22 March 1937 (Mortlock, BRG 213/65/9).
23. Statement made in evidence to the Tariff Board (AA Vic. MP394 Series 1 IC 44/106).
24. 'French from Ford most emphatic in his opposition to the government proposals as also were Chrysler, the latter going so far as to definitely inform the Board they would not enter into a manufacturing program.' Memorandum from Hartnett to Riley, 5 May 1937 (Mortlock, BRG 213/65/9).
25. *Sydney Morning Herald*, 18 February 1937.
26. Memo from Hartnett to Riley, 22 March 1937 (Mortlock, BRG 213/65/9).
27. The reason for French's apparent ability to ignore the interests of Ford USA stemmed from the pattern of ownership of the various Ford Companies. Henry and Edsel Ford and some Canadian shareholders owned Ford Canada. Ford USA held no shares, except through Henry and Edsel Ford (memo from Hartnett to Riley in New York, 10 December 1936 (Mortlock, BRG 213/65/9)).
28. Memorandum to E.C. Riley from R.A. May, assistant to General Manager, GM 6 May 1937 (Mortlock, BRG 213/65/9).
29. H.B. Phillips, Regional Director, General Motors to Hartnett, 16 July 1937 (Mortlock BRG 213/65/9).
30. Briefing note to the GM Board of Directors: 'Resume of Deliberations re Motor Car Manufacture in Australia', 15 March 1937, signed by H.B. Phillips, Regional Director, Australasian Region, and L.J. Hartnett, Managing Director, GM-H (Mortlock, BRG 213/65/9).
31. Imperial Chemical Industries and the Orient Steamship Co. subsequently joined these firms (internal historical review of GM-H's operations in Australia to May 1944 (Mortlock, BRG 213/65/6)).
32. Hartnett memo to Riley in New York, 10 December 1936 (Mortlock, BRG 213/65/9). As is so often the case in matters of industry policy, preferential treatment is considered 'fair' treatment.
33. Hansard, 7 December 1937, p. 300.
34. 'Resume of deliberations re Motor Car Manufacture in Australia', 15 July 1937 (Mortlock, BRG 213/65/9).
35. Phillips to Hartnett, 3 July 1940 (Mortlock, BRG 213/65/8).

36. Hartnett to E. Riley, General Manager GM Export Division, 10 December 1936 (Mortlock, BRG 213/65/9).
37. Hansard, 7 December 1937, p. 301.
38. F. Forde, Hansard, 7 December 1937, p. 309.
39. F. Forde, Hansard, 16 November 1938, p. 1530.
40. H. Gullett, Hansard, 11 November 1938, p. 1543.
41. F. Forde, Hansard, 16 November 1938, p. 1527, and 11 December 1938, p. 2542.
42. H. Gullett, Hansard, 11 May 1938.
43. F. Forde, Hansard, 16 November 1938, p. 1529.
44. Letter from Hartnett to Ed Riley, General Manager General Motors, New York, 10 December 1936 (Mortlock, BRG 213/65/9). Hartnett's information regarding Casey's appointment to the London post, replacing Stanley Bruce, proved to be correct. The two Ministers to whom Hartnett refers were presumably Menzies and Page.
45. *Sydney Morning Herald*, 26 November 1938.
46. AA A461/1 D418/1/6 Part 6.
    While it was reported that 'two or three Australian manufacturing firms' were interested in the project (*Sydney Morning Herald*, 8 December 1939), no firm proposal was ever made. One firm, however, Pengana Motor Industries, was successful in attracting publicity and some (albeit lightweight) political support. According to a Mr Dillon an M.L.A. in the Victorian Parliament, the complete manufacture of eight and four cylinder motor car engines and chassis in Australia by 1941 was assured. The firm had, he said, completed negotiations for the purchase of one of the most modern car engine manufacturing plants (the Hupmobile 'eight' plant) in the United States, and that arrangements had been made for its immediate dismantlement and shipment to Australia (*Sydney Morning Herald*, 16 January 1940).
    Pengana claimed to have built two successful experimental cars and paid deposit on purchase of a portion of the Hupmobile plant in Detroit. Subsequent events demonstrated Pengana's lack of financial backing, and dubious business methods. Attempts were made to associate the names of J.B. Were & Son (Melbourne stockbrokers) and B.S.B. Stevens (an ex-Premier of New South Wales) with Pengana. J. B.Were threatened legal action unless Pengana refrained from using Were's name, while Stevens denied that he had offered financial backing and claimed to have been misrepresented by Pegana (AA Vic. MP394 Series 1 IC44/106).
47. H. Gullett, Hansard, 11 November 1938, p. 1543.
48. AA Vic. MP394 Series 1 IC 44/106.
49. The Menzies Ministry met Parliament for the first time on 3 May 1939, succeeding the government of J.A. Lyons who had died in April 1939 (E. Page, *Truant Surgeon* (Sydney, 1963), p. 281).
50. AA ACT A461/1 D418/1/6 Part 3.
51. Hartnett noted 'Practically every evening cocktails/dinner talks, almost every Minister of the Cabinet and most State Premiers. Two instances, Sir Archdale Parkhill, the Minister for defense and Menzies. I was able to get into long pow wow with them in private homes – much more behind tariff move than meets the eye' (Hartnett to Riley, 10 December 1936 (Mortlock, BRG 213/65/9)).
52. Tariff Board, *Engines and Chassis*, p. 22.
53. Evidence given on 4 March 1937, by L. Shepherd, and quoted in Tariff Board, *Engines and Chassis*, p. 22, and AA Vic, CRS B1535 File 931/2/239.
54. G.A. Street, Hansard, 9 May 1939, p. 250.

55. The rates to be payable in the 1936 proposal were revised under the 1939 Act. The new rates were £30 for the first 20,000 units; £25 for the second 20,000; and £20 for the third 20,000 (s.8., Motor Vehicle Engine Bounty Act 1939).

56. J.V. Lawson, Minister for Trade and Customs, Hansard, 6 December 1939, p. 2211.

57. E.J. Holloway, Hansard, 7 December 1939, p. 2466.

58. Ibid.

59. The Federal Country Party had refused to participate in the Menzies government formed in May 1939 (Page, *Truant Surgeon*, p. 279).

60. McEwan had first referred to the original terms of reference to the Tariff Board in noting 'from the very outset strange circumstances have appeared in connection with this proposal. [It was only after speeches and representations by Country Party members that] the originally proposed terms of reference to the Tariff Board [were] altered, but rather grudgingly, by the addition of the words "with consideration given to the general national and economic aspects". Prior to that the Government appeared to be determined to manufacture motor cars in Australia irrespective of the economics of the proposal' (Hansard, 7 and 8 December 1939, pp. 2473–4).

61. Hansard, 7 and 8 December 1939, p. 2473.

62. Hansard, 7 and 8 December 1939, p. 2478. The Bill passed its first reading in the House of Representatives on 8 December 1939 with the vote 46 to 11 in favour, members of the Country Party opposing (Hansard, 8 December 1939, p. 2480).

63. Briefing note to the GM Board of Directors: 'Resume of Deliberations re Motor Car Manufacture in Australia', 15 March 1937, signed by H.B. Phillips, Regional Director, Australasian Region, and L.J. Hartnett, Managing Director, GM-H (Mortlock, BRG 213/65/9).

64. H.B. Phillips to G.K. Howard, General Manager, GM Overseas Operations, New York, 5 January 1940 (Mortlock, BRG 213/65/8).

65. Report of Smith's comments at ACI's annual general meeting, on 26 June 1940, in *Sydney Morning Herald*, 27 June 1940.

66. During the course of the second reading debate on the Bounty Bill, Mr Archie Cameron, Leader of the Country Party, mentioned that, 'vague rumors are current on the question of whether a big Australian company is prepared to take part in this venture, but I do not know if there is any truth in them' (Hansard, 7 and 8 December 1939, p. 2465).

67. Production was estimated to start 18 months later, with a hoped for annual production of 8,000 vehicles in the first year, rising to 20,000 vehicles in five years. The car to be produced would be of a popular American type of between 18 and 25 hp, and it was hoped that as far as possible, the company would obtain its bodies from existing body manufacturers. While the site of the proposed factory was not announced, it was 'learned authoritatively that it [was to be] in or near Sydney' (*Sydney Morning Herald*, 23 December 1939).

68. *Sydney Morning Herald*, 18 May 1939.

69. 'The Government, in its prolonged endeavor to get this industry established in Australia, found that Australian industrialists were disinclined to invest capital without an assurance from the Commonwealth Government that their investments would be protected against unfair competition from foreign motor car manufacturers. ... It is generally recognized that if several manufacturers equip factories to produce motor cars, the industry would be uneconomic. In this case severe capital losses would result, while the price of the Australian car would

be unnecessarily high. ... [the Government] did not desire to bring about a major dislocation to the existing industry, which could only have resulted in unemployment and capital losses. [Thus, the Government concluded] that it would be preferable during the period of the establishment to limit production ... to one factory in order that the industry accustom itself to the changed conditions' (J.N. Lawson, *Sydney Morning Herald*, 28 December 1939). Other complementary measures are described in AA ACT A461/1 M418/1/6 Part 1.

70. *Sydney Morning Herald*, 28 December 1939.
71. *Sydney Morning Herald*, 1 March 1940.
72. *The Age*, 5 January 1940.
73. *Adelaide Advertiser*, 4 and 8 January 1940. On the opposition to the monopoly elements of the proposal, B.S.B. Stevens, who had been Premier of New South Wales during the period from the introduction of the bounty proposal in 1936 until 1939, ascribed an important influence to South Australia. 'One cannot help feeling that much of the criticism has been caused partly by the resentment of South Australia, whose antagonism to any progress which may affect that State has been frequently voiced by its political leaders.' Stevens, an avid proponent of full manufacture, had made strenuous efforts to attract the industry to New South Wales.
74. From archival material we now know the representatives were Hartnett and Phillips from General Motors.
75. Mortlock, BRG 213 65/9.
76. J. Curtin, quoted in *Sydney Morning Herald*, 28 February 1940.
77. Ibid.
78. H.L. Anthony, Hansard, 30 & 31 May 1940, p. 1631.
79. J. Curtin, quoted in *Sydney Morning Herald*, 28 February 1940.
80. The government assured the company that it would:
'1. use its powers to safeguard the industry from competition from foreign companies;
2. use its best endeavors to limit production of engines of 15 h.p. or over to ACI for 5 years;
3. would purchase a substantial portion of its requirements from the company;
4. for machinery which could not be commercially made in Australia, it would ask the United Kingdom to waive its rights under the Ottawa Agreement; or if the machinery was not obtainable in Britain, it would admit it duty-free in other countries;
5. retain import control, and use it if necessary to counteract unfair competition; and
6. make available the usual cooperation of the Council for Scientific Research and the Aeronautical Laboratories' (AA Vic. MP394 Series 1 IC44/106).
81. *Sydney Morning Herald*, 28 February 1940. The scheme was not without its supporters outside the Federal Parliament: B.S.B. Stevens had been a strong proponent of the manufacture of the 'Australian car' and the grant of an initial monopoly as a means of providing impetus to the establishment of the industry. In a letter to F.J. Smith on 16 March 1940, Stevens stated his belief that 'The Pioneers of motor manufacture have right [*sic*] to be undisturbed by competition, and such wrecking tactics as might be expected from importers and special interests who do not want to see complete cars manufactured in Australia.' In studying the possibility of forming an Australian Company to manufacture 'the complete car', according to Stevens, 'There was no doubt ..., either in the minds of the underwriters or Mr Hartnett [the Head of GM-H] that, *provided the license to manufacture cars could be secured*, and irritating competition in the

developing stages eliminated, success was attainable' (Mortlock, MLK 4701 ML MSS 5146 Item 2).

82. *Sydney Morning Herald*, 23 December 1939.

83. *Sydney Morning Herald*, 18 January 1940. Following an interview with Smith, Menzies, in a cable on 4 January 1940, reassured South Australian parliamentarians and the South Australian motor bodybuilders T.J. Richards and Sons that ACI would obtain its supplies of motor bodies from South Australia, provided 'the quality is right and the price is reasonable' (AA ACT A461/1 M418/1/6 Part 1).

84. *Sydney Morning Herald*, 31 December 1939.

85. J.N. Lawson, quoted in *Sydney Morning Herald*, 4 January 1940.

86. Such a reference could be made under s.15 (h) of the Tariff Board Act.

87. *Sydney Morning Herald*, 1 February 1940.

88. AA ACT A461/1 M418/1/6 Part 1.

89. Private and confidential letter from Hartnett to H.B. Phillips, GM Regional Director, New York, 5 January 1940 (Mortlock, BRG 213/65/8). In a formal reply to Menzies, expressing its interest in the agreement, T.J. Richards and Sons indicated that it was negotiating a manufacturing arrangement with the Chrysler company in the United States, and noted, 'We are informed that the Minister for Trade and Customs sent telegrams to certain motor organizations [on 15 December 1939], asking whether such organizations were interested in motor engine and chassis manufacture under the provisions of the Motor Vehicle Bounty Act. We are surprised that no such telegram was sent to this company although we have capital of £250,000, every penny of which is Australian. ... Unless there is some special explanation, we consider that we have not had fair treatment' (AA ACT A461/1 M418/1/6 Part 1).

90. It is not certain whether Smith left on 5 or 6 January. Smith's prospective departure 'tomorrow' is mentioned in a telegram to the Premier of South Australia on 4 January and a press release on 5 January (AA ACT A461/1 O418/1/6 Part 2).

91. AA ACT A461/1 D418/1/6 Part 4.

92. AA Vic. MP394 Series 1 IC44/10.

93. *Sydney Morning Herald*, 1 February 1940.

94. Letter from F.J. Smith to S.G. Garnsworthy of ACI, reporting details of a telephone conversation between the two brothers. When W.J. Smith told his brother that withdrawal of the company 'would be the weakest possible attitude to take, and might well be misunderstood', F.J. Smith informed Lawson, the Customs Minister, who told him the government understood ACI's unwillingness to withdraw (Mortlock, MLK 4701 ML MSS 5146 Item 5).

95. AA ACT A461/1 O418/1/6 Part 2.

96. *Sydney Morning Herald*, 13 February 1940.

97. *Sydney Morning Herald*, 1 April 1940.

98. Internal memorandum to General H.W. Grimwade, from S.G. Garnworthy of ACI.

99. It was reported that such an amendment may well be passed, but should it do so, that ACI would abandon the project (*Sydney Morning Herald*, 4 May 1940).

100. *Sydney Morning Herald*, 31 May 1940.

101. Menzies dealt with the split in the coalition by noting that the amended Bill was not a government measure, 'but as a measure to which I ... am committed. It is well known that some of my colleagues are opposed to this measure and that, upon joining the Ministry, they retained the right to vote against it. ... My colleagues in the Cabinet will ... remain free to vote [on the amended Bill] as they

please in accordance with the arrangement that has been made with them' (Hansard, 30 May 1940, p. 1621).

102. The Act received assent on 3 June 1940. In it the Commonwealth would use its 'best endeavors' for a period of five years to limit production to any suitable 'Australian' companies (this effectively excluded Ford and GM-H) which gave satisfactory undertakings to the Commonwealth similar to those given by ACI (AA Vic. 44/106).

103. Later the Act would be seen as a plot by local bureaucrats against overseas interests. A letter intercepted by the Commonwealth censor from the local representative of Rootes, the British manufacturer, to his principals in the United Kingdom suggested 'there are certain Government officials permanently occupied with bringing to fulfillment the Commonwealth's ambition to establish its own Motor Industry. The officials in question, Mr Arthur Moore – Assistant Comptroller General of Customs – and his assistant Mr Marcusson, have little or no technical knowledge of modern motor manufacture. Their tactics throughout have been to play off one potential manufacturer against another until finally they succeeded in pushing through the A.C.I. Agreement Act [sic] at a time [June 1940] when overseas interests were too preoccupied to offer effective resistance' (AA Vic. IC 44/106).

104. Hartnett to Phillips, 1 July 1940 (Mortlock, BRG 213/65/9).

105. Ibid.

106. *Sydney Morning Herald*, 27 June, 1940.

107. Excepting conscription for overseas service. The amendments were passed on 20 June 1940.

108. Phillips to Hartnett, 3 July 1940 (Mortlock, BRG 213/65/9).

109. Opinion was sought on 6 June 1940. Solicitors Malleson Stewart Stawall and Nankivell advised on 14 June that manufacturing was an example of trade and commerce within a state (even if spread over two or more States) and thus was outside the power of the Commonwealth (Mortlock, BRG 213/65/6).

110. Dedman went on to say ' I mention this, because I understood the Prime Minister to say that [ACI] was to be commended for having agreed to suspend the operation of the contract. There is no contract; consequently it ought not to be commended for what it has not done' (Hansard, 29 May 1940, p. 1480).

111. The post-war future of the industry was referred to the Tariff Board, which reported on 13 April 1943 (Tariff Board, *Post-War Reconstruction, Motor Vehicles* (Canberra, 1943)).

112. GM-H in particular was worried about the two Acts and ACI's position, and was seeking more freedom of action from its United States parent. 'Implications motor vehicles agreement and motor engine bounty acts are such that early aggressive move by strong known local interests concerned could perhaps forestall and certainly be detrimental to so-called foreign companies if definite action by these companies delayed too long. Important to realize company named in act is powerful amply supplied funds aggressive faster moving than we and has a comprehensive range manufacturing facilities. We should have clear cut understanding scope and nature of program New York willing to approve and authority to make preliminary moves and commitments whenever necessary protect our position' (confidential cable from GM-H Melbourne (signed Hartnett and Phillips) to GM New York (Board of Directors), 10 October 1942). A Department of Trade and Customs Liaison Officer obtained a copy of the cable (AA Vic. IC 44/106).

113. Reported by Commonwealth censor. Memo from C.H. Hordern representing

Rootes in Australia to J.G. Chaldecott, Rootes UK, 23 January 1943 (AA Vic. IC 44/106).

114. The correspondence between Morris and Knowles took place in April 1943 (AA ACT 432/57 40/357).
115. AA Vic. IC 44/106.
116. Ibid.
117. J.B. Chifley, Minister for Post-War Reconstruction, 15 January 1944 (AA ACT A461 OP418/1/6 Part 2).
118. AA ACT A461 OP418/1/6 Part 2.
119. The firms 'before the war were engaged in the importation of chassis and in the assembly and distribution of complete vehicles in Australia'. They would certainly have included Ford and GM-H, and are likely to have included Chrysler (AA Vic. IC 44/106).
120. *Sydney Morning Herald*, 3 August, 1944.
121. Smith's letter was dated 18 August 1943 (AA ACT A461 OP418/1/6 Part 2).
122. *Sydney Morning Herald*, 22 August 1944.
123. The sub-committee comprised Mr Dedman (Minister for War Organization of Industry), the Treasurer (Mr Chifley), the Minister for Munitions (Mr Makin), and the Minister for Trade and Customs (Senator Keane) (AA ACT A461/1 O418/1/6 Part 2).
124. Press release by Prime Minister Curtin, 14 September 1944 (AA ACT A461/1 O418/1/6 Part 2).
125. *Sydney Morning Herald*, 14 September 1944.
126. *Sydney Morning Herald*, 5 October 1944.
127. Letter dated 3 February 1945 (AA ACT A461/1/6 U418/1/6).
128. *Sydney Morning Herald*, 14 September 1944.
129. In anticipation of the repeal of the two Acts, GM-H and Ford submitted proposals to the Secondary Industries Commission for the manufacture of motor vehicles in Australia. Subsequently Chrysler-Dodge Distributors submitted a proposal to manufacture, and Nuffield (Aust.) Pty Ltd submitted plans for the manufacture of coachwork and the assembly of vehicles, with the ultimate objective of building complete cars (AA Vic. MP394 5/81/15A).
130. AA ACT A461/1 O418/1/6 Part 2.
131. Question without notice to J.B. Chifley, 21 October 1947 (AA ACT A461/1 O418/1/6 Part 2).
132. Sir Henry Gullett, quoted by Mr F. Forde, Hansard, 7 December 1939, p. 2546.
133. AA ACT A425/1 36/10700.
134. AA Vic. MP394/1 5/81/107 Part 5.

# 5   The Canadian Connection

The governments of Australia and Canada have both had long-standing policies of assistance to stimulate manufacturing. Broadly, their motives were similar, with tariffs being an important means of accomplishing the task of nation building. Within the respective manufacturing sectors of both countries, the automobile industry has been a significant beneficiary.

Canada was a strong influence on the pre-Second World War development of automobile production in Australia. In some important respects the industry developed in a similar environment in both countries where it was shaped by geography, trade barriers and foreign ownership. Tariff protection and proximity to the United States resulted in the emergence of a Canadian industry dominated by US firms. Tariff preference and distance contributed to the domination of the Australian market by United States and (increasingly) Canadian interests – as exporters, and as 'Australian' producers. Canada played a major role in the emergence of the industry in Australia not only as a conduit for United States exports to Australia, but as the apparent source of ownership of the Ford Company's Australian subsidiaries.

## Early development of the industry in Canada

The origins of the Canadian automobile industry date from 1904, when in partnership with Henry Ford, a group of businessmen from Windsor, Ontario, set up the Ford Motor Company of Canada to manufacture and sell Ford products in the British Empire (excluding Britain itself). Bodybuilding played a central role in the early development of the Canadian industry as it did in Australia.[1] In Canada, in the first year 117 motor vehicles were produced,[2] 'but little more was done beyond putting bodies and wheels on chassis ferried across the river from Detroit'.[3] Three years after Ford was established, R. Samuel McLauglin, the proprietor of Canada's largest carriage manufacturing company, of Oshawa, Ontario, set up the McLauglin Motor Car Company. He had first approached the Jackson Automobile Company of Southern Michigan, buying two of Jackson's cars to assess their suitability for Canadian production. The Jackson Company, while known for producing excellent cars had a reputation for letting business opportunities slip, and this was no exception.[4]

William Durant, who was largely responsible for the creation of General Motors in the United States, had quite the contrary reputation.[5] Durant, who had made his fortune as the largest wagon maker in the United States, offered to sell Buick engines and other components to McLauglins. The offer was accepted, and in 1908 Durant concluded a 15-year agreement with McLauglin's son, Robert, to sell Buick engines and other parts for McLauglin's locally produced automobiles. Robert S. McLauglin became a Director of General Motors (GM), and following Durant's (temporary) fall from power in GM, in 1915 he agreed to build Chevrolets when it was a company independent of General Motors and under Durant's control.[6] In the process, McLauglin organized the Chevrolet Motor Company of Canada. Durant regained control of GM in 1916, and in 1918, Chevrolet Canada was sold to, and merged with the US General Motors Corporation. However, McLauglin's connection with Buick was maintained throughout Durant's break with GM, and was continued as a joint venture after the formation of General Motors-Canada.[7] This produced the McLauglin-Buick that was successfully exported throughout the world.[8] By 1921, when the Chrysler Corporation of Canada began production at Windsor, the 'big three' US car producers had become established in Canada.[9]

## Market conditions

In the period for which reasonably comparable data are available, Canada's production in most years far outstripped Australia's, especially during the worst of the Depression (1931–35) when it was more than three times higher.[10] In many respects, however, there were important similarities in market conditions in the two countries. There was comparatively little difference between their per capita incomes and income distributions (major determinants of demand for motor vehicles). Canada's population was greater (by about one-third to one half over the interwar period), but both countries were sparsely populated, with populations concentrated along the 'fringes': in Canada, the United States border; in Australia, the eastern seaboard.[11]

While Canada's larger population provided greater potential to exploit economies of scale in its domestic market, until the 1930s, economies of scale were not all that important in motor vehicle assembly.[12] Even in the United States, assembly was dispersed beyond Detroit. Relatively high freight costs for assembled vehicles outweighed any scale economies from centralized assembly there, and it is unlikely that the difference in populations between Canada and Australia would itself have made any great difference to production costs in the two countries. There is evidence, however, that high Australian labour costs, and the high level of labour unrest, especially in the 1920s, were inhibiting influences on potential foreign investors in the industry, and on its early post-war development. For example, in mid-1924, after Ford had decided to establish assembly plants in the major Australian cities, M.C. French, then visiting from Ford Canada (and who eventually was appointed to manage Ford's Australian operations), expressed the view that 'Australian labour conditions were not favorable at the present time to engage in an extension of manufacturing'.[13] Moreover, on the demand side, the costs of operating a vehicle were substantially lower in Canada: cars there were cheaper to buy, and cheaper to run.[14] Despite this, while per capita ownership of motor vehicles was higher in Canada than in Australia, the difference was not great.[15]

Nevertheless, in establishing automobile manufacturing and promoting its growth, on balance, the influences so far discussed provided an advantage to Canada over Australia, and were likely contributors to the disparity in the outputs of the industries of the two countries. However, when exports are subtracted from Canadian production, a large part of the disparity disappears. It suggests a fundamental difference between the two countries' industries: producers in Canada were outward looking; those in Australia were not.

## Trade barriers and foreign ownership

The contemporary Australian literature placed considerable emphasis on what it saw as the Canadian advantage of geographical proximity to the United States and, in particular, Detroit. As the *Australian Motorist* observed in its issue of August 1929, 'It has often been pointed out that Canada produces motor cars, but Canada would not have done so had there not been a big manufacturing centre ... across the river.' There is no doubt that geography – and transport costs – are important determinants of production location. In the present context, tariffs may be viewed as artificial transport costs, which provide an incentive to locate production where the aggregate cost of production and sale is minimized.[16] A consequence of high levels of protection characteristic of both the Australian and Canadian economies, together with their openness to foreign direct investment, was that foreign enterprises often overcame the protective barriers to their direct exports by means of local production by subsidiary firms. In particular, they looked to dominate industries characterized by large capital requirements, the potential exploitation of economies of scale, the development and use of new technologies, and skill in product marketing. The nascent automobile industries in Australia and Canada were therefore obvious candidates for foreign and particularly United States domination.

Ford and General Motors were the most important of these foreign investors, and Canada has played a central role in the overseas activities (particularly concerning Australia) of both these companies.[17] For example, Ford's Australian manufacturing/assembly operations, begun in Geelong in 1925, were subsidiaries of Ford Canada, which in turn was owned by Henry and Edsel Ford and some Canadian shareholders.[18] The Australian operations followed Ford's practice in the United States of keeping 'in house' as much of the production process – body construction and chassis assembly – as possible. Like Ford, GMA also followed the practice of its parent company by commonly using sources of supply outside the firm.[19] The relationship between GMA and Holden's, which built its bodies, continued until the Depression when the downturn in car sales brought Holden's to the brink of collapse. In the circumstances it was apparent that a merger would be mutually beneficial, and the result was the formation of GM-H in 1931.

Direct foreign participation in the Australian market had its vigorous opponents. When the entry of Ford Canada was proposed it was attacked on a number of grounds, most notably by the *Australian Motorist* under the editorship of H.W. Harrison. Ford's stated intention of moving rapidly towards establishing its own motor bodybuilding facility threatened the interests of Australian firms that hitherto had found constructing bodies for imported Ford chassis to be highly profitable.[20] It would involve the substitution of 'foreign' for Australian capital, with the profits being repatriated to Canada. As the editor observed, 'If Australians are to be fleeced behind a high tariff, the right policy is to keep the loot in Australia.' A likely increase in the price of the Model T was also a matter of concern, as the costs of producing the chassis were estimated to be one-third more in Canada than at Ford's Dearborn plant in Michigan.[21]

The entry of Ford also threatened local dealers with control over their operations and the prospect of 'American' methods of doing business. Before this, Ford dealers had made easy profits from Model T sales. They were afraid the comfortable arrangement in Australia seemed destined for radical change having seen what had happened in Britain after Ford had set up its plant in 1911 at Trafford Park, Manchester. For British dealers, Ford had 'laid down hard and fast conditions on contract quantities, [required an] exclusive Ford showroom, repair shop and spare parts, plus insistence that every agent must contract for some of every line produced, that is roadsters, tourers, sedans, and even Fordson tractors'.[22] Sedans at the time were rapidly declining in popularity, and the prospect of having to sell tractors would presumably have horrified inner-city dealers in Sydney and Melbourne. There was an added concern that Ford intended to establish its own distribution network.[23] This may have been a response to what was beginning to be discerned as a practice among emerging transnationals: initially employing local agents to explore the market before deciding whether to establish a local subsidiary to manufacture and market the product. Such forward integration did not occur, but it was for Australian dealers, nevertheless, a real fear in the 1920s.

Furthermore, in the motor trade and other press, reports began to appear to the effect that US manufacturers were exploiting imperial preference through their Canadian subsidiaries. The Prime Minister of New Zealand, a dominion with even closer ties to Britain than Australia, apparently first raised the subject. According to Prime Minister Massey:

> such articles as motor cars ... were of United States manufacture substantially, and that the one-fourth British workmanship was made up of Canadian work, such as assembling, painting, finishing and packing, and that freight and other handling charges were included in the proportion allotted to British workmanship.[24]

In Australia, concern regarding 'foreign' influence on the motor industry peaked in the second half of the 1930s, and Canadian influence was at the centre of the controversy. At issue was the Lyons government's plan to promote the local production of automobile engines. This was one of a number of measures comprising the policy of 'trade diversion' – switching the sources of imports from 'unfavorable' to 'favorable trading countries', while stopping the importation of certain products, and promoting their local manufacture. Canada was on the list of undesirables.[25]

By most conventional definitions, by 1936 Australia had acquired a motor vehicle manufacturing industry. According to Sir Henry Gullett, Minister directing negotiations for trade treaties, 'four fifths of almost every car on the Australian roads today is already the product of Australian material and Australian labour'. However, in an important sense the industry was incomplete: many of the most important chassis components – including the engine – were still not manufactured in Australia. As a remedy, Gullett told Parliament that,

> The [Lyons] Government intends to proceed ... to strengthen Australian secondary industries by halting some imports of commodities with a view to their manufacture in Australia. The chief of these ... is the motor chassis [including the engine] which we hope will be manufactured in Australia on a large scale in a very short time.[26]

The means was to be through the Motor Vehicle Engine Bounty Act and the events surrounding the Act described in Chapter 4.

The period from 1936 when the bounty measure was first proposed, to 1940, when it (and the related measures) were effectively scrapped, was witness to bitter dispute by the various interest groups concerned. The three leading producers, Chrysler, Ford and GM-H, were all strongly opposed to the idea, but Ford led the opposition – to the detriment of their joint cause. The company's Canadian ties were fully exploited by supporters of the bounty when Ford's tactics became apparent. The lobbying efforts of H.C. French, a Canadian and the Managing Director of Ford Australia, were disastrous: 'practically every newspaper in Australia came out with the headline, "Dirty Lobbying Accusations by Minister Against Canadian Car Company"'.[27] Sir Henry Gullett, who had introduced the scheme to Parliament, later attributed delays in its implementation to foreign, and particularly Canadian interests: 'the chief ... being the Ford Company of Canada [sic]'.[28]

### Trade barriers, automobile production and exports

Nearly 80,000 passenger automobiles were produced in Canada in 1919; by 1926 production had increased to 167,000, rising to its pre-Second World War high of 203,000 in 1929 (see Table 5.1). That in Canada, unlike Australia, a large part of production – about 30 per cent – was for export was a result of two primary influences. First, the restructuring of the automobile tariff in 1926 not only lowered rates on automobiles from 35 per cent to 27.5 per cent (20 per cent on vehicles valued at $1,200 or less), it effectively lowered or eliminated duties on many components. Thus, subject to certain conditions – among them, a 'Canadian content' requirement[29] – the industry in Canada could import

**Table 5.1**　Canada – automobile industry, 1918–1939

| Year | Prod'n (,000) | Imports (,000) | Exports (,000) | Domestic supplies (%) | Export/ dom. supp. (%) | Closed cars (%) | Engines made (,000) |
|------|------|------|------|------|------|------|------|
| 1918 | 75.1 | 9.2 | 9.0 | 175.3 | 12.0 | – | – |
| 1919 | 79.3 | 9.6 | 19.6 | 69.3 | 28.3 | – | – |
| 1920 | 84.0 | 7.2 | 18.1 | 73.1 | 24.8 | 10 | – |
| 1921 | 61.1 | 6.3 | 9.3 | 58.1 | 16.0 | 16 | 44.6 |
| 1922 | 92.8 | 10.7 | 35.4 | 68.1 | 52.0 | 20 | 52.3 |
| 1923 | 128.0 | 10.5 | 57.5 | 81.0 | 71.0 | 26 | 88.4 |
| 1924 | 114.6 | 8.3 | 43.9 | 79.0 | 55.6 | 32 | 80.6 |
| 1925 | 135.6 | 13.5 | 58.0 | 91.1 | 63.7 | 40 | 96.1 |
| 1926 | 166.9 | 26.0 | 53.6 | 139.3 | 32.1 | 55 | 119.8 |
| 1927 | 146.4 | 32.4 | 39.9 | 138.9 | 27.3 | 75 | 49.3 |
| 1928 | 197.8 | 39.8 | 55.7 | 181.9 | 28.2 | 77 | 97.3 |
| 1929 | 203.3 | 38.8 | 64.9 | 177.3 | 31.9 | 82 | 165.4 |
| 1930 | 121.3 | 18.9 | 28.8 | 111.4 | 23.8 | 83 | 114.9 |
| 1931 | 65.1 | 6.8 | 9.3 | 62.6 | 14.3 | 88 | 56.0 |
| 1932 | 50.7 | 6.7 | 9.8 | 47.6 | 19.3 | 93 | 29.5 |
| 1933 | 53.8 | 6.3 | 15.8 | 44.3 | 29.4 | 94 | 34.7 |
| 1934 | 92.6 | 1.6 | 31.3 | 62.9 | 33.8 | 95 | 83.0 |
| 1935 | 135.6 | 2.8 | 47.6 | 90.8 | 35.1 | 97 | 140.9 |
| 1936 | 128.4 | 7.7 | 42.3 | 93.8 | 33.0 | 98 | 121.8 |
| 1937 | 153.0 | 16.8 | 43.8 | 126.0 | 28.6 | – | 149.6 |
| 1938 | 123.8 | 13.6 | 40.4 | 97.0 | 32.6 | – | 155.3 |
| 1939 | 108.4 | 16.4 | 38.5 | 86.2 | 35.6 | – | 149.2 |

*Sources*: Calculated from Statistics Canada, *Historical Statistics of Canada* (1983); Dominion Bureau of Statistics, *Automobile Statistics for Canada* (various years); Motor Vehicle Manufacturers' Association, *Facts and Figures*, Toronto (various years); National Automobile Chamber of Commerce, *Automobile Facts and Figures*, Detroit (various years).
*Note*:
– Not available.

relatively cheap components, receiving the benefit of United States scale economies. Second, reinforcing the advantage to the assembly process resulting from these essentially pecuniary economies were any 'real' economies of scale resulting from levels of annual output almost one-third again as high as they would have been in the absence of exports. For these exports the Canadian industry had available the assistance of tariff preferences in certain British Empire markets, including Australia.[30]

In all of this, an obvious question arises: if tariff preference was a significant determinant of Canada's exports, why weren't British producers (who received even greater preference) more successful in exporting to the Australian market? An important part of the answer is that the American designs (whether produced in the United States or Canada)

> were popular because of price, appearance and horsepower in relation to weight. Chevrolets and Fords have the largest sales in Australia. In both these makes the purchaser gets a relatively low priced car of good appearance and high power. A British car of equal power is usually much heavier and more expensive. The British car may of course last longer, but this fact does not appear to carry very much weight with the Australian purchaser.[31]

Quite simply American/Canadian cars were perceived by consumers to be better suited to Australian conditions and to be better value for money than British cars, and they made their purchases accordingly. The same was apparently true in Canada where in 1932 duty-free entry of all motor vehicles from the United Kingdom was allowed. 'So unimportant did this concession appear to be for the Canadian automobile industry that little attention was paid to it in the Canadian Tariff Board Inquiry of 1936.'[32]

For much of the interwar period, the Canadian motor vehicle industry had a far greater (relative) export orientation than any of its major foreign counterparts (see Table 5.2). Over the period 1926–38, Canada was second only to the United States in terms of the number of motor vehicles (including trucks and buses) it exported, and Australia was by far its major market.[33] Exports accounted for one-third of Canada's production, compared with 17 per cent for the United Kingdom and 16 per cent for France. Over the same period the industry in the United States exported only 8.5 per cent of the vehicles it produced, though of course in terms of absolute numbers of vehicles exported it far outstripped Canada.

As an important consequence of its role as an exporter, the industry in Canada expanded rapidly and by the mid-1920s it was a major employer. By 1926, about 12,000 persons were directly employed in assembly/manufacture, excluding employment in the production of materials and parts. As V.W. Bladen, the 1961 Royal Commissioner, observed '[For the time this] was a substantial industrial development for Canada',[34] and this development continued for the remainder of the decade. By 1928 there were more than

16,000 people employed in motor vehicle manufacturing,[35] while another 3,500 were employed in the production of automobile parts and accessories (see Tables 5.3 and 5.4). The industry, however, suffered a severe and prolonged setback from the Depression: one that was longer lasting and far more severe than for Canadian manufacturing as a whole. The level of motor vehicle manufacturing employment in 1932–33 was only one-half that of 1929, and it did not regain its pre-Depression peak of nearly 17,000 employees in the remaining years of the interwar period. Motor vehicle production and exports were even harder hit, with 1932 levels respectively being one-quarter and one-eighth those of the levels in 1929.[36] Automobile parts and accessories producers fared better: while in 1931 employment had fallen by nearly 40 per cent compared with 1929, by 1934 it exceeded its 1929 level, and by 1937 it was

**Table 5.2**  Major countries – motor vehicle exports and production, 1918–1939 (,000)

| Year | Canada | | USA | | UK | | France | |
|------|--------|---------|--------|-------------|--------|---------|--------|---------|
|      | Prod'n | Exports | Prod'n | Exports[a] | Prod'n | Exports | Prod'n | Exports |
| 1918 | 82.4   | 10.4    | 1088.3 | –      | –     | –    | –      | –     |
| 1919 | 87.8   | 22.9    | 1845.8 | –      | –     | –    | –      | –     |
| 1920 | 94.4   | 23.0    | 2132.9 | –      | –     | –    | –      | –     |
| 1921 | 66.3   | 10.7    | 1616.1 | 41.4   | –     | –    | –      | –     |
| 1922 | 101.0  | 38.0    | 2545.2 | 81.6   | –     | –    | –      | –     |
| 1923 | 147.2  | 69.9    | 4033.2 | 159.1  | –     | –    | –      | –     |
| 1924 | 132.6  | 56.6    | 3605.2 | 187.7  | –     | –    | –      | –     |
| 1925 | 162.0  | 74.2    | 4265.8 | 330.0  | 167.0 | 29.1 | 179.0  | 57.5  |
| 1926 | 204.7  | 74.3    | 4300.9 | 313.6  | 198.0 | 33.4 | 192.0  | 59.8  |
| 1927 | 179.1  | 57.4    | 3401.3 | 393.1  | 211.8 | 36.3 | 191.3  | 52.0  |
| 1928 | 242.1  | 79.4    | 4358.8 | 515.8  | 211.9 | 32.8 | 223.6  | 46.0  |
| 1929 | 262.6  | 101.7   | 5337.1 | 546.2  | 238.8 | 42.2 | 253.0  | 49.2  |
| 1930 | 153.4  | 44.6    | 3362.8 | 245.2  | 236.5 | 30.0 | 230.0  | 31.1  |
| 1931 | 82.6   | 13.8    | 2380.4 | 135.8  | 226.3 | 24.4 | 201.0  | 26.3  |
| 1932 | 60.8   | 12.5    | 1331.9 | 70.1   | 232.7 | 40.3 | 163.0  | 19.2  |
| 1933 | 65.9   | 20.4    | 1889.8 | 111.5  | 286.3 | 51.9 | 189.0  | 25.5  |
| 1934 | 116.9  | 43.4    | 2737.1 | 242.2  | 342.5 | 57.9 | 181.0  | 25.0  |
| 1935 | 172.9  | 64.3    | 3971.2 | 271.4  | 416.9 | 68.6 | 165.0  | 18.9  |
| 1936 | 162.2  | 55.6    | 4461.5 | 285.8  | 481.5 | 82.3 | 204.0  | 21.2  |
| 1937 | 207.5  | 65.9    | 4820.2 | 395.2  | 493.3 | 99.2 | 201.0  | 25.1  |
| 1938 | 166.1  | 57.8    | 2508.4 | 276.7  | 444.9 | 83.7 | 227.0  | 23.8  |
| 1939 | 155.4  | 58.5    | 3577.3 | 254.3  | 402.5 | 62.8[b] | 173.8[b] | 20.9[c] |

*Sources*: See Table 5.1.
*Notes*:
[a]  Does not include 'foreign assemblies' (i.e., CKD kits).
[b]  8 months.     [c]  7 months.
–  Not available.

almost 80 per cent higher than its pre-Depression peak. By 1934, exports of parts and accessories had also regained their 1929 level, but in the remainder of the 1930s did not approach the interwar peak attained in 1925.

Unlike its Canadian counterpart, the horizons of Australia's industry remained firmly onshore. The inward-looking orientation of Australia's industry may be seen as at least a partial by-product of foreign ownership and the high transport costs caused by geographic isolation.[37] Even within the United States, the high cost of transport for completely built-up (CBU) vehicles was enough to provide the spur for the geographic dispersion of assembly during the 1920s (components production remained centralized). Compared with completely knocked down (CKD) vehicles, CBUs suffered a twofold transport cost disadvantage: they were bulky, and comparatively fragile. Between three and four vehicles could be shipped CKD in the same space as

**Table 5.3**   Canada – motor vehicle manufacturing, 1918–1939

| Year | Plants | Employees | Wholesale Value | | | Exports | Imports[a] |
| | | | Cars (C$m) | Trucks (C$m) | Total (C$m) | (No.) | (No.) |
|---|---|---|---|---|---|---|---|
| 1918 | 10 | 5362 | – | – | – | 10.4 | 10.8 |
| 1919 | 11 | 6771 | – | – | – | 22.9 | 11.7 |
| 1920 | 17 | 8281 | – | – | – | 23.0 | 9.1 |
| 1921 | 14 | 5475 | 53.6 | 3.8 | 57.4 | 10.7 | 7.3 |
| 1922 | 15 | 9344 | 67.2 | 5.2 | 72.5 | 38.0 | 11.6 |
| 1923 | 10 | 9305 | 78.3 | 8.9 | 87.2 | 69.9 | 11.8 |
| 1924 | 12 | 9277 | 70.6 | 8.1 | 78.7 | 56.6 | 9.3 |
| 1925 | 11 | 10301 | 86.2 | 12.2 | 98.4 | 74.2 | 14.6 |
| 1926 | 11 | 11905 | 106.0 | 16.6 | 122.6 | 74.3 | 28.6 |
| 1927 | 11 | 11063 | 100.9 | 14.9 | 115.9 | 57.4 | 36.6 |
| 1928 | 14 | 16749 | 127.3 | 21.9 | 149.2 | 79.4 | 47.4 |
| 1929 | 17 | 16435 | 134.0 | 29.5 | 163.5 | 101.7 | 44.7 |
| 1930 | 16 | 12541 | 75.3 | 16.5 | 91.8 | 44.6 | 23.2 |
| 1931 | 26 | 9545 | 42.6 | 10.3 | 53.0 | 13.8 | 8.7 |
| 1932 | 25 | 8810 | 32.5 | 6.1 | 38.6 | 12.5 | 1.4 |
| 1933 | 22 | 8134 | 32.6 | 6.1 | 38.6 | 20.4 | 1.8 |
| 1934 | 21 | 9674 | 57.3 | 12.8 | 70.0 | 43.4 | 2.9 |
| 1935 | 20 | 13095 | 79.2 | 19.8 | 99.0 | 64.3 | 4.1 |
| 1936 | 16 | 12933 | 76.8 | 19.1 | 96.0 | 55.6 | 9.9 |
| 1937 | 15 | 14946 | 93.4 | 30.4 | 123.8 | 65.9 | 20.1 |
| 1938 | 12 | 14872 | 81.7 | 26.5 | 108.2 | 57.9 | 15.2 |
| 1939 | 12 | 14427 | 71.1 | 28.1 | 99.2 | 58.7 | 18.3 |

*Sources*: See Table 5.1
*Notes*:
a    Excludes engines.
–    Not available.

a single CBU, and, for a given volume/weight, railways in the United States imposed a freight surcharge (about 10 per cent) for the shipment of CBUs, which were difficult to load and unload, and easily damaged.[38]

In Australia, isolation and the transport costs associated with it affected the industry in conflicting ways. They assisted the process of final assembly of the automobile by providing a margin of protection against fully built imports; conversely they provided penalties by inflating the cost of importable components, and providing a barrier to exports. Thus, production costs were higher than they would otherwise have been, and there were high costs entailed in transporting the bulky, easily damaged final product to foreign markets. Empire tariff preference was not enough to overcome these barriers to any potential Australian exporters, especially when combined with the influence of foreign ownership. As the two major firms of the industries in both countries had the same ultimate ties – Ford and General Motors in the United States –

**Table 5.4**   Canada – auto parts and accessories, 1918–1939

| Year | Plants | Employees | Wholesale Value of Production (C$m) | Exports (C$m) | Imports[a] (C$m) |
|---|---|---|---|---|---|
| 1918 | – | – | – | 0.9 | 6.6 |
| 1919 | – | – | – | 3.5 | 10.0 |
| 1920 | – | – | – | 4.3 | 14.4 |
| 1921 | – | – | – | 1.1 | 8.4 |
| 1922 | – | – | – | 1.9 | 13.7 |
| 1923 | – | – | – | 3.5 | 15.0 |
| 1924 | – | – | – | 5.0 | 15.2 |
| 1925 | – | – | – | 6.4 | 20.7 |
| 1926 | – | – | – | 5.5 | 27.5 |
| 1927 | – | – | – | 3.4 | 31.9 |
| 1928 | 77 | 3509 | 17.0 | 2.1 | 48.8 |
| 1929 | 65 | 4708 | 32.0 | 2.3 | 44.8 |
| 1930 | 57 | 3580 | 18.4 | 1.6 | 23.4 |
| 1931 | 73 | 2899 | 12.6 | 0.8 | 14.4 |
| 1932 | 76 | 3832 | 12.2 | 1.8 | 11.6 |
| 1933 | 83 | 3776 | 13.0 | 1.3 | 10.8 |
| 1934 | 80 | 5172 | 24.4 | 2.4 | 19.5 |
| 1935 | 82 | 6614 | 32.7 | 2.9 | 24.5 |
| 1936 | 85 | 6842 | 33.4 | 2.9 | 24.0 |
| 1937 | 88 | 8416 | 46.6 | 2.9 | 32.8 |
| 1938 | 97 | 7900 | 37.0 | 2.7 | 24.7 |
| 1939 | 97 | 8119 | 38.7 | 3.3 | 25.3 |

*Sources*: See Table 5.1.
*Notes*: See Table 5.3.

from their points of view, Canada's advantages of geographic proximity, including the relative ease of communication and control, favourable tariff treatment of inputs and tariff preference for the sales of its subsidiaries made it an ideal conduit for indirect US exports to British Empire markets. In fact, producers in the United States treated these 'Canadian' exports as their own. Thus, in the statistics provided by the United States National Automobile Chamber of Commerce, for much of the interwar period, production and international trade data for Canada and the United States were not separately recorded. Moreover 'Canadian output' is included in a table headed 'sales of American motor vehicles outside United States'.[39] The clear inference is that parent firms in the United States viewed as equivalents exports from the home country and production by their 'foreign' subsidiaries in Canada.

In the same way, their Australian activities may be viewed as outposts of North America. Unfortunately the picture of the industry which is now available to us is clouded by a lack of consistent statistics. An important reason for this is that automobile design and production methods of the time viewed

**Table 5.5**  Australia – motor industry, 1919/20–1929/30

| Year | Factories | Hands employed | Factories | Hands employed | Motor body production | Chassis unassembled imports |
|------|-----------|----------------|-----------|----------------|-----------------------|-----------------------------|
| 1919–20 | 622 | 6599 | | | – | – |
| 1920–21 | 784 | 8225 | | | – | – |
| 1921–22 | 917 | 8895 | | | – | – |
| 1922–23 | 1021[a] | 11420[a] | | | 46.9[b] | – |
| 1923–24 | 1300 | 14718 | | | 25.0[c] | – |
| 1924–25 | 1496 | 17235 | | | 32.8[c] | – |
| 1925–26 | 1712 | 19401 | | | 41.3[c] | – |
| 1926–27 | 1754[d] | 13739[d] | 156[e] | 9283[e] | 88.9 | 91.0 |
| 1927–28 | 1896 | 13809 | 158 | 7842 | 58.9 | 56.2 |
| 1928–29 | 2199[e] | 22841[f] | | | 72.2 | 92.2 |
| 1929–30 | 2300 | 19423 | | | 46.4 | 58.6 |

*Sources*:  Commonwealth Bureau of Census and Statistics, *Production Bulletin, Annual 1919–20 to 1938–39*; AA ACT A461/1 1418/1/6 Pt 1; *Australian Motorist*, May 1, p. 466. Further sources – see Table 5.6.

*Notes*:
a   Cycles and motors (production).
b   Calendar year.
c   South Australia only (i.e. including Holdens and T.J. Richards).
d   Motors and motor cycle and bicycle building and repair.
e   Motor bodybuilding and repairing.
f   Motor vehicles and accessories (production).
–   Not available.

automobile production as two separate activities: bodybuilding and chassis assembly.[40] However, examination of the statistics for the production of motor bodies and the import statistics for unassembled chassis (see Tables 5.5, 5.6 and 5.7) provides a guide to the magnitude of what would now be classified as automobile production. Notable are the growth of the industry during the 1920s, the effect of the Depression from 1929 to 1934, and the recovery of the industry in the second half of the 1930s. From just over 2,000 people in 1932, by 1936 the industry employed 12,000 people in the manufacture and repair of bodies, and 4,000 in the assembly of chassis and the fitting of bodies, four times the number in 1932 (see Table 5.6).[41]

The importance of the North American influence on the Australian industry (see Table 5.7) is also notable. For the greater part of the interwar period the United States and Canada dominated Australian chassis imports, with the United Kingdom third – and in the 1920s, often a distant third. Until the mid-1930s, most of the motor cars sold in Australia were based on chassis imported from North America.

The influence of the trade diversion measures of 1936, an aim of which

**Table 5.6**   Australia – motor industry, 1926/27–1938/39

| Year | Motor body construction and repair | | | Motor vehicles and cycles constr. and assembly | | Imports |
|------|-----------|-------------------|-------------------|-----------|-------------------|------------------------------|
|      | Factories | Hands employed | Production (,000) | Factories | Hands employed | Unassembled chassis (,000) |
| 1926–27 | 156[a] | 9283[a] | 88.9 | – | – | 91.0 |
| 1927–28 | 158[a] | 7242[a] | 58.9 | – | – | 56.2 |
| 1928–29 | – | – | 72.2 | – | – | 92.2 |
| 1929–30 | – | – | 46.4 | – | – | 58.6 |
| 1930–31 | 160 | 2777 | 10.4 | 70 | 1522 | 9.2 |
| 1931–32 | 153 | 2176 | 6.3 | 60 | 974 | 4.1 |
| 1932–33 | 159 | 3654 | 13.5 | 59 | 1150 | 15.6 |
| 1933–34 | 170 | 6214 | 26.3 | 55 | 1728 | 32.4 |
| 1934–35 | 177 | 9526 | 45.4 | 66 | 2713 | 52.7 |
| 1935–36 | 180 | 12008 | 67.3 | 77 | 4007 | 74.1 |
| 1936–37 | 201 | 12267 | 77.2 | 85 | 4626 | 54.1 |
| 1937–38 | 205 | 12795 | 92.1 | 86 | 4908 | 70.1 |
| 1938–39 | 232 | 11742 | 79.0 | 89 | 4279 | 60.7 |

*Sources*: Commonwealth Bureau of Census and Statistics, *Trade and Customs and Excise Revenue of the Commonwealth of Australia*, Melbourne (various years); Commonwealth Bureau of Census and Statistics, *Australian Statistics of Overseas Imports and Exports*, Melbourne (various years); Commonwealth Bureau of Census and Statistics, *Overseas Trade and Customs and Excise Revenue*, Canberra (various years).
*Notes*:
a    Motor bodybuilding and repair.
–    Not available.

was to switch the source of Australian imports from 'unfavorable trading countries', may also be discerned. The relative importance of (direct) imports from the USA declined to be overtaken by Canada and the United Kingdom. An inference from these data is that increasingly United States producers were using Canada as an avenue for avoiding the impact of Australia's trade measures.

The Depression damaged the industry severely in both countries, and as they slowly emerged from it, the mid-1930s brought the introduction of far more interventionist policies towards the industry. In Canada, the Tariff Revision of 1936 lowered tariffs on most US imports, explicitly recognized the tax-effect of tariffs on inputs not produced in Canada, and provided for tariff concessions on automotive components if 'content' rules were satisfied.[42] These provisions

**Table 5.7** Australia – chassis imports, 1919/20–1938/39

| Year | Main sources of unassembled chassis | | | Total all sources | Assembled chassis | Total chassis |
|------|--------|--------|--------|------|------|------|
| | Canada | USA | UK | | | |
| 1919–20 | 2450 | 11000 | 1210 | – | – | 15100 |
| 1920–21 | 4150[a] | 14200[a] | 5800[a] | – | – | 25200[a] |
| 1921–22 | 4810 | 7170 | 2740 | – | – | 18000 |
| 1922–23 | 17933 | 15919 | 1406 | – | – | 37632 |
| 1923–24 | 22951 | 41372 | 2680 | – | – | 70478 |
| 1924–25 | 15735[b] | 48909[b] | 6017[b] | – | – | 74940[b] |
| 1925–26 | 12251 | 58512 | 13403 | – | – | 88591 |
| 1926–27 | 16118 | 52226 | 21212 | 91026 | 27928 | 118954 |
| 1927–28 | 2738 | 45992 | 7131 | 56234 | 11641 | 67875 |
| 1928–29 | 23028 | 59375 | 9427 | 92198 | 7302 | 99500 |
| 1929–30 | 9422 | 40339 | 8663 | 58647 | 3334 | 61981 |
| 1930–31 | 2375 | 4807 | 1973 | 9220 | 147 | 9367 |
| 1931–32 | 9 | 1599 | 2447 | 4059 | 87 | 4146 |
| 1932–33 | 4065 | 4296 | 7200 | 15629 | 147 | 15776 |
| 1933–34 | 12223 | 8723 | 11337 | 32354 | 570 | 32924 |
| 1934–35 | 18692 | 23530 | 10363 | 52656 | 1319 | 53975 |
| 1935–36 | 30809 | 29270 | 13989 | 74120 | 1532 | 75652 |
| 1936–37 | 19708 | 18010 | 16235 | 54105 | 1082 | 55187 |
| 1937–38 | 24425 | 21365 | 23946 | 70146 | 1133 | 71279 |
| 1938–39 | 20630 | 15553 | 23493 | 60675 | 732 | 61407 |

*Sources*: See Table 5.6.
*Notes*:
[a] Estimated by dividing total import values by average unit value of chassis imported in 1922–23 (£151). The total number of unassembled chassis so estimated was then apportioned to Canada, USA and UK on the basis of their relative values of imports as a proportion of the total value of chassis imports in each year.
[b] Data refers to total chassis imports, that is both assembled and unassembled.

laid the foundations for later local content schemes that since then have been features of automotive industry policy in both countries.

## Evaluation

In both Australia and Canada the automobile industry has been a major beneficiary of long-standing efforts to develop manufacturing bases as part of their respective governments' programmes of national development. Tariffs have been a significant instrument of their policies, and an important determinant of foreign direct investment.

In the case of the automobile industry in Canada, before the First World War it is almost inconceivable that the large-scale assembly of motor vehicles would have been undertaken without the assistance of tariffs. However, an amalgam of the influences of location, distance and transport costs have also played important roles in the industry's development. With the major US car producers just across the Detroit river from Windsor, Ontario, it was no coincidence that it was businessmen in that city who perceived the opportunity provided by the tariff, and thus determined the site of Ford's first Canadian plant. That Oshawa, Ontario, was chosen as the initial site of General Motors Canada was determined by the location of McLauglin's facilities there. While further from Detroit than Windsor, it is nevertheless still close, and with the added advantage of proximity to the major Canadian markets of Toronto and Montreal.

A similar amalgam has played the same role in Australia. Tariffs and transport costs are additive barriers to trade and inducements to local (subsidiary) production. In the case of automobile production, transport costs were a most important determinant of the structure of production in Australia. Bodies were bulky, fragile and expensive to ship. They were therefore obvious candidates for local production. Chassis (including engines and transmissions) were relatively compact and not so easily damaged. Moreover, the economic production of chassis components relied on the exploitation of scale economies, while their assembly on a small scale could be undertaken fairly cheaply. For much of the interwar period the structure of the Australian tariff reinforced the pattern of production encouraged by transport costs. It provided high protective rates for body building, but low revenue duties on chassis.

The form and importance of Canadian participation in the Australian industry was also determined by tariffs. The Canadian tariff encouraged United States producers to manufacture and assemble behind the Canadian tariff wall. The preference offered by the Australian tariff to 'Canadian' producers (compared with the duties that would be charged on the same goods of US origin) encouraged United States producers to use their Canadian subsidiaries as conduits for their operations in Australia. A result was that for much of the interwar period Canada was a dominant if indirect force in the formation of the industry in Australia. However, by the 1930s the major US producers had established a presence in Australia that was extending in the direction of increased local content and reduced imports. As local content increased, the influence of Canada on the Australian industry inevitably declined.

## Notes

1. In Canada, motor vehicle manufacture inherited the (nominal) tariff protection of the carriage-building industry – 35 per cent, *ad valorem* (V.W. Bladen, *Report of the Royal Commission on the Automotive Industry* (Ottawa, 1962), p. 5).
2. Motor Vehicle Manufacturers Association, *Facts and Figures of the Automotive Industry* (Toronto, 1969), p. 4.
3. Bladen, *Report of the Royal Commission*, p. 5.
    Ford Canada's location in Windsor, Ontario, was a function of Ford's location and the industry's concentration in and near Detroit. However, during the 1890s more than half of US automobile producers had been located elsewhere – mainly in the northeast of the United States, between Philadelphia and Boston. During the first decade of the twentieth century, most production shifted to southeast Michigan. While in the second decade most assembly operations relocated to other regions, production of parts continued to be concentrated in southeast Michigan and remained there until the 1980s.
    It is often suggested that the early locational concentration in Michigan was a historical accident. Certainly the presence there of Henry Ford was a very large influence. However, Michigan was the production centre for carriages and petrol engines – two of the products contributing most heavily to early automotive technology. (The bicycle was a third.) Moreover, the area offered a surplus of unskilled labour and the availability of venture capital (northeast bankers had proven reluctant to lend to potential motor vehicle manufacturers). The success of Ford's Model T, which captured nearly half of the US market, was pivotal. Ford's first plant was located in Detroit and the company relocated (as it expanded) four times within the Detroit area within its first 15 years (see J.M. Rubinstein, *The Changing US Auto Industry, A Geographical Analysis* (New York, 1992), Chapters 2 and 3.)
4. See G.S. May, 'Jackson Automobile Company' in G. May (ed.), *Encyclopedia of American Business History and Biography*, 'The Automobile, 1896–1920' (New York, 1990), pp. 269–71.
5. Durant was an empire-building financier, with little or no management skill. However, he knew a good deal when he saw one, and had the skill and charm to carry it off. According to Walter Chrysler (the automobile maker), Durant had 'the most winning personality of anyone I've ever known. He could coax a bird right down out of a tree' (W.P. Chrysler, *Life of an American Workman* (New York, 1937), p. 143).
6. Durant had overextended GM in the course of its rapid early expansion. He was forced out of GM's management in 1910 and formed the Chevrolet Company in 1911.
7. Robert McLauglin ran General Motors' Canadian operations until 1924 when his

brother George succeeded him as president. George remained as a director of
General Motors until he retired in 1967 at the age of 96. See Rubinstein, *The
Changing US Auto Industry*, pp. 72–7.

8.  In 1927 two special McLauglin-Buicks were built for the then Prince of Wales
    (General Motors, *The First Seventy-five Years of Transportation Products* (Auto-
    mobile Quarterly in association with the Princeton Institute for Historic Research,
    1983), p. 52).

9.  Chrysler took over the assets of Maxwell-Chalmers Motor Company of Canada.
    In its first year of operations, Chrysler produced nearly 8,000 vehicles. By 1929
    it had built a new passenger car assembly plant, and had absorbed Dodge
    Bros, Canada (cars), and Graham Bros, (trucks) (Bladen, *Report of the Royal
    Commission*, p. 5; Motor Vehicle Manufacturers Association, *Facts and Figures
    of the Automotive Industry*, p. 5).

10. See Tables 5.1 and 5.6.

11. Australia's population in 1920 was about 5.4 million people, Canada's about
    7 million; in 1936 Australia's was nearly 6.9 million people, Canada's just over
    11 million (Commonwealth Bureau of Census and Statistics, *Official Yearbook of
    the Commonwealth of Australia* (Canberra, 1939), pp. 317–18).

12. The dissemination of mass production methods outside the United States was
    quite slow. In Europe, for example, the methods associated with Henry Ford were
    not widely adopted until well into the 1930s. (For a brief description of the rise
    (and fall) of mass production in the industry, see J.P. Womack, D.T. Jones and
    D. Roos, *The Machine that Changed the World* (New York, 1990), Chapter 2.)

13. *Coach and Motor Builder*, June 1924. An example of labour relations determining
    industry location, was the decision of the British firm, Cadbury Brothers, to
    manufacture milk chocolate in Tasmania, at some distance from the major
    markets, in part because of the lower labour costs, and fewer days lost through
    strikes compared with the mainland.

14. For example, in 1936, the retail price of a Ford 30 hp V8 was A£234.13.10 in
    Canada, and A£355 in Australia (Tariff Board, *Engines and Chassis for Motor
    Vehicles* (Canberra, 1938)). According to a 1930s calculation, in Canada, the cost
    of running a 1,500 cc car for 8,000 miles (registration tax, petrol (including fuel
    tax) and compulsory insurance) was only slightly over one-third the cost in
    Australia. The cost of running a car in Canada was estimated to be 84 per cent of
    that of the USA (G. Maxcy and A. Silberston, *The Motor Industry* (London,
    1959), p. 48).

15. In 1931, Australia had one motor vehicle for every 11 persons; for Canada the
    ratio was 1:8; for USA 1:4.6. By 1939 the corresponding ratios were 1:9, 1:8
    and 1:4 (Automobile Manufacturers Association, *Automobile Facts and Figures*
    (Detroit, 1931 and 1939)).

16. Alfred Weber's 1909 work (in German) *Theory of the Location of Industries*
    (trans. C.J. Friedrich, Chicago, 1929), provides the framework for modern
    industrial location theory.

17. In this chapter we concentrate on Ford and General Motors, the two principal
    foreign firms. Chrysler was also an important market participant.

18. Ford USA held no shares except through Henry and Edsel Ford (Mortlock, BRG
    213/65/9).

19. The early development of the industry in Australia reflected the differences in the
    organizational philosophies of Ford and General Motors. In the United States,
    Ford provided the archetype of the vertically integrated, centrally controlled
    firm. By the 1930s it obtained virtually all its components 'in house'. An

important reason (aside from Henry Ford's distrust of outsiders) was that with the development of mass production methods there was a need for complete interchangeability of parts. Ford required components manufactured to closer tolerances and tighter delivery schedules than had ever been required before. Henry Ford did not believe that arm's-length purchases in the open market could provide these needs. As described in the text, Ford also pursued this 'in-house' strategy in Australia by setting up both body production and chassis assembly operations in 1925.

General Motors' approach was different. Under Alfred Sloan, General Motors' decision-making was decentralized, allowing its foreign subsidiaries (and its domestic divisions) high degrees of autonomy. Purchasing outside the firm was commonplace and in this respect General Motors' Australian subsidiary was no exception when it obtained its bodies externally from Holden's (see Womack, Jones and Roos, *The Machine that Changed the World*, Chapter 2).

20. In the opinion of the *Australian Motorist* (November 1924) the entry of Ford could be 'disastrous for Australians who have invested Australian capital in the automobile business'.
21. *Australian Motorist*, November 1924.
22. Ibid. The issue also saw the revival of an Australian gripe over war debt against a sister dominion. 'Canada supplied the men, but Great Britain equipped them, found them ammunition, and paid them. Australians, on the other hand, found the men and the money too' (*Australian Motorist*, May 1925). On the issue of the form of its participation, Ford Canada was unfavourably compared with US companies, including GM, which, as noted in the text, bought bodies (and other components, including tyres) from local producers (*Australian Motorist*, May 1925).
23. The May 1925 issue of the *Australian Motorist* reported that 'On July 1, the Ford Co. will take over unsold cars and spare parts from Australian distributors, but not the buildings or plants.'
24. *Coach and Motor Builder*, September 1924.
25. 'Unfavorable trading countries' (mainly the USA and Japan) were those which were considered to be poor customers for Australia's exports; 'favorable countries' included Britain and many of the Empire countries. On balance Canada was not viewed favourably by the Government of the day. According to L.J. Hartnett, Managing Director of GM-H, 'the Australian government is not sympathetically inclined towards the Canadian government because of the treatment that has been meted out [the Australian exports of citrus fruits and other items] where the Canadian government favored the US over Australia'. (Briefing Memorandum dated December 1936, from Hartnett to E. Riley, General Manager General Motors, New York (Mortlock, BSR 213/65/9). The trade diversion measures were a diplomatic and economic disaster, and most of them were abandoned in 1937, though not the major measures affecting the automobile industry. See B. Dyster and D. Meredith, *Australia in the International Economy in the Twentieth Century* (Cambridge, 1990), pp. 150–53.
26. Hansard, 22 May 1936, p. 211.
27. L.J. Hartnett to E. Riley, Managing Director, General Motors Export Division, New York, 10 December 1936 (Mortlock, BRG 213/65/9).
28. Hansard, 11 May 1938.
29. Components 'of a class or kind not manufactured in Canada' could be imported duty-free. As well, partial drawback (refund) of duty on some components was allowed, provided at least 50 per cent of the factory cost of the completed vehicle

was incurred in the British Empire (Bladen, *Report of the Royal Commission*, p. 7).

30. For most of the interwar period, Canadian automotive exports to Australia were subject to intermediate tariff rates, about halfway between the general and the British preferential rates.
31. AA ACT A461/1 048/1/6 Part 2.
32. Bladen, *Report of the Royal Commission*, p. 8.
33. During the second half of the 1930s, for example, more than 50 per cent of Canadian automobile exports were to Australia (Dominion Bureau of Statistics, *Automobile Statistics for Canada* (Ottawa, various years). See also AA ACT 1418/1/6, Part 2).
34. Bladen, *Report of the Royal Commission*, pp. 6–7.
35. This figure includes those employed in truck and bus manufacture.
36. These figures compare with total employment in the manufacturing sector which declined by about 30 per cent compared with its 1929 level in 1932 and 1933, and regained its 1929 level by 1937. See Statistics Canada, *Historical Statistics of Canada*, 2nd edition, Series R1–22 (1983).
37. In 1929 it was reported that a car shipped f.o.b. (free on board) from the USA for A£206, was valued at A£400 c.i.f. (cost, insurance, freight) when landed in Australia (*Sydney Morning Herald*, 26 August 1929).
38. That transport costs may be a determinant of industry location and the form of activity undertaken is hardly new. In the present context, Henry Ford has taken the credit for the 'branch assembly' of motor cars. 'Only a small percentage of our automobiles are used in or around Detroit and so we quit being automobile makers excepting for the district and instead began to make automobile parts and ship them out to assembly points through the country. This saved the cost of final assembly at the factory, of testing, of knocking down the automobile and crating it, and of paying the extra freight on a bulky piece of machinery' (H. Ford, 'What I have learnt about management in the last 25 years', *System, The Magazine of Business* (January, 1926), p. 40; Henry Ford Museum Archives and Library, Dearborn, Michigan, Accession 96 Box 18).

    However, some observers suggest the credit is more accurately attributed to Charles Couzens and Norval Hawkins, two senior Ford employees. In particular, '[Hawkins] conceived the idea of making a freight car pay its way, by the establishment of assembly plants all over the world, and shipping in knock-down condition from the plant in Detroit the pieces and parts that went to make up the car' (L.W. Goodenough, Henry Ford Museum Archives and Library, Dearborn, Michigan, Accession 84 Box 2, p. 183).

    The savings were significant. 'The assembly plants permitted Ford to fill freight cars completely with [components]. The equivalent of twenty-six automobiles could be shipped in knocked-down form, compared to seven or eight fully assembled vehicles.' Moreover, in addition to the saving of space, the freight rate for components was lower than for relatively fragile, fully built automobiles (Rubenstein, *The Changing US Auto Industry*, p. 54).
39. National Automobile Chamber of Commerce, *Facts and Figures of the Automobile Industry* (New York, 1939), p. 30.
40. There are no statistics available for Australian 'automobile' production for the interwar period. This is the result of the nature of the then production process and of the product itself. Automobiles were seen as comprising two fundamental and separable components: the chassis and the body, and each was produced separately. It was only with the development and introduction (in Australia,

after the Second World War) of the integrated body/chassis design and unitary construction that the two 'components' were viewed for statistical purposes as part of the same process of manufacture.

Another important reason is the swift post-First World War growth of the importance of the automobile and the concomitant decline of such activities as the manufacture of saddlery, coaches and wagons. There was an understandable failure of the Commonwealth Statistician immediately to accommodate these swift structural changes in the economy in the published statistics.

41. Moreover, in 1936, according to the Tariff Board, 2,000 people were also engaged in the manufacture of original equipment and replacement parts, and a further 2,000 in the manufacture of replacement parts only (Tariff Board, *Engines and Chassis*, pp. 9, 12).

42. The tariff revisions made changes to the intermediate tariff rates that in 1931 applied to imports from the United States. These rates were lowered to 17.5 per cent, irrespective of value. The intermediate rates of 1931 were 17.5 per cent on automobiles valued at not more than $1,200, 22.5 per cent on those valued at more than $1,200, and not more than $2,100, and 30 per cent on those valued at more than $2,100. Before that general rates of 20 per cent, 30 per cent and 40 per cent, respectively, had applied to imports from the US.

While in 1926, partial drawback of duty on components had been allowed subject to a British Empire content requirement, this later measure went further and provided duty-free access to automobile assemblers for parts of 'a class or kind not made in Canada', and for some parts there was a further condition that a certain proportion of factory cost (varying between 40 and 60 per cent, depending on the level of output) was of Empire origin (Bladen, *Report of the Royal Commission*, pp. 8, 9).

# 6    Britain and Empire

When war broke out in 1914, most cars in Australia were British-made. The war brought the effective cessation of car imports from Britain and a clear field for American producers. By war's end Britain's pre-war dominance of the Australian market for motor cars had ended. The war had paupered Britain and much of its industry. The slump of 1921 and the strikes that followed left British car manufacturers with few resources, and a local market, 85 per cent of which had been taken by United States producers. From the British point of view, it was a matter of starting all over again. As W.E. Rootes, the founder of one of Britain's most important car manufacturers, put it, 'we had to regain our own markets at home, and then make some money before we [could regain our export markets]'.[1]

## Regaining the Australian market

Even before the war, however, there had been signs of trouble for British producers. 'The *Australian Motorist* in 1912 and 1913 and up to the outbreak of war warned the British motor manufacturers in almost every issue of his [*sic*] falling export trade, and earned this paper the reputation of being anti British.'[2] Most Australians, however, were far from anti-British and receptive to a reassertion of British influence and market dominance. Indeed, 'it was the natural instinct for every Australian to give preference to all things British, particularly if it was a matter of trading'.[3] Nevertheless, for much of the inter-war period, any such instinct was suppressed by the perception that British cars were generally expensive and often unsuitable for local conditions. Moreover, spares were in short supply, and British producers and their Australian distributors were often seen as ignorant of and unresponsive to conditions in the local market.

While British producers recognized the unfavourable perceptions of their products in the Australian market, little of substance was done to change them, despite the British car industry delegations that between the wars were periodically sent to Australia pledging to deal with any problems and recover the lost ground. Major R.E. Goddard headed the first in 1919 with the aim of having 'The British manufacturer in future endeavour to supply Australia with what it wanted.'[4] Adding to the difficulties was the gradual reduction in Australian tariff preference for imports of British motor vehicles, which according to the Federation of British Industries would result in 'Australia [becoming] completely closed to makers of any British motor car'.[5] Such a statement proved to be exaggerated, but nevertheless, British producers still faced considerable consumer resistance to their products during the 1920s. The reason was not just the partial loss of tariff preference and its effect on consumer prices, however. Rather, the product itself was perceived to be at fault, and endeavours to improve it apparently came to little. Although Britain's share of new registrations had risen to about 15 per cent in the second half of the 1920s from very low figures in the years immediately after the war, sales were far from acceptable to British producers.[6] As a consequence, in 1927 W.E. Rootes visited Australia to 'investigate conditions and to combine with our representatives [to] launch a definite policy which will give us a large volume of business in due course'.[7] Just a month later, Sir Archibald Boyd-Carpenter headed a British motor industry delegation on a fact-finding mission, and one 'fact' was immediately obvious: its products were still not meeting the needs of the market. The delegation was faced with complaints regarding types and styles of British cars, but when it came to specifics,

> [it] experienced difficulty in Australia in obtaining a consensus of opinion as to alleged defects of British cars. ... The delegation wanted to know which particular details of manufactures wrong, and hoped to learn how it might be rectified [but] could get no comprehensive information by a large body on any specific point.[8]

From the British point of view, the whole business was highly frustrating, with one British visitor quoted as commenting that

> the Australian market was most difficult to satisfy. It had been said that British motor manufacturers did not consider Australian conditions, and so failed to place a suitable vehicle on the Australian market. However he considered that Australian conditions were more thoroughly studied than those elsewhere. Australians, he thought were decidedly conservative where the purchase of motor vehicles were concerned.[9]

If Australians were 'conservative' in not buying British cars, some Australian importers had good reason to be wary of the British product.

> Under the banner of patriotism Australians rallied and got anything but a profitable deal [from selling British cars] ... and many Australians went out of business as a consequence. It was not a consequence of American competition that smashed these Australians, but failure to give Australians British goods that could not [sic] be merchandised with a profit, because they would not stand up to the Australian requirements, the expense of servicing, and in some cases partial reconstruction, created colossal expense to Australians.[10]

It was apparent that at least some representatives of British industry did not hear, or were just not listening to the complaints. According to Lt. Colonel

Hacking, a member of Boyd-Carpenter's delegation, 'British cars were always synonymous with quality, and in spite of the temptations to sacrifice quality in order to secure cheaper production, he agreed with the view that it was essential that British quality should be maintained.' For Vice-Regal users the image of British quality may well have been justified. At a dinner for the delegation, Sir Dudley de Chair, Governor of New South Wales, told an appreciative audience that 'while in Australia he had always used British cars and had always found them most satisfactory'.[11] One may expect, however, that Sir Dudley may have been insulated from some of the problems experienced by the *hoi polloi*, and indeed, satisfaction with British cars seemed to be higher especially during and after a good dinner. Moreover, telling an audience what they want to hear is usually an infallible guide to successful speech-making and the South Australian Agent-General apparently knew it. British engineering inspectors at a dinner in London in 1928 received his opinion most favourably that 'Australian motorist's preference was changing form Uncle Sam to John Bull, because Britain was now building cars suitable for the Australian market'.[12] Unfortunately for British producers few, if any Australian car buyers were there to listen.

By the end of the 1920s, Britons were losing patience. Sir Herbert Austin commented 'I sometimes feel annoyed with the Dominions, for example Australia, where there are eight foreign cars to one British', and spoke of the need for 'reciprocity' for Britain which was Australia's best customer.[13] That Britain was Australia's best customer was quite true, but at the same time the balance of trade and payments was firmly in Britain's favour. Austin's comments on reciprocity were followed just two days later by a formal request by the Australian Association of British Manufacturers for favourable tariff and primage treatment for their products.[14]

Despite more than 10 years of apparent effort, British cars in the eyes of most Australian buyers still did not come up to the mark. Some models had quite specific and well-known shortcomings. For example, Morris cars were notorious for the failure of their rear axles.[15] In terms of broad segments of the market, low-priced British cars suffered from their light construction and small size.[16] However, not all of the blame for the failures of British cars could be placed directly on their manufacturers. Engine design in Britain for much of the interwar period was perverted by a tax regime which encouraged designers to use small cylinder bores with long piston strokes, which minimized the tax, but adversely affected engine performance.[17]

> It is true that British cars would be bought more readily if sold at lower prices, but the reason for their higher cost in Australia is the tariff. The politicians in Great Britain have also dealt a severe blow to the motor industry there by the H.P. [horse-power] tax, so the British motor manufacturers has been hard hit by politicians in two places.[18]

To the extent that regaining a dominant share of the market was a measure of success of British efforts to improve the image and performance of their products in Australia, the available data suggest that for most of the interwar period the efforts were a failure. Nevertheless, some progress was made, albeit with the assistance of increased tariff preferences provided to British imports from 1929.[19] In the period 1926 to 1929 British cars comprised about 15 per cent of annual new car registrations in Australia (see Table 6.1). From 1930 to 1936 the British share averaged 24 per cent of new registrations, but it was a market which had been devastated by the Depression.[20] As a further reflection of the hard economic times, most of British sales over the period were of 'baby cars', production of which was eschewed by United States manufacturers. These vehicles (mostly Austins and Morrises) comprised about 40 per cent of British-origin new car registrations in 1929 and this figure rose to nearly 85 per cent in 1936. In terms of the overall share of the Australian market, British baby cars comprised 6 per cent of new registrations in 1929 and over 20 per cent in 1936.[21] Those (fewer) Australians still buying cars during the worst of the Depression, were mainly seeking cheap, basic transport and for them the

**Table 6.1**  New car registrations in Australia, 1926–1939

| Year | Total number | US & Canada | Continental[a] | British[b c] No. | % |
|------|-------------|-------------|----------------|------------------|-----|
| 1926 | 80655 | 64889 | 3411 | 12355 | (15.3) |
| 1927 | 82570 | 67497 | 1986 | 13087 | (15.8) |
| 1928 | 72568 | 61089 | 1033 | 10446 | (14.4) |
| 1929 | 65720 | 55403 | 985 | 9332 | (15.0) |
| 1930 | 29571 | 24171 | 372 | 5028 | (17.0) |
| 1931 | 10299 | 8078 | 177 | 2044 | (19.8) |
| 1932 | 10684 | 6898 | 98 | 3688 | (34.5) |
| 1933 | 15679 | 9672 | 185 | 5922 | (37.8) |
| 1934 | 27868 | 20030 | 189 | 7649 | (27.4) |
| 1935 | 39955 | 31242 | 129 | 8584 | (21.5) |
| 1936 | 48206 | 36766 | 37 | 11403 | (23.7) |
| 1937 | 58064 | – | – | – | |
| 1938 | 58201 | – | – | – | |
| 1939 | 52995 | – | – | – | |

*Sources*: General Motors' market research for the period 1926–36 (AA ACT, BI/1, 850 Bundle 5). Total registrations for 1937–39: Industries Assistance Commission, *Australian Market for PMVs*, Mimeo (June 1974), p. 5.
*Notes*:
[a] Citroen and Fiat only.
[b] British and Continental imports less Citroen and Fiat.
[c] Estimate.
– Not available.

British babies were virtually their only resort. Any observed improvement in the market position of British cars in the first half of the 1930s was therefore largely illusory, and ascribing any such 'improvements' to the availability of better and more suitable British vehicles would be misleading.

Despite their increasing sales in each year from 1931, it was still apparent that Australian consumers were unhappy with British-produced cars. In 1936 the Minister for Trade and Customs, T.W. White, suggested the reason British manufacturers did not enjoy a larger share of the Australian market was 'that they do not supply cars of a type suitable for Australian requirements as do their American competitors'.[22] There were fundamental reasons for the dominance of North American vehicles over those made in Britain. In addition to good appearance, they were relatively cheap and powerful. Any superior durability of British cars carried little weight with Australian buyers.[23]

By the mid-1930s British producers had had more than 15 years to solve the problems in supplying the appropriate types and qualities of vehicles, sufficient spare parts and technical backup. They had failed on almost every count. Why? At least part of the reason was the failure of British management. According to one observer, with its autocratic style and purely engineering outlook, 'British motor management [failed] to progress beyond the stage of enthusiastic pioneering engineer, running a one man band, to the commercial management of a large, complex mass-producing organization engaged in large scale competition.'[24]

If there were fundamental problems for British producers and their Australian representatives, they were of attitude and ignorance. They are well illustrated in correspondence from Marcus Bell, a representative of the Department of Defence Laboratories to R. Russell Grimwade of Australian Consolidated Industries, one of the country's largest industrial companies.[25] In his letter dated 27 January 1932, Bell first noted the favourable Australian reaction to the use of locally produced components by GM-H, observing: 'people [suppliers] who are getting business from GM[-H] are propagandists for their vehicles and their number in increasing all the time'. Bell's further remarks are worth quoting at length, because they go to the heart of the British problem.

> Contrast [GM-H] with British methods – the other day the representative of a British Coy. came here with twelve springs for testing: The matter was quite serious I understand, a dispute with a customer. Our fee for [the] test was 2/6d. each – almost a nominal charge which GM[-H] has paid many a time. The British man took them away untested sooner than pay it, spent as much time and driving as the test was worth, and doesn't now know whether his springs are good or bad. [Before that we] took the opportunity of ... talking of local production. He said it was no good – he had tried it. On being pressed, he admitted that he has no drawings and specifications to put up to manufacturers and had apparently never thought how products were to be checked.

On another occasion Bell

> had a word with an official of the Association of British manufacturers; he assured
> me no car parts are made here, everyone is importing them in spite of heavy duties, in
> any case they cannot be made here and are not likely to be for some considerable
> time. When I told him shortly what the position is, he was surprised. ... The position
> is unfortunately typical of British trade here ... where we have direct dealings and
> know the facts. The results are deplorable; it was bad enough for Britain's trade to be
> lost to her by the War ... but here we have business being deliberately given away and
> a position which should never have been allowed getting progressively worse.[26]

## Australian trade policy in the 1930s

The Scullin government's emergency measures of April 1930 were a response
to the onset of the Great Depression. They brought unprecedented increases in
tariffs. The rationale for their introduction was not protectionism, however, but
as measures for saving the international financial viability of the country, which
even before late 1928 had suffered falling export prices, and a highly adverse
balance of trade. Imports of British goods were caught in the net, with British
preference tariffs increased in proportion to the general tariff increases. Scullin
then urged British manufacturers to establish local facilities behind the tariff
wall.[27] Canada had also raised protective barriers and as a result of the declining
position of Britain in Empire trade, and its deteriorating economy at home,
the British government sent a delegation to Ottawa in July 1932, to negotiate
a series of bilateral trade agreements with Empire countries. In effect, the
agreements that commenced on 20 August 1932 provided a secure market in
Britain for wheat and other foodstuffs, mainly from Canada and Australia, and
in return the Empire countries offered tariff reductions on their imports of
manufactures from Britain. For Australia, the eventual result was a three-
column tariff comprising British Preferential, Intermediate (MFN) and General
rates.

Nevertheless, Lord Nuffield on arrival in Australia on a 1935 visit
complained 'from the British car manufacturer's point of view, the export of
cars to Australia was fast becoming entirely uneconomic. Owing to tariffs and
body-building costs, the Australian public cannot obtain our open cars, and this
class of business is therefore completely denied to us.'[28] But this was only a
part of the automotive market. In the market for inputs, Britons had far less to
complain about as

> a significant fact, not generally realized is that of the materials imported because they
> are not yet available in Australia, the great proportion is purchased in England. ...
> Thus, while bodies are not imported into Australia in any real volume, nevertheless a
> high percentage of the materials not procurable in Australia for body manufacture,
> and which provides employment for Australians, actually come from the United
> Kingdom.[29]

These remarks point to the sensitivities of many Australians to the views of Nuffield and others who suggested that Australia was not pulling its weight as a member of the Empire. The *Australian Motorist* provided a broader rebuttal to the Nuffield view in publishing figures indicating 'the measure of Australia's contribution to the material wellbeing of Great Britain in the post-war period. ... We believe our readers ... have justification for feeling satisfied that Australians are Empire builders, and that we are not importunate members of the British family that some would make us believe.'[30]

Much of Australia's contribution to Britain and Empire in the 1930s was a result of the Ottawa Agreement.

> From Australia's point of view there was a realization that the very strength of Britain depends upon its widely diverse secondary industries and its export of manufactured goods. ... In the main, Britain's capacity to sell to the Empire and to foreign countries depends on her capacity to purchase the exports of those countries. Putting it plainly, there is room for a substantial increase of Australian exports of primary products to Britain, provided we are able to give Britain an increased share of the Australian market. If we would sell to the United Kingdom more of those things which we can sell nowhere else, we must buy more from the United Kingdom.[31]

In addition to the benefits flowing to British producers from the Ottawa tariff preferences, sales of some General Motors motor vehicles produced in Britain had also been given a fillip from intracompany pricing arrangements. They effectively provided a further margin of preference for GM's British products. The arrangements were described to Prime Minister Lyons in 1936 by L.J. Hartnett, GM-H's British-born Managing Director.

> [W]e subsidize or take a very much lower profit margin in the course of importing and merchandising English products [Vauxhall and Bedford] compared with American products we handle. ... we actually subsidize and aid United Kingdom motor car manufacturers to a very large degree as compared with United States manufacturers. ... if we were to price Vauxhall and Bedford products on the same basis as our American products and if we priced our bodies to United Kingdom motor car chassis importers in Australia on the same basis as bodies for American chassis, then the United Kingdom car and truck registrations in Australia would contract by at least forty or fifty per cent.[32]

The trade diversion measures introduced in mid-1936 were a further turning point in Australia's trade relations. According to Sir Henry Gullett, Minister for Trade Treaties, the policy aimed

> simultaneously to increase our exports, to expand industry and employment, and also to guard and enhance our financial credit abroad. ... We have decided that circumstance compels us, however reluctantly, to follow the policy adopted by a large number of countries throughout the world, and divert a certain amount of our import trade from countries which are very indifferent purchasers of Australian exports, first as far as practicable with respect to Australian secondary industry, and next, to countries which are, or recently have been heavy purchasers of our exports. In other words, we have resolved to give more room in this market to those

who are our great buyers, and somewhat less room to those who are indifferent buyers.[33]

It was, of course, Britain which mainly comprised the former; the USA the latter. The idea was simple. If Britain were to buy more of Australia's agricultural exports which had been badly affected by Depression-caused trade restrictions imposed by many previously good customers, Australia would have to buy more of Britain's manufactures in return – and a strong Britain had a greater capacity to soak up Australia's agricultural surpluses. In this respect,

> From Australia's point of view there was a realisation that the very strength of Britain depends upon its widely diverse secondary industries and its export of manufactured goods. ... Putting it plainly, there is room for a substantial increase of Australian exports of primary products to Britain, provided we are able to give Britain an increased share of the Australian market.[34]

Of the measures, the one most directly affecting automobile production was aimed at stimulating engine manufacture through the Bounty Act.[35] However another aspect of it was potentially of great benefit to British automobile producers. In a system of import licensing which was introduced as part of trade diversion, all goods of British Empire origin would be exempted except motor chassis. There was an important exception to the exception, however. 'The restriction ... will not apply to motor chassis from the United Kingdom.'[36]

The government requiring import licences for motor chassis from Empire sources (aside from Britain) may seem odd at first glance, but here Canada was the target. There were two main reasons for this: Australia's large adverse balance of trade with Canada (largely accounted for by chassis imports); and the fact that 'Canadian' chassis exports were in effect indirect exports from the USA, taking advantage of Canada's preferential treatment in the Australian tariff. (The latter was discussed in Chapter 5.) The special place cars assumed in the government's new policy had been foreshadowed earlier in 1936. 'In particular [the government holds] the view that Australia is buying just about as much as she can from overseas, but we think that a considerable proportion of our motor car imports could be deflected from our worst customer to our best.'[37] As Table 6.2 shows, this is exactly what happened.

Total unassembled chassis imports reached their lowest level in the period between the wars in 1931/32 when just over 4,000 were imported. Of this number, imports from the United Kingdom (mainly 'baby cars') comprised 60 per cent. As the effects of the Depression slowly waned, Britain's share fell consistently, reaching a low of 19 per cent (about 14,000 of a total of 74,000 units) in 1935/36 – at the end of which period the trade diversion policy was instituted. The effects of trade diversion were felt in the following year. Overall imports fell by more than one-quarter (to 54,000) as a result of implementing direct import controls. Of these imports, however, Britain's share increased to 30 per cent (the absolute number of British imports also increased from nearly

14,000 to more than 16,000) while the numbers and shares of Canadian and US imports fell.[38] Britain's share continued to increase at the expense of Canada and the United States until the outbreak of the Second World War.

## British producers and Australian production

Proposals for local production by British producers dated from well before the trade diversion measures of the mid-1930s, but despite numerous promises in the interwar period (usually conditional on their being granted significant concessions) nothing came of them. The apparent position of British manufacturers was well summarized by Ford's Managing Director, H.C. French, when he stated in evidence to the Tariff Board in 1937 that 'United Kingdom chassis manufacturers have never shown a desire to establish the industry in Australia. They evidently preferred to operate under the heavy preferences without assuming the risks that were incidental to the founding of a local industry.'[39]

French's comments were made in the light of promises by British producers – or at least statements of good intent – over the previous 15 years or more. For while the subject of local manufacture came up often, that was as far as it went. In 1921 there were proposals for several leading British manufacturers to export components for assembly into complete vehicles in the overseas Dominions. It would be 'the first step towards the establishment of local manufacturing industries financed and staffed by British subjects [acting] as a material inducement to British manufacturers to proceed with proposals of this kind'.[40] By 1929 the British Economic Commission reported after investigation, 'It should be the aim of both countries that Australia should produce ... further parts of a car, until possibly the whole manufacture is carried out in

**Table 6.2**   Sources of unassembled chassis imports, 1931/32–1938/39 (%)

| Year | Canada | USA | UK | Total[a] |
|---|---|---|---|---|
| 1931/32 | <1 | 39 | 60 | 100 |
| 1932/33 | 26 | 27 | 46 | 100 |
| 1933/34 | 38 | 27 | ·35 | 100 |
| 1934/35 | 35 | 45 | 20 | 100 |
| 1935/36 | 42 | 39 | 19 | 100 |
| 1936/37 | 36 | 33 | 30 | 100 |
| 1937/38 | 35 | 30 | 34 | 100 |
| 1938/39 | 34 | 26 | 39 | 100 |

*Sources*: See Table 5.6.
*Note*:
[a]   Totals have been rounded.

Australia, thus finding work for more people, probably British immigrants and British capital.'[41] British capital, however, remained reluctant.

Just prior to the introduction of the trade diversion measures in mid-1936, the British government requested of the Australian government a number of concessions for United Kingdom producers. Among them were the remission of primage duties on parts, bodies and panels; free entry of British bodies for high-priced cars which were uneconomic to make in Australia; and to prevent dumping by foreign competitors, replacing *ad valorem* duties with specific rates based on the weight of vehicle components. Of the requested concessions, the most important was for an increase in the British content of Australian motor imports from 50 to 75 per cent. This supposedly would have made it profitable for British manufacturers to set up bodybuilding works in Australia, for according to British producers it was the availability (or rather the lack) of bodies that was their major problem.

Virtually all of the requested concessions were granted.[42] British producers were also particular beneficiaries when trade diversion was implemented.

> [I]n order to treat the motor industry of the United Kingdom as fairly as possible and at the same time to expedite engine manufacture in Australia, the imports of chassis from the principal suppliers other than the UK would be restricted to the same level of imports of chassis for the year ended April 30 1936. British manufacturers would be particularly invited to participate in the new manufacture within the Commonwealth and during the period of progressive diversion to Australian manufacture existing British interests would be preferentially considered.[43]

By 22 May 1936, the result was a seemingly firm – indeed unequivocal – commitment to local manufacture. The leading British manufacturers told the Australian government that they had examined local participation, and 'a definite assurance that extensive new plants for the building of bodies for United Kingdom cars to be sold in the coming season will be set up in connection with established chassis assembly plants, within the shortest possible time after remission of the fabricated panel duty'.[44]

In the meantime British producers could continue to obtain them from local producers. But here was the problem: local bodybuilders were unable to guarantee delivery – even for cars already sold. The apparent crux was that Ford and GM-H had largely tied up sources of supply and were making life difficult for other producers – and not just British makes. It was also alleged there existed a bodybuilding 'combine' comprising GM-H, T.J. Richards & Sons (suppliers of Chrysler Dodge) and Ruskins Motor Bodies Pty Ltd. In a letter to Prime Minister Lyons from Automobiles (W.A.) Ltd it was alleged these companies often refused to give quotations, and even when orders had been accepted, deliveries failed to materialize or were long delayed.[45]

Of the concessions it had been given, the British industry was 'most appreciative that the Australian government in amending the tariff has incorporated changes desired by the United Kingdom manufacturers'. However the producers further 'asked to be placed in a position of attaining the volume of sales which alone can lead to the economic manufacture of chassis parts', and noted that 'Tariff amendments while distinctly advantageous, cannot themselves lead to volume of sales. Full benefit cannot be secured unless steps are taken to remove the difficulties experienced by the United Kingdom manufacturers in obtaining bodies.'[46] It was apparent that while British producers were duly grateful for all the concessions they had received, their gratitude did not extend to local production.

Their lack of interest in Australian manufacture, despite numerous invitations by Australian government representatives, was an embarrassment to local proponents of British participation. Aside from the valid and important complaint about the lack of available bodies, the reasons for the reluctance of British producers to commit themselves to local manufacture were many. They were well put by successive Ministers for Trade and Customs, and none of them were to do with the motor body problem. First, on a visit to Britain in 1938, T.W. White

> interviewed the principal motor car manufacturers, but most of them gave reasons for not undertaking manufacture in Australia. Some said that they preferred to manufacture in England and export to Australia; others said that an Australian [manufacturing operation] would be too far away from England for proper control, whilst others declared that they feared American competition. Still others gave different reasons.[47]

White's successor, John Lawson, also had disappointing reactions from British producers to his efforts to encourage their local participation: 'they mostly felt that the Australian market was not large enough to justify undertaking the expense of setting up factories here. Others recognised that there would be opposition from foreign countries and they did not felt like taking the risk.'[48]

For the interwar period, that was the end of the matter as far as 'complete' Australian manufacture by British producers was concerned. It was to be more than a decade after the Second World War before a British producer – the British Motor Corporation (essentially formed by the merger of Austin and Morris) – decided that the risk of Australian production was worth taking.

### Notes

1. *Sydney Morning Herald*, 26 May 1927.
2. *Australian Motorist*, January 1927.
3. M. Cann, Minister representing the New South Wales government at a reception held for the British Motor Delegation, 1927 (*Sydney Morning Herald*, 18 May 1927).
4. *Coach and Motor Builder*, 15 October 1919.
5. AA ACT A457/1 NA 300/17.

6. Detailed registration figures are not available for the early 1920s. However, imports of chassis provide an indication of their magnitude. In 1922–23, of a total of 37,632 chassis imports, only 1,406 (or 3 per cent) were of British origin. See Table 5.7.

7. *Sydney Morning Herald*, 26 April 1927.

8. *Sydney Morning Herald*, 20 May 1927.

9. Lt. Commander J.W. Thorneycroft of the London Engineering and Shipbuilding firm Thorneycroft and Co. in *Sydney Morning Herald*, 20 May 1927.

10. *Australian Motorist*, October 1929.

11. *Sydney Morning Herald*, 18 May 1927.

12. *Sydney Morning Herald*, 28 March 1928.

13. According to Austin, the issue was one of reciprocity: 'Australia should remember that Britain is the Commonwealth's best customer. Actual reciprocity is more valuable than theory. In New Zealand British cars rank second in number compared with other makes, whereas in Australia they are sixth of seventh. Do not let us talk about Imperial trade reciprocity, let us act' (*Sydney Morning Herald*, 5 July 1929).

14. Memorandum to Prime Minister Joseph Scullin, 7 July 1931 (AA ACT A461/6/1 Part 2). Primage was in effect a revenue-raising tariff surcharge imposed during the Depression.

15. S.A. Cheney, *From Horse to Horse Power* (Adelaide, 1965), pp. 214–15.

16. According to the *Australian Motorist*, 'small, light cars of British construction cannot possibly supply the needs of Australians, for the reason that the Australian averages a greater height of stature, needing more body room, and his motoring conditions are entirely different, and, what is more important, our roads are so bad that only the chassis of stout construction can withstand the frightful impacts created by miles upon miles of pothole metal roads. Many Australians have looked at these low-priced English light cars, and realized at the first glance that they would not run 1000 miles upon Australian roads without serious upkeep costs' (*Australian Motorist*, January 1927).

17. The tax was based on the Royal Automobile Club system that assessed horse-power simply as a function of piston area. See T.S. Watson, 'Government Policy and Two World Wars – Shapers of the Automotive Industry?', Thesis (School of Social Sciences, Deakin University, 1990), p. 48. The tax was modified in the mid-1930s, to mitigate its adverse effects on engine design (Tariff Board, *Engines and Chassis for Motor Vehicles* (Canberra, 1938), p. 14).

18. *Australian Motorist*, January 1927.

19. 'Glowing references were made to the new tariff and its assistance to English motor car manufacturers by [the representative of] Armstrong-Siddeley Motors' (*Sydney Morning Herald*, 7 September 1929).

20. To highlight the point, in 1928 72,568 cars were registered in Australia of which 10,446 (14.4 per cent) were of British origin. In 1932 only 10,684 cars were registered, 3,688 of which were British (34.5 per cent). See Table 6.1.

21. These data were derived from an analysis of the Australian market conducted for GM-H in 1937 (AA ACT B1/1 850 Bundle 5). See notes to Table 6.1.

22. AA ACT A461/1 B418/1/6 Part 2.

23. Memo, 8 April 1935 (AA ACT A461/1 I418/1/6 Part 2).

24. D.H. Rhys 'Concentration in the Inter-War Motor Industry', *Journal of Transport History*, New Series, III, 4 (1976), pp. 245, 253.

25. In 1939 ACI would be invited by the Commonwealth Government to produce an 'Australian Car' assisted by bounty payments for engine production and a monopoly on the local production of cars.

26. AA Vic. MP1118/2 43/1/225.

27. A. Capling and B. Galligan, *Beyond the Protective State* (Cambridge, 1992), pp. 97–9.
28. *Sydney Morning Herald*, 25 February 1935.
29. L.J. Hartnett in *Sydney Morning Herald*, 28 December 1935.
30. The *Australian Motorist*, July 1936, provided the following figures for the 15 years, 1920–1934.

|  | £m |
|---|---|
| Australian purchases of British goods | 693.3 |
| Australian exports to Britain | 680.7 |
| Balance of trade to Britain | 12.6 |
| Interest on loans [paid] to Britain | 328.3 |
| Estimated invisibles payments to Britain | 60.0 |
| Balance in Britain's favour | 400.9 |

31. Sir Henry Gullett, Hansard, 22 May 1936, pp. 2212–13.
32. Letter from Hartnett to Prime Minister Lyons, 27 April 1936 (AA ACT A461/1).
33. Hansard, 12 May 1936, pp. 2212–13.
34. Sir Henry Gullett, Hansard, 12 May 1936, p. 2213.
35. See Chapter 4.
36. Sir Henry Gullett, Hansard, 12 May 1936, p. 2213.
37. Mr J. Fairbairn, government MP in *Sydney Morning Herald*, 21 March 1936.
38. From a total for both countries of 60,000 units in 1935–36, to 38,000 in 1936–37. See Table 5.7.
39. *Sydney Morning Herald*, 18 February 1937.
40. AA ACT A457/1 NA 300/17.
41. AA Vic. MP394 Series 1 IC44/106.
42. AA ACT A461/1 B418/1/6 Part 2.
43. *Sydney Morning Herald*, 23 May 1936.
44. Letter dated 22 May 1936 (AA ACT A425/127 45/3666).
45. Nash, an American make, had great difficulties obtaining bodies from Ford and GM-H. In response to one order for bodies in 1936, Nash received the reply that GM-H had 'no intention to supply' (Letter dated 16 May 1936 (AA ACT A461/1/6 Part 2)).
46. AA ACT A461/1 B418/1/6 Part 2.
47. Hansard, 7 and 8 December 1939, p. 2467.
48. Hansard, 20 September 1939, p. 809.

# 7 Post-Second World War

The Second World War brought an end to the 'complete' car project. By the end of hostilities, however, conditions were ideal for the emergence of an 'Australian' car. The war considerably boosted Australia's manufacturing capacity, especially in the metal trades. There was widespread concern that the war would be followed by a return to the high levels of unemployment of the 1930s unless practical steps were taken to sustain and increase employment in manufacturing. The war also exposed the vulnerability of Australia to invasion by an Asian power. It provoked the response of the post-war immigration programme, combined with measures to promote the further development of the manufacturing sector as a means of substantially increasing the European population and defence capability of the country. A local motor vehicle manufacturing capacity was central to those aims.

Moreover, six years of war with the natural attrition of private vehicles, few new car registrations to replace them and shortages of spare parts left fewer private vehicles on the nation's roads at war's end than at the beginning.[1] Those that remained were worn and outdated. After years of austerity and pent-up demand the conditions were right for a boom in car ownership – cars for mass private motoring – and the emergence of an 'Australian' car. The two became the aspirations of both politicians and the electorate.

Even during the war the government had not lost sight of the aim of a post-war car manufacturing industry. It asked the Tariff Board in 1942 to inquire into the 'motor vehicles' industry. In its report submitted to the Minister in April 1943, the Board concluded, 'that [the] manufacture of a complete motor vehicle in Australia as a post-war measure is desirable'. It was of the opinion that with careful planning 'production costs would not represent an undue burden on users' and if chassis imports were to continue, overseas suppliers should be encouraged to ship them totally unassembled. 'The assembly would at least provide additional employment.' As usual consumers got short shrift. The Board accepted that unless the industry received government assistance, an Australian Car while 'sound and useful' would 'lack requirements in design and equipment'. Purchasers would also have the choice of a smaller range of models, and model changes would be less frequent than overseas.[2]

After its appointment to oversee post-war industrial development in October 1943, the Secondary Industries Commission considered the case of car production, concluding that the manufacture of a complete car would present no insurmountable technical problems.[3] However, the two pieces of Commonwealth legislation which had caused so much controversy in the late 1930s – the Motor Vehicle Engines Bounty Act, 1939 and the Motor Vehicles Agreement Act, 1940 – provided major barriers to local production. In a cabinet submission dated 20 March 1944, the Commission recommended their immediate repeal, and an Act to that effect was passed by Parliament in May 1945.[4] In the same submission the Commission noted 'potential manufacturers ... should now be engaged in post war planning of car production'. It also suggested that, 'Failing presentation to the Commission by commercial industry of suitable plans for motor manufacture (and a proof of intention to implement them), it will have to be considered whether the Commonwealth can undertake the manufacture of motor car engines and chassis either as a government, or joint Government/commercial venture.'[5] It was a threat the pre-war market leaders, Ford and GM-H, could not afford to ignore.

Immediately after the war while planning for production was taking place, car imports boomed. Most were British – models from Austin, Morris, Hillman, Vauxhall and Ford. The 'dollar shortage' – the acute shortage of dollars to buy goods from the United States – meant that many popular American cars were virtually unobtainable in Australia.[6] One of the results was a renewed stimulus for local assembly – of British cars. GM-H began importing CKD Vauxhalls for assembly in 1945. The following year Rootes Australia began assembly of Hillman, Humber and Singer cars at Port Melbourne; while in 1948 Austin acquired an assembly plant in Melbourne and in 1949 the Standard Motor Co. was formed to assemble and distribute its Standard cars – mainly the Vanguard.[7]

However, it was the proposals for complete manufacture that concentrated the minds of the politicians, the bureaucracy and the public during the immediate post-war years. In anticipation of the repeal of the Bounty and Agreement Acts, four firms had put forward serious proposals for local manufacture.[8] Three of them, Chrysler Dodge de Soto Distributors, Ford Motor Co., and GM-H, proposed full manufacture of motor vehicles. The fourth, Nuffield (Aust.) Pty Ltd submitted plans for the manufacture of 'coachwork' and for the assembly of vehicles with the ultimate object of building a complete car in Australia.[9] Having received the proposals the Secondary Industries Commission requested the appointment of an inter-departmental committee to consider them.

## From proposal to manufacture: the establishment of an industry

*Ford*

The most ambitious (and first) of the plans submitted was Ford's. The company had been invited to do so by Prime Minister John Curtin in August 1944.[10] The proposal entailed producing a V8 30 hp engine and an appropriate chassis. Complete manufacture would be attained after five years with the aim of producing 20,000 cars per year.[11] In return Ford required more generous government assistance than its competitors. It sought a number of concessions. Among them were exemption from sales tax and customs duties on imported plant, equipment and some components; whole or partial exemption from sales tax on sales of vehicles with a locally manufactured chassis; provision of overseas exchange; additional tariff protection; and a 'capital contribution' by the government of £850,000. Despite strong support from the interdepartmental committee (among the advantages it saw Ford providing 'greater value from the defense point of view' than the GM-H plan) the government did not accede to a number of Ford's crucial requests. In particular the government refused to pay the capital contribution, increase tariff protection or provide exemptions from sales taxes.[12] In reply to the letter from Prime Minister Chifley informing Ford of the government's decision, Ford's Managing Director, H.C. French, expressed his deep regret at the government's refusal and stated that the 'situation thus created [has] caused us to reconsider the whole question'.[13] In the meantime in the early post-war years, Ford turned mainly to assembly of such British cars as the small Prefect and Anglia, and importing fully built the large, but old fashioned Pilot V8. In those car-starved years, the company sold as many of these models as it could obtain.

When the plan for local manufacture was reconsidered after the war the result was a more cautious approach by Ford. In a revised proposal submitted in May 1946, capital expenditure of £750,000 was to be found from Ford's own resources, and no Commonwealth assistance was sought. The tentative plan for the production of a 'super de luxe V8 sedan' (a truck was also part of the proposal) had three stages. At the end of the first stage (which was then partially complete with a local content of 61 per cent) local content would be 72 per cent, completion of the second stage would see local content of 83 per cent, and the third stage 93 per cent.[14]

Ford Managing Director French explained the choice of car for local production to Prime Minister Chifley:

> while original plans gave equal emphasis to our English and Canadian vehicles ... it is now apparent that our chief attention must be centred on our Canadian product, and every effort made to build as much of the Canadian chassis in Australia as is dictated by business economics. ... [T]he market for the English- and Continental-type vehicle is a fairly limited one, public demand being largely for the heavier duty

vehicles of North American origin. This is exemplified by our own order position. – 7800 for English type and 26,151 for the Canadian type.[15]

However, there was a problem. Foreign exchange was rationed owing to the 'dollar shortage' (and Canada was included as part of the dollar problem). Completion of the plan needed dollars for the purchase of capital equipment and components, and 'Ford considered itself at a disadvantage vis à vis GMH in regard to its current quota from the appropriate Dollar "bank".' The company asked the Committee to make representations to the government to increase Ford's allocation despite the plan being tentative. The Committee, however, was 'unable to undertake this' without a concrete proposal.[16] As a consequence Ford through its Canadian Executive Vice President undertook to submit a firm plan for consideration not later than 1 April 1949. (It was finally received on 20 June 1949.)

The new plan envisaged a four-stage process and by November 1948 'of these the first two could be said to have almost been completed'. The third was expected to bring Australian content up to about 85 per cent and would include the manufacture of a number of engine components. Stage 4 would entail the manufacture of cylinder blocks and heads, crankshafts, camshafts, transmissions and rear axles, bringing local content up to about 95 per cent.[17]

Having received the revised proposal, J.J. Dedman, Minister for Post-War Reconstruction, was of the view that Ford's need for foreign exchange could be met, and indeed it 'should be possible to make the dollar allocations to enable Ford to proceed'. Some requests by the company were still to be considered, 'but as the company's firm plan makes provision for an Australian content of approximately 85 per cent in Ford cars and trucks by mid-1952, the plan could be approved "in principle"'.[18] Dedman acquired a further interest in Ford's project in his later portfolio. '[A]s Minister for Defense I am interested in the defense potentialities of this sort of industrial expansion. The greater the extent and variety of the productive capacity of the company, the greater the role it can play in Australia's future defense should the need arise.'[19]

## GM-H

GM-H's proposal was submitted to the Secondary Industries Commission on 5 January 1945.[20] It involved full manufacture of a 'low priced' 5-seater 18 hp sedan car and a related utility, 'especially designed for Australian conditions'.[21] It would be marketed together with the company's American-designed types.[22] Anticipated production was 25,000 vehicles per annum, with manufacture beginning two years after the decision and agreement to proceed. The aim was to sell in competition with imported vehicles without subsidy and without an increase in the tariff rate prevailing in 1939. In return, the government was requested by GM-H to give 'favourable consideration' to duty, primage and sales tax-free importation of machinery, equipment and components not locally available. (The final agreement settled in 1945 stipulated that the value of imported components should not exceed 10 per cent of the ex-factory price of the vehicles or 5 per cent of the weight.)

The car (model 48-215) was the product of a joint American-Australian design team that had been chosen for the project in 1944. Three prototypes of the new car produced in North America were tested on General Motors' proving grounds in Michigan and shipped from Vancouver on the *Wanganella* on 4 December 1946, arriving in Sydney on 28 December.[23] The final design, of 'unitary' body construction (body and chassis in one all-steel unit) was a 'medium' sized car, its size a compromise between the larger American cars and the smaller English vehicles then on Australian roads.

The gestation was far from smooth. In the period immediately after the war there were shortages of sheet steel at home and abroad. The Victorian government was not helping matters either. The company was finding difficulty in obtaining the necessary building permits for factory extensions. Skilled labour was in short supply, there was industrial unrest (particularly in the year prior to the release of the new car), and the senior engineers and other professionals who were brought for the project from Britain and the United States were unable to get accommodation in Australia. In a letter to the Secondary Industries Committee, L.J. Hartnett, then Managing Director of GM-H, complained, 'Some members of this organisation, including myself, have taken some of these men into our own homes, but there is a limit to this expedient.' Hartnett even used his own garage as a temporary 'sleepout' for the men.[24]

The method of finance chosen for the project by GM-H's US parent was also causing local disquiet. English-born Hartnett, a key and active proponent of the scheme, wanted it 'to be a really Australian project'. General Motors, however, opposed the issuing of local share capital which Hartnett avidly supported, stipulating the money for the project had to be raised as loan funds.[25] Though there had been a number of issues that had caused tension between Hartnett and the parent company since his appointment in 1934, it was this conflict that finally brought his removal as managing director.[26] In 1946 an executive from General Motors arrived in Australia with two letters: one formally appointed H.E. Bettle as Managing Director of GM-H; the other advised Hartnett that he was being transferred to New York.[27] By Hartnett's account he resigned in protest and it was Bettle who launched the Holden 48-215.[28]

Even naming the new car provoked controversy within the company and it was delayed almost until the first car left the assembly line in November 1948. Before choosing 'Holden' the names on the short list included Anzac, Canbra (the early favourite and, yes, this was the proposed spelling), Chevrolet and GMH.[29] 'Holden' was eventually chosen to honour Sir Edward Holden, who had died in 1947. He had negotiated the merger of Holden's with the General Motors Corporation in Australia to form GM-H in 1931, had become the new company's first chairman and had been manager of its Woodville plant.

Once on the market, the Holden's price, £733 (including sales tax), proved highly competitive.[30] From the beginning the car was a huge success. Now if there was a problem it was one of insufficient production capacity. Only 112 cars were produced in 1948, but within months of starting production, thousands of orders had been taken. Buyers were placed on a waiting list, with places at the head of the queue selling for more than £100. It was not until 1950 that daily production reached 80 cars. In 1951 production reached 100 cars per day by which time it was Australia's top selling car, overtaking the four-cylinder 1.2 litre Austin A40. There was no secret to the Holden's popularity: it was simple, had good performance and turned out to be highly durable. Experience showed its 'engine happily ran past 80,000 miles without so much as a "decoke" while [English] four-cylinder models of the day rarely ran 30,000 without giving trouble'. [31]

### Chrysler Dodge de Soto Distributors

Chrysler Dodge de Soto Distributors Ltd (Adelaide) (CDD) was an Australian company distinct from the American Chrysler Corporation. An arrangement between the two firms had existed since the mid-1930s in which Chrysler sold components to CDD at a profit for local assembly. Immediately after the war CDD absorbed the Adelaide bodybuilding firm Richards Industries and proposed to build 30 hp cars of the types manufactured by the Chrysler Corporation of the US.[32] The aim was to eventually produce 20,000 vehicles annually.

The plan submitted in May 1946 was indicative of the firm's cautious approach to full motor vehicle manufacturing: it would only go ahead 'when the time was ripe'. '[C]ertain specified parts' would be made locally in the three years from the start of initial production, but no percentage local content was specified to be attained at the end of the period. 'The Company's objective [was] to produce a 100 per cent Australian vehicle as soon as it becomes practicable and economically possible. The proposal [was] not one for producing a substantially complete motor vehicle in Australia at an early date.' From the government the company sought the elimination of import restrictions on some components, and in common with the other firms CDD sought the remission of duty on imports of plant, machinery and components.

There the matter rested until August 1949, when CDD made a new and more detailed proposal. A new agreement was negotiated with Chrysler Corporation in the United States. It provided for the US company to sell at a net export selling price required components, and make available the fruits of its research and development so that CDD was in a position to manufacture all the necessary components for a selected range of Chrysler vehicles. Manufacture was to be implemented in four planned stages with a view to eventual 100 per cent local content.[33]

Stage 1 was to be completed by the end of 1949 by which time 60 per cent local content would be achieved. Local content on completion of stage 2 would be 75 per cent; stage 3 – 85 per cent and stage 4 – 100 per cent. As part of the arrangement with the US Chrysler Corporation, CDD undertook for the currency of the agreement (initially 10 years) to pay Chrysler a 'service fee' on each completed vehicle, though the amount of the fee was not then specified. After examining the proposal the reaction of the Secondary Industry Committee was favourable even though CDD 'will copy models designed and produced overseas'. Far more important, the firm was 'completely Australian and autonomous' and consequently the committee was of the opinion that the plan merited 'general approval although no final judgement is possible until the amount of the service fee is known'.[34]

This concern was soon overtaken by events. In June 1951 Chrysler Corporation (USA) bought a controlling interest in the CDD plant in South Australia. It changed the firm's name to Chrysler Australia Ltd and began a vigorous plan of expansion, aiming to eventually achieve a local content of 90 per cent for its product range.

*Nuffield*

Nuffield's plans for its post-war operations were outlined in a meeting between Nuffield/Morris and the Secondary Industries Commission in Sydney on 25 May 1945. 'Our first intentions are to endeavor to produce coachwork ... going from there to the progressive development of the chassis.' Nuffield proposed eventual manufacture with increasing local content of 'popular models such as the small, low horse-power car, and to continue importing larger models to meet the limited demand for them'. Minimum anticipated production was 10,000 cars annually but no starting date was given. Unlike its three competitors, Nuffield raised the issue of the grant of concessions by the government quite circumspectly. It proposed the importation of parts until local production became economic and was 'anxious to learn of any proposed alteration in existing tariffs'. It 'inquired' if duty-free admission could be granted for plant which could not be made in Australia, and 'raised the question' of exemption from sales tax for any vehicles locally produced.[35]

Nuffield was certainly in a favourable position to carry out its comparatively unambitious proposal. The sales infrastructure for the Morris range of cars (these included the Morris, MG, Riley and Wolseley) had been well established before the war, and many of those cars had been at least partially assembled in Australia. Potential manufacturing infrastructure was there too. When William Morris made his first post-war visit to Australia in late 1945 he proposed that Nuffield buy the Victoria Park racecourse in Sydney to build a manufacturing facility. The Board of directors in Britain, however, refused to sanction the purchase. Nuffield/Morris who knew a good deal when he saw one, bought the property himself and sold part of it to firms in the motor trade such as Olympic Tyres and Lucas-Girling for an amount sufficient to cover his initial cost of purchase. With the early post-war import boom, by 1947 demand for Nuffield cars had increased so much that the company's board in Britain decided an assembly plant was needed and bought the rest of the land from Morris for that purpose. The plant opened in 1950, becoming the group headquarters when the British Motor Corporation was formed (essentially a merger between Austin and Morris) in 1953.

### The development of the industry in the 1950s

In the years immediately after the war a combination of the dollar shortage and the 1949 devaluation of sterling gave British cars a significant price advantage over their American rivals leading to the dominance of the Australian market by British producers. In 1949 they had about 80 per cent of the market, around twice their pre-war share. From then it was all downhill. By 1951 models marketed by GM-H, including Vauxhall and Chevrolet, had 23 per cent of new car sales compared with a total of 30 per cent for Austin and Morris, 15 per cent for Ford, 10 per cent for CDD, while Rootes and Standard shared about 14 per cent.[36] The relative dominance of Austin and Morris came to an end as the capacity constraints that had hampered Holden production were overcome. When the successor to the 48-215 was released in 1953 – the FJ Holden then priced at £1,023 – the Holden alone had 36.5 per cent of the Australian market, with plans to boost production to 400 cars per day by 1958 – a fourfold increase over the 1951 figure.[37]

In this environment of change – particularly the industry's increasing local content and production – the Menzies government referred to the Tariff Board for inquiry, 'tariffs, and their protective effects on the automotive industry', but events overtook the process. The country was experiencing continued foreign exchange shortages and in 1952 licensing controls were introduced to cover all countries, severely limiting imports of CKD kits for local assembly.[38] Quotas were established for imports of automotive parts from non-dollar countries, and imports from dollar areas limited to parts not available from non-dollar countries. The effects on the local industry were almost immediate. Following their implementation, in just three years to 1954/55 the value of imported car bodies fell by 50 per cent and assembled chassis by just over 60 per cent.[39] The new regime of import licensing and quantitative restrictions became the binding constraint on imports: tariffs were effectively redundant as a means of protection. In the new environment the Tariff Board's inquiry into the industry was deferred until 1954. The direct import restrictions provided significantly greater protection and encouragement for the local manufacture of a wide range of automotive products than tariffs alone. Ford, for example, moved toward the production of complete vehicles. Having seen the popularity of the big V8s in the late 1940s and early 1950s, the company decided to build a V8 production line at the manufacturing plant at Geelong and, from 1955, to produce large Customline sedans and its utility equivalent, the Mainline. Chrysler began increasing local content at its assembly plant in South Australia and like Ford saw the future in large cars. Using some locally-produced body panels, it began assembly of large Chrysler Royal and Dodge Phoenix six- and eight-cylinder vehicles based on US designs.[40]

The changed import regime which now involved restrictions on imports from the sterling area provided the impetus for British firms to expand their assembly operations, and a stimulus to the merger of the two main British rivals, Austin and Morris. Like Morris, Austin had had a well-established pre-war distribution organisation. Immediately after the war the company moved quickly to re-establish its pre-war position in the market by initially fully importing cars, while laying the groundwork for later local manufacture. In 1948 the company bought the former Ruskin Works in Melbourne as a basis for bodybuilding, while the Pressed Metal Corporation in Sydney started to assemble CKD Austin A40s – then the best-selling car on the market – under contract.[41] In Australia the union between Austin and Morris took place in 1953 (in Britain the merger had taken place the previous year), with Nuffield's Sydney plant becoming the headquarters of the new firm, the British Motor Corporation (BMC).

The success of the Holden (in the mid-1950s GM-H held a total of 50 per cent of the market for its range of models; Ford just 10 per cent) saw Ford take the decision in 1955 to expand local production with a new design from the United States – the Falcon. The decision turned out to anticipate another tightening of import restrictions in the following year when the permissible number of fully imported cars was reduced by 25 per cent, and the number of CKD packs and components by 12.5 per cent. The government also announced a long-term plan to raise significantly the local content of all new cars sold, leading to the acceleration of schemes by established firms to assemble or fully manufacture cars. This, and the accelerating sales of Holdens saw GM-H discontinue assembly of Vauxhalls leaving 'Holden' as its sole brand name.[42] Meanwhile Ford built a modern assembly plant at Broadmeadows in Victoria where it assembled Consuls and Zephyrs (models succeeding the Customline range), both British designs of similar size to the Holden, and American models larger than the Holden including the Fairlane and Custom, until the Falcon began production in 1960.[43] Chrysler was also active. Following the acquisition by the Chrysler Corporation of 30 per cent of the French Simca Automobile in 1958, the local firm extended its product range to smaller cars by assembling Simca models.

In all of this BMC had been largely left behind. During the 1950s Australian buyers showed a clear preference for larger cars – the six- (particularly the Holden) and eight-cylinder cars produced by their rivals. Despite this Austin and Morris spent large sums on modern capital equipment enabling them to wholly manufacture four-cylinder cars derived from British designs. The result was an almost catastrophic decline in its share of an expanding market: from nearly one-third of the market in 1953 to just over one-eighth in 1958. The company's reaction to falling sales was to build a modern plant at Victoria Park in New South Wales with an annual production capacity of 50,000 vehicles (this, in a market with total sales of about 155,000 cars). The plant produced four-cylinder Austin Lancers and Morris Majors with 96 per cent local content. However, BMC's market share continued to fall. By the end of the 1950s the company was in deep trouble, resorting to a proliferation of British designs, including, belatedly and unsuccessfully, a six-cylinder car. The Morris Marshal was not competitively priced against the more durable Holden, and production ceased in 1960 after just three years. For a reprieve BMC had to wait for the introduction of the revolutionary Mini Minor in 1961.

By the mid- to late 1950s it was apparent to the Tariff Board at least that the largely *ad hoc* tariff regime sheltering the industry was overdue for reform. When the report of the revived Tariff Board inquiry was finally published in 1957[44] it concluded 'any action at this time to raise tariffs, even with the objective of simplification of the tariff schedule, beyond the safe minimum required to sustain and consolidate the automotive industry would be inadvisable and not in the best interests of the Australian economy'.[45] At the end of 1958 the government accepted the Board's recommendations to restructure the tariffs sheltering the industry's products from import competition. Fully assembled vehicles were dutiable at 35 per cent, while the new tariff structure grouped automotive components into three categories. Goods in the first two were afforded protective duties ranging from 22.5 per cent to 62.5 per cent. Group X included components that when locally produced were deemed to have a price disadvantage against imports.[46] Included in group Y were components that were made 'economically and efficiently' in Australia. Group Z components were to be admitted under standing by-law at non-protective rates. The last group included components, 'the manufacture of which had not developed to the extent that local manufacturers were capable of supplying a reasonable portion for original equipment'.[47] As the industry developed, the standing by-law was amended to exclude the additional components produced, imports of which would then be subject to the substantive duty rate.

At the end of the 1950s the result of 15 years of post-war protectionism was there for all to see. The development of the industry was the opposite of that overseas, where increasing economies of scale promoted mergers, takeovers and the disappearance of a number of smaller makers. Instead, Australia with average annual new car registrations of about 140,000 vehicles in the 1950s, acquired a number of assemblers – including Rootes, Rover, Standard and Volkswagen – and four vehicle manufacturers competing in a market which at best was capable of sustaining one at near optimum scale of output.[48]

By the end of the decade the composition of the market had changed greatly. The pre-war family cars – the Chevrolet and the Plymouth – had moved into the luxury market. Their places had been taken by the medium-sized Holden which came to dominate the Australian market, accounting for 51 per cent of new registrations in 1959.[49] It was joined in 1960 by the Ford Falcon, and in 1962 by the Chrysler Valiant. The small car segment was expanding with BMC, Volkswagen, Rootes, Ford and Standard the major competitors. The influence of Japanese producers had yet to be felt.

When import licensing controls were lifted in 1960, the tariff once more became the predominant device protecting the industry. Having been sheltered by the almost prohibitively high barriers provided by import licensing, the new rules came as a shock to local producers who now faced stiff competition from imported cars and components. The 'solution' to their problem was to again make the tariff irrelevant as a protective measure – this time though a series of local content plans.

## The local content plans, 1964–1983

The boom in imports followed by the 'credit squeeze' induced recession of 1960–61 put the Australian manufacturing sector under considerable pressure and the automotive industry was no exception. For the car producers the start of the decade was a rather mixed experience. The sellers' market of the 1950s had gone. The local producers were competing vigorously among themselves and with imports.

While GM-H continued to dominate with about 45 per cent of the market at the beginning of the decade, Ford got off to a bad start. The first Falcon model (in Australia called the XK) began local production in 1960. The Falcon had been extremely successful when earlier introduced to the United States market and it was transplanted to Australia with its design virtually unchanged. Unfortunately it was initially plagued by durability problems. Its relative fragility was quickly exposed by poor Australian roads, and the necessary modifications cost Ford dearly. By some accounts the firm came close to withdrawing from local production.[50] Chrysler was also under pressure. Its large Royal series of cars was of dated design and sales were falling though it had a high local content. Chrysler had to wait until 1962 for the introduction of the highly successful United States-designed Valiant (with a far lower local content than the Royal it eventually replaced) to retrieve its fortunes. BMC had introduced two cars specifically designed for the Australian market: the four-cylinder Major Elite and the six-cylinder Austin Freeway. Neither was successful. Fortunately for the company, the Mini Minor, introduced in Australia in 1961, proved an enormous success enabling BMC to overtake Ford and Chrysler sales the following year.

The origins of the local content plans implemented during the 1960s are unclear. Ostensibly the surge in imported components following the relaxation of direct import controls was the precipitating influence. Capling and Galligan describe how Charles McGrath the owner of Repco, Australia's largest components manufacturer, lobbied Sir John McEwan, then Minister for Trade and Industry, for what was then the novel idea of introducing a formal local content requirement for locally produced cars to reduce imports and boost the use of local components.[51] However, by Stubbs' account, a senior public servant speaking off the record told him the policy was developed in response to a proposal by one of the multinational producers to include Australia in a system of 'world wide sourcing'. The proposal would have the company's subsidiaries in different countries specialize in the production of particular components. The subsidiary would then be source of those components for the company's operations throughout the world.[52] Whatever its origins and these explanations are not mutually exclusive, the Menzies government introduced the local content plans in May 1964. The idea was to encourage vehicle manufacturers to increase local content by providing an attractive carrot: duty concessions for imported components.

There were two basic plans – 'A' and 'B' – derived from a proposed Canadian local content scheme.[53] Under the plans, producers were provided with duty concessions on components, provided they achieved a specified level of local content in their vehicles. Plan A involved participants raising local content to 95 per cent over five years and provided that residual components entered under the plan could be imported free of duty or at nominal rates under the by-law provisions of the tariff. Plan A benefits were guaranteed until the end of 1974. Plan B (sub-divided into B1 and B2) was for low-volume producers who could obtain by-law concessions for more limited increases in local content.[54] These plans, however, were to operate as an interim arrangement, pending the government's decision on the Tariff Board's 1965 report. When the decision came, while accepting the thrust of the Board's recommendations the government modified the original plans, taking a less finely graduated approach between volume of output and the required minimum local content than the Board suggested. When the plan was first implemented, to receive duty concessions for models with annual production of 1–2,500 vehicles, a producer would require 45 per cent local content; annual production of 2,501–5,000 vehicles, 50 per cent local content; and 5,001–7,500 vehicles, 60 per cent local content. Components were to be regarded as local content 'only if they were subject to some degree of local manufacture going beyond mere assembly of imported parts'.[55]

Ten vehicle models were entered under Plan A. At the time, the Holden held just over 40 per cent of the Australian market, leaving the remaining nine models to share the remainder. Not surprisingly, the Tariff Board, when asked by the government to evaluate the plans, had 'considerable doubts as to the possibility of some [models] obtaining economic volumes of production – at least in the foreseeable future'.[56] In addition to an examination of the plans, the Board's terms of reference included consideration of the duties on completely built-up (CBU) vehicles. Following its report in 1965, the government accepted the Board's recommendation that if imports of CBU vehicles exceeded 7.5 per cent of the market, the tariff would be automatically raised from 35 to 45 per cent, general, and from 25 to 35 per cent, preferential. This step was taken in August 1966, mainly because of the increasing popularity of comparatively small, very well-equipped vehicles produced in Japan.

Despite the increased tariffs, Japanese producers were able to maintain their competitiveness in the Australian market and their share continued to grow. As a result, Volkswagen, an assembler, could not fulfil its plan obligations. The Tariff Board's doubts had turned out to be justified. Volkswagen terminated a local expansion programme, withdrew from Plan A, sold off much of its plant and became purely an assembler.[57]

The plans in their original form did not last long. Modifications to Plan A were made in November 1966, just five months after its introduction,[58] but more important were the concessions granted in December 1968 as a result of the difficulties some Plan A manufacturers had been experiencing in meeting the local content requirements. Among them was the introduction of an optional 85 per cent local content plan for vehicles with a sales volume of less than 25,000 units per year.[59]

The easing of the rules of the original plans (and the rules themselves) came in for justified criticism by those who were able and had abided by them. In evidence to the Industries Assistance Commission, E.N. Clark representing GM-H complained,

> When local content plans were introduced in January 1965, it was established at that time that the plans as written would remain in force until December 1974. Such has not been the case. Over the intervening years many separate changes, some of which have involved significant modifications, have been made to these plans. We believe these changes were generally brought about by companies being unable or unwilling

to achieve their local content undertakings ... G.M Holden's has never requested any relaxation of our undertakings under the local content plans.[60]

Moreover, the administration of the schemes was the subject of considerable 'administrative discretion' and secrecy. Even the measurement of local content – the wholesale price less the landed duty paid value of imported components – was itself deeply flawed. Merely by increasing the wholesale price local content could be increased without any change in the physical make-up of the vehicle.

By 1971 the effects of more than half a decade of plan-production were clear. Rather than a small model range with high local content, it had resulted in model proliferation, and in particular, the fragmentation of the small car market, the market segment showing the highest rate of growth. In fact, the plans actually *encouraged* small-scale manufacture. The duty concessions were highest for vehicles with the lowest local content, and in being so, compensated small-scale producers for being just that – at the expense of larger scale, more efficient production. Achieving the required levels of local content under the low volume plans was easy. Simply assembling a CKD packaged vehicle would almost achieve 45 per cent local content; just a few deletions from the pack and the substitution of locally produced components would satisfy the 60 per cent requirement. However, the extra 25 or 35 per cent required to achieve 85 or 95 per cent local content was far more difficult and expensive than achieving the earlier increments. The last increments required investment in plant and equipment; the duty concessions were less valuable, and as local content increased, local components became progressively more expensive compared with imported equivalents.[61] Moreover, the plans encouraged the fragmentation of the components industry. A proliferation of models brought with it a proliferation of required local components to suit. As well, local vehicle manufacturers who had committed themselves to the plans also encouraged manufacture by more than one components producer to promote competition and reduce the risk of disrupting supplies. The net result of all these was a disastrous influence on the efficiency of all parts of the industry.[62]

The decision was therefore made to phase out the low-volume plans by the end of 1974. The 85 and 95 per cent plans would be retained (with amendments) until 1979.[63] The general tariff on cars remained at 45 per cent, until it was reduced to 33.75 per cent as part of the government's 25 per cent across-the-board tariff cut in July 1973.[64] Despite the still high levels of assistance, the competitive position of the Australian industry – dependent largely on six-cylinder 'family' vehicles: Falcon, Holden and Valiant – continued to deteriorate from the mid- to late 1960s, largely as a result of the switch to smaller, cheaper cars, mainly Japanese. The share of registrations of 'small' cars rose consistently during the 1960s and early 1970s – from 29 per cent in 1961 to 47 per cent in 1973, mostly at the expense of locally produced cars.[65]

By 1974, the situation for the local producers was critical – Chrysler, Ford and GMH announced they would retrench more than 7,000 employees. Not for the first time (nor for the last) the government responded to the car makers 'persuasion'. In November the government announced a policy of preserving for local producers 80 per cent of the Australian market. This 80/20 market sharing arrangement to prevent the job losses was supposed to be a 'short-term' stabilization measure. Initially the market sharing was to be implemented by a trigger tariff mechanism. CBU passenger vehicles would be dutiable at 35 per cent if imports comprised up to 20 per cent of the market, and 45 per cent if they exceeded this market share – but by the time it was introduced imports already exceeded 20 per cent. The trigger therefore came into effect immediately. It was not enough to do the job, however, and 80/20 market sharing was implemented – as a 'temporary' measure – by direct quantitative restrictions on imports.

The 'temporary' measure was extended in 1976, 1977 and 1979 and was due to terminate finally at the end of 1984. During the period of its operation the restrictions were lifted for a short period after the devaluation of the Australian dollar in November 1976. The suspension was made in the mistaken belief that the devaluation would make local producers sufficiently competitive as to make the direct restrictions redundant. It did not take long to show how uncompetitive the local producers were, even with the devaluation. The restrictions were re-imposed in July 1977 to 'prevent severe disruption to employment in the local industry'.[66]

Meanwhile Nissan and Australian Motor Industries (Toyota), which for a number of years had been locally assembling small vehicles, were invited by the government to become full plan producers. Both firms accepted the invitation, joining Chrysler, Ford and GM-H in a new plan implemented in September 1976 that was to run until 1984. By the second half of the 1970s there were five plan producers in a market, the local share of which could only be maintained by stringent import controls. The rationale for Nissan's and Toyota's entry was provided by the Minister for Business and Consumer Affairs, John Howard. 'Because of strong demand in the Australia for Toyota and Nissan products, their exclusion from local manufacture would create a continuing need for import restrictions [contrary to GATT and damaging Australia's relationship with Japan].'[67] The government obviously thought it was better to have the Japanese producers on the inside looking out than on the outside looking in.

Any expectation of certainty and continuity of government policy in the period from the implementation of the 1976 plan to its scheduled expiry in 1984 would certainly have been disappointed. Aside from the on-again/ off-again 80/ 20 market sharing over the period, tariff rates changed in response to essentially short-term exigencies. In 1977 the duty rate on CKDs was increased (to 35 per cent from the 25 per cent that applied two years earlier), while in the following year the tariff on CBU vehicles was increased by 12.5 per cent as part of a budgetary measure applying to all goods which were subject to quantitative restrictions. This brought the duty rate of CBUs to 57.5 per cent though this was not a binding constraint on imports. As an illustration, in October 1979, the government decided to sell by tender 10,000 units of the available quota in two lots of 5,000 units. When in November 1979 the first sale of 5,000 units took place the tender 'price' was 50.5 per cent. When added to the base duty rate of 45 per cent this made a total duty rate payable on these imports of 95.5 per cent. The total duty rate for the second 5,000 units sold in March 1980 was 131.5 per cent.[68]

The entry of a further two firms – Nissan and Toyota – had the entirely predictable effect of further fragmenting the market and contributing to a further deterioration of the local industry's competitive position. The problem was that 'traditional' barrier controls had reached their limits as a means of maintaining a viable industry. Plan producers were already allowed to import 15 per cent of the total value of their production duty-free under by-law. Export facilitation – an extension of the 1976–84 automotive plan – was seen as a way for local producers to participate in an increasingly integrated world industry. The scheme was announced in 1979, initially for vehicle producers and later for components producers, both of which came into operation in 1982.

When first introduced, the scheme enabled producers to earn 'credits' for any exports that could be used for the duty-free importation (under by-law) of components or CBU vehicles up to a value of 7.5 per cent of their plan production. For components producers the limit was 20 per cent of their original equipment (oe) component sales for use in plan vehicles. Both plan producers and specialist components producers could trade credits, so for example plan producers could acquire credits by exporting goods produced by other firms, including specialist components producers. The objective was to achieve industry rationalization, the exploitation of scale economies and as a consequence, greater international competitiveness.[69]

Export facilitation was introduced as a result of representations by GM-H which had plans ready to take advantage of the scheme with its participation in General Motors Corporation's 'world car' plan involving exports from a world-scale four-cylinder engine plant in Victoria. The other plan producers and specialist components producers were far less enthusiastic, Ford in particular stating 'we have not yet been able to devise a system under which we can take any sort of sizeable advantage of export facilitation'.[70]

All of this was a part of the government's assistance arrangements for the industry to operate after the scheduled expiry of the 1976 plan in 1984. Following the Industries Assistance Commission's Report in 1981 the government announced that the local content scheme would continue, and export facilitation would be extended.[71] The 80/20 market sharing arrangement was to be replaced by a tariff quota system in which an unlimited number of vehicles could be imported outside the quota at a penalty duty rate set initially at 150 per cent, to be reduced to 125 per cent in 1992.

In the March 1983 election the coalition government was defeated, and the new Labor government reviewed the proposed post-1984 arrangements. The substance of the revised arrangements have become known as the 'Button' Car Plan, which was to take the industry into the 1990s.

## Notes

1. In 1938–39 there were about 820,000 motor vehicles (including commercial vehicles, but excluding motor cycles) on Australian roads.The total vehicle population fell to just under 730,000 in 1942–43, rising to about 800,000 at the end of the war, about the same number as in mid-1938. (P. Stubbs, *The Australian Motor Industry* (Sydney, 1972) pp. 21–2.) See Table 7.1 for annual new passenger motor vehicle registrations.
2. AA Vic. MP394 Series 1 5/81/107 ATT4.
3. The Secondary Industries Commission was formed to oversee policies for the post-war development of a broader industrial base to reduce Australia's dependence on primary industries.
4. ACI was paid £55,000 as compensation. 'In an informal arbitration ... his Honour Mr. Justice Roper found that the Commonwealth had a moral obligation to the company by reason of the correspondence which passed between the two parties in 1939 and expressed the view that the sum of £55,000 should reasonably be paid to the company in respect thereof' (Treasury minute 29 December 1948 (AA ACT A461/1 D418/1/6 Part 5)).
5. AA Vic. MP394 Series 1 5/81/14.
6. Essentially this meant that as there was a fixed and overvalued exchange rate against dollar countries, it was necessary for Australian governments to institute a system of rationing scarce foreign (dollar) exchange.
7. See Stubbs, *The Australian Motor Industry*, pp. 26–27; P. Davis, *Wheels Across Australia* (Sydney, 1987), p. 103; Automotive Industry Authority (AIA), *State of the Australian Automotive Industry* (Canberra, 1997), p. 107.
8. According to the Secondary Industries Commission, in February 1945, 23 companies and organizations had 'definite claims to manufacture' (AA Vic. MP394 Series 1 5/81/15A).
9. The outline of manufacturing proposals following is based on the Draft report from the Interdepartmental Committee to the Secondary Industries Commission regarding Proposals for Motor Car Manufacture, 20 August 1945 (AA Vic. MP 394 Series 1 5/81/15A).
10. AA Vic. MP394 Series 1 5/81/151 Part 3.
11. At the beginning, Ford's aim was to manufacture the complete range of the company's products.
12. Letter to H.C. French, Managing Director Ford Motor Company of Australia, from Prime Minister J.B. Chifley, 28 November 1945 (AA Vic. MP394 Series 1 5/81/151 Part 2).
13. French to Chifley, 13 December 1945 (AA Vic. MP394 Series 1 5/81/151 Part 2).
14. AA Vic. MP394 Series 1 5/81/151 Part 2.

15. French to Chifley, 14 May 1948 (AA Vic. MP394 Series 1 5/81/151 Part 3).
16. Secret submission 37/48, Cabinet sub-committee on secondary industries (AA Vic. MP394 Series 1 5/81/151 Part 3).
17. Ibid.
18. Ibid.
19. *The Age*, 19 October 1949.
20. AA Vic. MP394 Series 1 5/81/151 Part 3.
21. There are several published accounts of the Holden story, and only a brief outline of it will be given here. A very good account may be found in J. Wright, *The Heart of the Lion – The Holden Story* (Sydney, 1998).
22. AA Vic. MP394 Series 1 5/81/151 Part 3.
23. *The Australian Magazine*, 25–26 July 1998.
24. AA Vic. MP394 Series 1 5/81/102 Part 2.
25. A total of £2.5 million was eventually borrowed from the Commonwealth Bank and the Bank of Adelaide.
26. Hartnett was formally elected as Managing Director by the Board of directors of GM-H on 27 March 1934 (J. Rich, *Hartnett: Portrait of a Technocratic Brigand* (Sydney, 1996), p. 71).
27. From an account of an interview with Hartnett by Pedr Davis, reported in *The Australian*, 14–15 November 1998.
28. Hartnett was prone to exaggeration, and was not above bending the truth to suit his ends. A good account of the circumstances of the severing of Hartnett's links with GM-H is given in Rich, *Hartnett*, pp. 129–35.
29. *Sydney Morning Herald*, 27 November 1998.
30. *The Australian*, 14–15 November 1998.
31. *Sydney Morning Herald*, 27 November 1998.
32. T.J. Richards & Sons Pty Ltd became Richard Industries in 1941.
33. AA Vic. MP394 Series 1 5/81/151 Part 3.
34. Ibid.
35. AA Vic. MP267/1 3 Number Series 5/81/158.
36. Davis, *Wheels Across Australia*, p. 234.
37. *The Australian*, 14–15 November 1998.
38. The measures covered about 98 per cent by value of Australian imports.
39. Tariff Board, *Report on the Automobile Industry* (Canberra, 1957), p. 59.
40. P.L. Swann, 'General Motors-Holden's – The Australian Automobile Industry in Economic Perspective', unpublished Ph.D. thesis (Monash University, 1972), p. 483.
41. Davis, *Wheels Across Australia*, p. 204.
42. Ibid., p. 215.
43. The Zephyr was about the same size as the Holden, but more luxurious and expensive. The two cars were not direct competitors.
44. The terms of reference included an inquiry into the means of overcoming any detriment to assemblers and Australian components producers caused by the system of deletion allowances operated by overseas suppliers of motor vehicles (Department of Industry Science and Technology, *State of the Australian Automotive Industry, 1997* (Canberra, 1999), p. 108).
45. Tariff Board, *Report on the Automobile Industry*. See also Department of Industry Science and Technology, *State of the Australian Automotive Industry*, p. 108.
46. Among the reasons for the disadvantage were the small scale of local production and inadequate deletion allowances. These were the price reductions allowed when certain imported parts were deleted from an imported vehicle and local parts substituted. In cases where the allowance was less than the cost of the import, it provided a disadvantage to local components producers.

**Table 7.1** Australia – new passenger motor vehicle registrations, 1921–1998

| Year | (No.) | Year | (No.) | Year | (No.) |
|------|-------|------|-------|------|-------|
| 1921 | 6200[a]   | 1951 | 125115 | 1981 | 457200[b] |
| 2    | 19500[a]  | 2    | 103717 | 2    | 462400[b] |
| 3    | 31000[a]  | 3    | 104533 | 3    | 403614 |
| 4    | 57000[a]  | 4    | 144813 | 4    | 442355 |
| 5    | 57800[a]  | 5    | 172064 | 5    | 509589 |
| 6    | 80655  | 6    | 145869 | 6    | 398739 |
| 7    | 82570  | 7    | 154949 | 7    | 363964 |
| 8    | 72568  | 8    | 175071 | 8    | 410473 |
| 9    | 65720  | 9    | 196989 | 9    | 448514 |
| 1930 | 29571  | 1960 | 244818 | 1990 | 464630 |
| 1    | 10299  | 1    | 188132 | 1    | 391529 |
| 2    | 10684  | 2    | 266789 | 2    | 406427 |
| 3    | 15679  | 3    | 307380 | 3    | 414425 |
| 4    | 27868  | 4    | 333063 | 4    | 460698 |
| 5    | 39955  | 5    | 331751 | 5    | 488372 |
| 6    | 48206  | 6    | 306688 | 6    | 492058 |
| 7    | 58064  | 7    | 335541 | 7    | 540353 |
| 8    | 58201  | 8    | 368836 | 8    | 584360 |
| 9    | 52995  | 9    | 400879 | 9    | –      |
| 1940 | 28740  | 1970 | 413061 |      |        |
| 1    | 12036  | 1    | 417224 |      |        |
| 2    | 3252   | 2    | 405852 |      |        |
| 3    | 1342   | 3    | 460509 |      |        |
| 4    | 453    | 4    | 475598 |      |        |
| 5    | 1239   | 5    | 472624 |      |        |
| 6    | 11228  | 6    | 468703 |      |        |
| 7    | 32337  | 7    | 430353 |      |        |
| 8    | 59736  | 8    | 451470 |      |        |
| 9    | 86117  | 9    | 461936 |      |        |
| 1950 | 139003 | 1980 | 466900[b] |   |        |

*Sources*: AA ACT B1/1 850 Bundle 5. AA ACT A461/1 D418/1/6 Part 2; Industries Assistance Commission, *Australian Market for Passenger Motor Vehicles*, mimeo (June 1974), pp. 5, 96; Industries Assistance Commission, *Draft Report on Passenger Motor Vehicles* (Canberra, 1981); Automotive Industry Authority, *Report on the State of the Automotive Industry* (Canberra, various years).
*Notes*:
These data are derived from a number of sources. Where two or more sources have registration figures for the same year, there are often small discrepancies. In early years, rarely is any discrepancy more than 100 vehicles and in the years after the Second World War, more than 1000 vehicles.
[a]  Estimated by taking total registered motor cars in (say) 1924 from those on the register in 1925. An adjustment has been made for scrappage.
[b]  Estimated from July to June data.
–  Not available.

47. See Industries Assistance Commission, *Passenger Motor Vehicles, etc* (Canberra, 1974), Chapter 7, for a comprehensive assessment of the system.

48. Rootes commenced assembly of the small Hillman Minx in 1946 at Port Melbourne and later Singer and Humber cars. Volkswagen began assembly of the 'Beetle' in 1954. Rover cars were always imported, but from 1949, Landrovers were assembled in Sydney. Standard Motor Company (Australia) was formed in 1949 to assemble and distribute Standard cars. The company became Standard Motor Products in 1952 following the local purchase of the 50 per cent British shareholding of the earlier company. In turn this company was renamed Australian Motor Industries (AMI) in 1958. By 1960 when AMI had acquired the Rambler Franchise from American Motors, its product range included Standard, Triumph and Rambler.

49. Stubbs, *The Australian Motor Industry*, p. 28.

50. Davis, *Wheels across Australia*, p. 212.

51. A. Capling and B. Galligan, *Beyond the Protective State* (Cambridge, 1992), p. 199.

52. Stubbs, *The Australian Motor Industry*, p. 79.

53. See H.G. Johnson, 'The Bladen Plan for Increased Protection of the Canadian Automotive Industry, *Canadian Journal of Economics* (May, 1963), pp. 212–38.

54. F.G. Davidson and B.R. Stewardson, *Economics and Australian Industry* (Melbourne, 1974), p. 155.

55. Tariff Board, *Motor Vehicles and Concessional Admission of Components* (Canberra, 1965), p. 129.

56. Ibid., p. 16.

57. F.G. Davidson and B.R. Stewardson, *Economics and Australian Industry* (Melbourne, 1974), p. 161. In 1968 Volkswagen (Australasia) became Motor Producers, a wholly owned subsidiary of the German Volkswagen company. Motor Producers assembled in Australia Volkswagen, Datsun (Nissan) and Volvo vehicles (IAC, *Passenger Motor Vehicles, etc.* (Canberra, 1974), p. 30).

58. Manufacturers of cars entered under Plan A with volume less than 25,000 units per year were given the option of a two-year extension (to seven years) of the time for achieving 95 per cent local content.

59. Another option for producers with more than one car under Plan A was to retain duty concessions by agreeing to reach a weighted average of 95 per cent local content for all their cars. The small volume plans were also modified allowing assemblers to retain some duty concessions even if their volume exceeded the limits set by the plans.

60. IAC, *Passenger Motor Vehicles, etc.*, pp. 140–41.

61. In substituting local for imported components producers would first choose those with the least price disadvantage. As local content increased, components with progressively higher price disadvantages would be used.

62. IAC, *Passenger Motor Vehicles, etc.*, pp. 135–7.

63. The amendments included modifying the time requirements of the 85 per cent plan; local content in exports to new markets could be considered as local content in nominated vehicles; and the 'no reversion rule' in which bought-in components once purchased from local manufacturers could not be displaced by imports which qualified for by-law admission (Ibid., p. 129).

64. The tariff cut was designed to increase imports at a time of high domestic demand, a shortage of domestic production capacity and high inflation.

65. IAC, *The Australian Market for Passenger Motor Vehicles* (Canberra, 1974), pp. 5, 8.

66. IAC, *Passenger Motor Vehicles and Components – Post-1984 Assistance Arrangements* (Canberra, 1981), pp. 73–4.

67. Hansard, 30 March 1976, p. 1130.
68. The bidding was in terms of an *ad valorem* duty rate that would be added to the base, 45 per cent rate. Under 'tender quota' the rate of duty applying was the lowest tender price (that is *ad valorem* duty rate) which cleared the tender allocation. IAC, *Passenger Motor Vehicles and Components*, pp. 73–4.
69. See W. Fife, Minister for Business and Consumer Affairs, *Commonwealth Record*, 3, 45, (1978), p. 1590; and IAC, *Passenger Motor Vehicles and Components*, p. 99.
70. Ford's evidence at IAC public hearing quoted in IAC, *Passenger Motor Vehicles and Components*, p. 100.
71. The Industries Assistance Commission had replaced the Tariff Board on 1 January 1974.

# 8 The 'Button' Car Plan and the Post-1992 Environment

The Button Plan (named after the then Minister for Industry, Technology and Commerce, Senator John Button) was introduced in May 1984, and was to operate until 1992.[1] The government's desire was that once the plan was completed, the industry would comprise no more than three manufacturers, producing no more than a total of six vehicle models.

The substance of the assistance package included the introduction of tariff quotas, which replaced the existing 80/20 market sharing arrangement. Imports under quota were dutiable at 57.5 per cent, general; out-of-quota imports were dutiable at 100 per cent, to be phased down to 57.5 per cent by 1992. The existing 85 per cent local content scheme was essentially retained, and access to export facilitation – in which producers received duty-free import entitlements in return for their (value-added) exports – was widened. An Automotive Industry Authority (AIA) was established to oversee the arrangements. In 1986 the government introduced penalties for low-volume production, and in early 1987, separate export facilitation provisions for vehicle importers.

The overall thrust of the arrangements was to increase gradually the pressure of import competition on local producers to encourage high-volume production of a limited number of models. However, these pressures were greatly reduced by the significant devaluation of the Australian dollar in 1985 and 1986, which precipitated a mid-term review of the plan in 1988. In it, the government abolished import quotas and reduced tariffs to 45 per cent, with phased reductions to 35 per cent in 1992. The local content scheme was abolished from 1 January 1989, eliminating any restriction on the proportion of components plan producers could source overseas, while paying duty on these imports at a rate no greater than the standard tariff applying at the time.

In 1989 the government requested the Industry Commission (the successor of the Industries Assistance Commission) to inquire and report on prospective assistance arrangements for the automotive industry from 1993 to 2000. In its 1990 report the majority of the Commission recommended, and the government accepted that the tariff be reduced from 35 per cent at the end of 1992 to 15 per cent by 2000, through eight annual reductions of 2.5 per cent. (The Commission's draft report had recommended annual reductions of five percentage points).[2] Automatic by-law entitlement, by which producers receive duty-free access to imported vehicles and/or components equal to 15 per cent of the value of their production, was retained.[3] Export facilitation was also retained and a number of previous restrictions on access to the scheme were removed, including eliminating differential treatment of vehicle assemblers, specialist component producers and pure importers.

## A selective look at the post-Button Plan industry

*Sales and market shares of local producers*

Table 8.1 and Figure 8.1 show aspects of the Australian market for passenger motor vehicles. Of the period shown in the table, the 80/20 market sharing arrangement operated from 1982 to 1984, and tariff quotas from 1985 to 1988. Both achieved their aims in preserving local producers' share of the Australian market at about 80 per cent. The abolition of tariff quotas in 1988 and the beginning of phased reductions in tariffs are also apparent from the table. The share of locally produced vehicles fell by a total of more than 15 percentage points over the next five years to about 62 per cent in 1993, and another 15 points to 47 per cent in 1998. Imports of CBU vehicles by local producers (mainly duty-free imports under the export facilitation scheme and the 15 per cent automatic by-law allowance) accounted for nearly 13 per cent of the market in 1996 (the last year for which such data are available). The remainder – about 34 per cent – was supplied by specialist importers. In 1997 and 1998, identifiable imports of CBU vehicles by producers comprised about 9 per cent of the market.

While the domestic/import mix of the market has changed in recent years (as policy has changed), the size of the market has changed relatively little though 1997 and 1998 were record years for the domestic market. Sales in 1997 were about 540,000 units, the first time since 1985 that the market had exceeded 500,000 vehicles. Nevertheless, since 1980, Australia's population had increased by about 25 per cent, but it is clear from Figure 8.1 that the local market has not reflected even a small part of that population growth. Markets for passenger motor vehicles in North America and Europe in recent years have shown the same pattern. With the exception of excellent sales (particularly in North America) in 1997 and 1998, those markets have been stable or even declining. It is difficult to foresee anything other than a relatively static local market for the first decade of the twenty-first century, so that any significant growth in sales by local producers will have to come from export markets – at a time of significant global excess capacity.

*Exports*

The aim of the export facilitation scheme (EFS) is to provide local producers with access to scale economies not otherwise achievable by supplying only the local market. It was also intended to reduce the cost penalties imposed by the local content plan, which itself aimed to ensure that the local industry developed as more than a purely assembly operation. In one form or another, export facilitation schemes have operated since 1982. Table 8.2 provides a record of their achievements. It shows the value of automotive exports, and export sales of vehicles over the period 1982–98.

In 1998 exports of automotive products in current dollars were more than

**Table 8.1**   Australia – estimated passenger motor vehicle sales volumes and market shares, 1982–1998

| Year | PMV locally produced | | | | PMV producer Imports CBU | | Other PMV Imports CBU | | Total |
|------|-------|---------|-----------|-----|-------|--------|--------|-------|-------|
|      | Total sales | Less exports | = Domestic sales (No.) | (%) | (No.) | (%) | (No.) | (%) | |
| 1982 | 362714 | 861 | 361853 | 81.2 | 29772 | 6.7 | 54079 | 12.1 | 445705 |
| 1983 | 323826 | 2897 | 320929 | 79.9 | 28836 | 7.2 | 51849 | 12.9 | 401614 |
| 1984 | 356747 | 1525 | 355222 | 80.3 | 27253 | 6.2 | 59880 | 13.5 | 442355 |
| 1985 | 393949 | 2541 | 391408 | 76.8 | 39406 | 7.7 | 78775 | 15.5 | 509589 |
| 1986 | 326613 | 4594 | 322019 | 80.8 | 26532 | 6.7 | 50188 | 12.6 | 398739 |
| 1987 | 317499 | 10119 | 307380 | 84.5 | 15122 | 4.2 | 41462 | 11.4 | 363963 |
| 1988 | 332337 | 1921 | 330416 | 80.5 | 26378 | 6.4 | 53685 | 13.1 | 410473 |
| 1989[a] | 344701 | 5370 | 339331 | 75.6 | 36271 | 8.1 | 72912 | 16.3 | 448514 |
| 1990 | 372438 | 22478 | 349960 | 74.9 | 38890 | 8.3 | 78643 | 16.8 | 467493 |
| 1991 | 298824 | 27604 | 271220 | 69.0 | 38127 | 9.7 | 83814 | 21.3 | 393161 |
| 1992 | 289218 | 25785 | 263433 | 64.7 | 45984 | 11.3 | 97907 | 24.0 | 407324 |
| 1993 | 287869 | 26328 | 261541 | 62.2 | 158663 | (37.8) | | | 420204 |
| 1994 | 397847 | 22253 | 285594 | 61.0 | 182256 | (39.0) | | | 467850 |
| 1995 | 297449 | 22693 | 274756 | 56.1 | 214843 | (43.9) | | | 489599 |
| 1996 | 304577 | 39631 | 264946 | 53.2 | 63260 | 12.7 | 170027 | 34.1 | 498239 |
| 1997 | 308715 | 55046 | 253669 | 46.9 | (47053)[b] | 286684 | (53.1) | – | 540353 |
| 1998 | 327721 | 54360 | 273361 | 46.8 | (51034)[b] | 310999 | (53.2) | – | 584360 |

*Sources*: Automotive Industry Authority *State of the Australian Automotive Industry* (various years); Industry Commission, *The Automotive Industry* (Canberra, 1991, 1996, 1997).

*Notes*: Over the period these data have undergone a number of revisions. Some years certain types of vehicles (for example utilities) may have been included or excluded. While any discrepancies are likely to be small, the data should be viewed as indicative.

[a]   From 1989, years ended December. Previous years ended June.

[b]   Total PMV producer imports were not available. This figure is the sum of identifiable models of producer imports and may be considered a minimum.

–   Not available

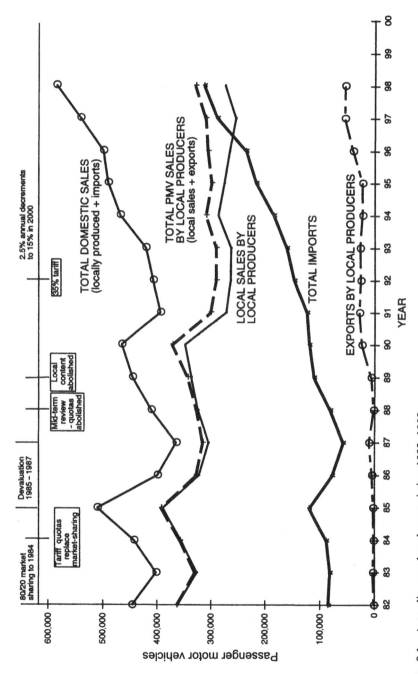

Fig. 8.1    Australia – market characteristics, 1982–1998

139

nine times the level of 1982 and more than six times the level of 1984, the beginning of the Button Plan. However, with the exception of 1987, 'real' exports (in 1984 A$) were fairly static until 1990, when Ford began exporting the Capri sports car to the United States.[4] When first introduced, US retail prices of this vehicle (a more highly specified model than the locally available car) were approximately A$16,000 to A$17,000, considerably below the Australian recommended retail price of about A$24,000 for the base model. While part of the price difference may be attributed to lower sales tax rates in the United States, this would have been at least partially offset by international transport costs from Australia. The result was a pricing arrangement that implied a considerable cross-subsidy from Australian purchasers and taxpayers to those buying Capris in the United States.[5] Since then Toyota and Mitsubishi have become major exporters of CBU and CKD vehicles: Mitsubishi exporting its Magna/Verada models to the US, Germany and the UK; Toyota exporting its Camry/Vienta models to countries of the Arabian Gulf. Both companies planned to double their 1996 exports of automobiles by 1999. Export sales

**Table 8.2**    Australia – automotive exports, 1982–1998

| Year | Total value of exports (A$m) | Index of 'raw' exports (1984 = 100) | Deflated value of exports[a] (A$m) (1984 A$) | Index of real exports (1984 = 100) | Exports of vehicles CBU (A$m) | CKD (A$m) | Export sales of vehicles (No.) |
|------|------|------|------|------|------|------|------|
| 1982 | 277.0 | 72.2 | 318.0 | 82.9 | – | – | 861 |
| 1983 | 357.4 | 93.2 | 379.0 | 98.9 | – | – | 2897 |
| 1984 | 383.4 | 100.0 | 383.4 | 100.0 | – | – | 1525 |
| 1985 | 442.3 | 115.4 | 401.0 | 104.6 | – | – | 2541 |
| 1986 | 463.3 | 120.8 | 348.9 | 91.0 | – | – | 4594 |
| 1987 | 754.9 | 196.9 | 510.8 | 133.2 | – | – | 10119 |
| 1988 | 613.4 | 160.0 | 392.2 | 102.3 | – | – | 1921 |
| 1989 | 649.1 | 169.3 | 391.7 | 102.2 | – | – | 5370 |
| 1990 | 1013.8 | 264.4 | 581.7 | 151.7 | 341.1 | 69.6 | 22478 |
| 1991 | 1157.3 | 301.9 | 635.5 | 165.8 | 390.7 | 30.4 | 27604 |
| 1992 | 1246.9 | 325.2 | 671.5 | 175.1 | 408.7 | 40.4 | 25785 |
| 1993 | 1474.3 | 384.5 | 736.4 | 192.1 | 562.3 | 13.8 | 26328 |
| 1994 | 1537.6 | 401.0 | 749.7 | 195.5 | 463.7 | – | 22253 |
| 1995 | 1775.9 | 463.2 | 823.3 | 214.7 | 485.4 | – | 22693 |
| 1996 | 2173.8 | 566.9 | 995.3 | 259.6 | 836.6 | 34.9 | 39631 |
| 1997 | 2647.2 | 690.5 | 1207.7 | 315.0 | 1077.2 | 187.1[b] | 55046 |
| 1998 | 2516.2 | 656.3 | 1151.6 | 300.4 | 1132.6 | – | 54360 |

*Sources*: See Table 8.1.
*Notes*:
[a]    As an approximation of 'real' export values, nominal values of export values were deflated by the price index of local cars. See Table 8.3.
[b]    Estimate.
–    Not available.

however, have been disappointing with Mitsubishi, for example, achieving only half the projected 1999 sales of 20,000 vehicles to the United States.

Another major contributor to automotive exports in recent years has been the export of engines and engine parts – mainly by General Motors to Europe and more recently to Korea. The value of exports of engines and parts in 1998 (the latest available year) was nearly A$400 million (down from almost A$580 million in the previous year), about 16 per cent of total automotive exports.[6] Other recent export programmes have included those for such automotive components as braking systems, instrumentation, cylinder heads and catalytic converters to overseas manufacturers including BMW, Chrysler, Mercedes (the last two now merged to become DaimlerChrysler), Rover and Peugeot.

Much of this export activity has been due to the EFS, but its 'success' has been far from costless. The scheme makes available a subsidy for exports: it will pay firms to subsidize exports as long the subsidy they pay is less than the value of the duty they save on imports. In 1992 when nominal duty rates were 35 per cent, the value of exports eligible to earn credits exceeded A$935 million and the duty foregone was A$418 million. However, as tariffs fell over the remainder of the decade, the available subsidy also fell. As an illustration, in 1998 when duty rates had fallen to 20 per cent, the value of eligible exports was about A$2 billion but the duty foregone under the scheme fell to A$280 million.[7] As assistance under the scheme declines and as present export contracts and manufacturing programmes come to an end, in the longer term this calls into doubt continued improvements in export performance.

*Prices and quality*

Table 8.3 shows indices of local and imported car prices, average weekly earnings (AWE) and the consumer price index (CPI). In terms of the CPI (all groups), clearly a new car, whether locally produced or imported became relatively more expensive over the period 1984–98. Overall, car prices outstripped the growth of the CPI over the period shown in the table, though the price index of locally produced cars increased by less than that of imported cars. If the CPI (motor vehicle expenditure class) is divided by the index of average weekly earnings, the resulting 'affordability index' for the period 1987–96 is in the mid-80s (base 1984 = 100). This indicates that compared with AWE, cars were about 15 per cent 'less affordable' during this period than in the base year. However, in December 1997 the index exceeded 100 (cars became more affordable than in the base year) for the first time. Moreover, it must be recognized that cars now are far more sophisticated and better equipped than their counterparts produced in 1984.

The major increases in car prices shown in the table, particularly of imports, took place over 1985–87 – the time of a significant devaluation of the Australian dollar against the major currencies. Over the eleven years to 1998, despite significant reductions in protection, the increase in local car prices (just under 48 per cent) exceeded that of imports (almost 36 per cent). The price increases between 1992 and 1993 of both local cars (7.8 per cent) and imports (11.0 per cent) were the highest since 1986–87 and again the devaluation of the Australian dollar, particularly against the Yen and the Won, was the prime cause. Since 1996 exchange rates have tended to move back in favour of imports. This, with continued phased reductions in tariffs, has placed considerable pressure on car producers in Australia. The index of local car prices has remained stable since 1996, while the import price index has fallen from 239 in 1996 to 230 in each of the following two years.

Prices of cars in Australia are no longer exorbitant when compared with prices of similar vehicles in other countries. In terms of the number of weeks of average weekly earnings, the prices of small cars such as Honda Civics and Toyota Corollas, and medium-sized Toyota Camrys are as cheap or cheaper in Australia than in the United States and Britain. Britain is especially expensive. There, in 1999 a medium-sized Vauxhall Vectra cost A$44,000; virtually the same car, until recently produced in Australia, may be bought for about A$25,000. The base models of the six-cylinder Ford Falcon and Holden Commodore are among the best equipped and largest cars for their price (less

**Table 8.3**  Australia – December quarter price indices, 1982–1998

| Year | Cars | | CPI | AWE |
| | Local | Imported | All groups | |
| --- | --- | --- | --- | --- |
| 1982 | 87.1 | 79.3 | 87.6 | 86.1 |
| 1983 | 94.3 | 92.6 | 95.0 | 91.7 |
| 1984 | 100.0 | 100.0 | 100.0 | 100.0 |
| 1985 | 110.3 | 117.3 | 108.2 | 106.3 |
| 1986 | 132.8 | 148.9 | 118.8 | 114.3 |
| 1987 | 147.8 | 169.5 | 127.3 | 120.5 |
| 1988 | 156.4 | 181.5 | 136.1 | 130.7 |
| 1989 | 165.7 | 186.6 | 147.7 | 139.1 |
| 1990 | 174.3 | 191.3 | 157.8 | 148.4 |
| 1991 | 182.1 | 196.3 | 160.2 | 153.3 |
| 1992 | 185.7 | 201.2 | 162.1 | 156.0 |
| 1993 | 200.2 | 223.3 | 163.7 | 161.7 |
| 1994 | 205.1 | 230.0 | 167.8 | 169.0 |
| 1995 | 215.7 | 244.2 | 176.3 | 176.8 |
| 1996 | 218.4 | 239.2 | 179.0 | 183.4 |
| 1997 | 219.2 | 230.5 | 178.6 | 189.2 |
| 1998 | 218.5 | 230.0 | 181.4 | 197.5 |

*Sources*: AIA (various years); IC, *The Automotive Industry*, (Draft Report) (Canberra, 1997).

than A\$35,000) available anywhere.[8] 'Luxury' cars are far more expensive in Australia than in these countries but that is mainly a result of an additional luxury-car sales tax which applies to vehicles with Australian selling prices roughly in excess of \$60,000. While prices in Japan are lower than in countries such as Australia, restrictive safety laws make it prohibitively expensive to maintain vehicles more than a few years old.

Table 8.4 summarizes the results of surveys of private buyers of new cars, several months after taking delivery of their vehicles. The surveys concern the number of faults detected and the overall level of satisfaction with the car after its delivery. Since 1988 (when the initially trouble prone EA model Ford Falcon and the slightly less troublesome VN model GM-H Commodore were released), the results show a clear trend of improvement for local cars.[9] In 1991, for the first time there was an overlap between the highest number of faults for imported Japanese cars, and lowest number of faults for locally produced cars.[10] The period 1992–94 saw further improvements in their quality, while local car producers reported substantial progress in raising the quality of components from their local suppliers.[11] The quality measures of both imports and locally produced cars until recently have remained much the same (the measures still overlapped, but the balance remained in favour of imports). The deterioration in the quality measure for the Commodore and the Falcon in 1998 reflects the introduction of completely new models by both GM-H and Ford. This aside, the improvement in the early 1990s and then the comparative stability in the quality measures since then suggest the 'easy' improvements in quality have been achieved and that further improvements in the long term are likely to be small.

*Profitability*

The available profit information does not provide an encouraging picture of the first years of the Button Plan. From 1985 until 1993 there were only two years of overall profits for the manufacturing operations of plan producers – 1985 and 1989 (see Table 8.5). Since 1993, while these overall profits have been positive, the figures obscure the fact that at times during the period both Mitsubishi and Toyota have incurred record losses, though in 1997 all four producers published profitable results. In the first half of 1999 Mitsubishi was again reported to be experiencing difficulties. While in January 2000, Mitsubishi's head office in Tokyo apparently committed the company to invest \$450 million to develop a locally produced car from 2005, there are still questions over the firm's long-run future as a manufacturer in Australia. The required funds are contingent upon 'extensive restructuring' of its Australian operations, with the further condition that the new car must be profitable solely from local sales. Export sales will not be taken into account. As the current model will continue in

**Table 8.4** Average number of owner detected faults for Australian and imported cars, 1985–1998

| | Average 1984–88 | 1985 | 1986 | 1987 | 1988 | 1989 | 1990 | 1991 | 1992 | 1993 | 1994 | 1995 | 1996 | 1997 | 1998 |
|---|---|---|---|---|---|---|---|---|---|---|---|---|---|---|---|
| **Australian** | | | | | | | | | | | | | | | |
| – High | | 3.3 | 3.5 | 2.9 | 4.4 | 3.3 | 2.9 | 2.5 | 2.2 | 2.1 | 2.2 | 1.9 | 1.9 | 2.1 | 2.4 |
| – Low | | 2.3 | 1.7 | 1.6 | 2.1 | 2.0 | 1.8 | 1.6 | 1.4 | 1.3 | 1.5 | 1.3 | 1.3 | 1.4 | 1.4 |
| **Imported** | | | | | | | | | | | | | | | |
| – High | | – | – | 2 | 1.6 | 1.7 | 1.6 | 1.7 | 1.6 | 1.6 | 1.9 | 1.9 | 1.7 | 2.1 | 1.9 |
| – Low | | – | – | 2 | 0.9 | 0.9 | 0.9 | 0.9 | 0.9 | 0.8 | 1.0 | 1.0 | 1.0 | 0.8 | 0.9 |
| Commodore[a] | 2.7 | 3.3 | 2.4 | 2.5 | 3.2 | 3.3 | 2.9 | 2.5 | 2.0 | 2.1 | 1.9 | 1.9 | 1.9 | 2.1 | 2.4 |
| Falcon[a] | 3.4 | 3.1 | 3.5 | 2.9 | 4.4 | 3.2 | 2.9 | 2.4 | 2.2 | 2.0 | 2.2 | 2.1 | 1.8 | 1.8 | 2.1 |
| Corona/Camry | 2.5 | 2.6 | 2.1 | 2.6 | 2.4 | 2.1 | 2.1 | 1.6 | 1.4 | 1.4 | 1.7 | 1.8 | 1.4 | 1.4 | 1.4 |
| Magna | 2.2[b] | 2.4 | 2.1 | 2.2 | 2.2 | 2.0 | 1.8 | 1.9 | 1.8 | 1.7 | 1.8 | 1.6 | 1.5 | 1.4 | 1.4 |

*Sources:* AIA, *The Automotive Industry* (various years).

*Notes:*

[a] Including derivatives.

[b] 1985–1988.

– Not available.

144

production (with two scheduled 'facelifts' before 2005) until the new model appears, achieving the reported break even output of 40,000 units (local sales in 1999 were about 30,000) will be difficult indeed.[12] The position of Mitsubishi in Australia has been further clouded by the proposal of an 'alliance' of Mitsubishi Motors Corporation in Japan with DaimlerChrysler. The proposed arrangement that was put before the board of Mitsubishi in March 2000 would entail DaimlerChrysler acquiring 33.4 per cent of the Japanese company. The alliance would produce the third largest car manufacturer with an annual output of 6.5 million vehicles.[13]

The bright spots for plan producers have been duty-free imports of CBU vehicles allowable under the automatic 15 per cent duty-free by-law

**Table 8.5**   Australia – profits (losses) as a return on sales (%)

| Year | PMV manf. operations | Total PMV activities[a] | Specialist component producers[b] | Import sector[b] |
|---|---|---|---|---|
| 1985 | 1.44 | – | – | – |
| 1986 | (4.89) | – | – | – |
| 1987 | (1.75) | – | – | – |
| 1988 | (0.23) | 2.63 | – | – |
| 1989 | 2.09 | 3.87 | 6.59 | 10.25 |
| 1990 | (3.48) | (1.27) | 6.13 | 6.69 |
|  |  |  | *6.1* | *6.9* |
| 1991 | (9.63) | (6.09) | 2.87 | (0.19) |
|  |  |  | *2.8* | *0.6* |
| 1992 | (3.73) | (1.08) | 3.29 | (1.51) |
|  |  |  | *3.4* | *1.5* |
| 1993 | 0.8 | 1.7 | 5.5 | 2.1 |
| 1994 | 4.9 | 5.4 | 8.3 | 0.0 |
| 1995 | 5.0 | 5.0 | 7.1 | 1.0 |
| 1996 | 4.9 | 5.7 | 6[e] | – |
| 1997 | 4.9 | 5.4 |  |  |
| 1998 | 5.0 | 4.6 |  |  |

*Sources*: AIA (various years); IC, *The Automotive Industry* (Draft Report) (Canberra, 1997).
*Notes*:
Companies which responded to surveys for all years (32 special component producers and 10 importers).
Data in italics are obtained from AIA (1994) and are derived from one more respondent firm for specialist components producers and two more firms for importers.
[a]    Calendar years.
[b]    Financial years ending June.
[e]    Estimate.
–    Not available.

entitlement, and the export facilitation scheme. Estimates of the duty foregone under both schemes are included in Table 8.6. The table has also been compiled in an effort to gauge the profitability of these import concessions. One point often overlooked, and highlighted in the table, is that plan producers' imports (most, or all of which are duty-free) have accounted for about one-third of total CBU imports in the years for which such data are available. For the period 1988–98, the table shows plan producers' profits for their manufacturing operations, their total passenger motor vehicle (PMV) activities, and the calculated difference between these two figures (the 'residual'). Most of the residual is the profit from their activities as importers of CBU vehicles, and clearly these activities are most lucrative. The data were first made available in 1988, and until 1998, the residual activities showed accumulated profits of A$1.47 billion compared with about A$1 billion in profits from manufacturing over the same period. More important, during 1988–92 producers accumulated losses of about A$800 million in manufacturing which were largely offset by residual profits of A$700 million.

The total of the estimated duty foregone under the export facilitation scheme alone for just three years, 1991–93 (A$814 million), exceeded 'residual' profits accumulated during 1988–93. Indeed, it appears that duty-free importation of CBU vehicles and components allowed overall losses for local producers in the six years to 1993 to be kept within tolerable levels (though not for Nissan which withdrew from local production in 1992). Without these imports (and the duty foregone) the remaining producers would clearly have faced far greater difficulty in maintaining their manufacturing operations in the 1980s and early 1990s. The duty waived under both schemes from 1991 to 1998 totalled more than A$4.1 billion, which by any standards is a concession of remarkable magnitude.

*Aspects of industry structure, productivity and employment*

Since the beginning of the Button Plan, the industry has undergone considerable rationalization. In 1988 Toyota and GM-H began what proved to be a short-lived joint venture – United Australian Automotive Industries (UAAI) – involving the sharing of facilities and models (for example Commodore/ Lexcen); while Ford and Nissan also entered a model-sharing arrangement (for example Corsair/Pintara). Only Mitsubishi stood alone. The Holden/Toyota joint venture and model sharing arrangements ceased in 1996. Of the five original plan producers only four – Ford, GM-H, Mitsubishi and Toyota – now continue as local producers following Nissan's withdrawal in 1992.

The number of models produced by the local industry has also declined: from 13 in 1985, to five at the end of 1996. Towards the end of 1998 GM-H brought the medium-sized Vectra into production, bringing the number of

**Table 8.6**  Sources of profits – passenger motor vehicles

| Year | Plan producers Imports (No.) | Plan producers Share of total imports (%) | Estimated av. value of total CBU imports f.o.b. A$ | Profit Manuf. (A$m) | Profit Total (A$m) | Resid. (A$m) | Duty rate (%) | Estimated duty waived (A$m)[a] | Duty foregone under the duty-free allowance (A$m) |
|---|---|---|---|---|---|---|---|---|---|
| 1984 | 27253 | 29.0 | 5758 | – | – | – | – | – | – |
| 1985 | 39406 | 34.4 | 6634 | – | – | – | – | – | – |
| 1986 | 26532 | 38.1 | 9525 | – | – | – | – | – | – |
| 1987 | 15122 | 28.7 | 10986 | – | – | – | – | – | – |
| 1988 | 26372 | 34.6 | 12131 | (12) | 174 | 186 | 45 | 114 | – |
| 1989 | 36271 | 28.7 | 10946 | 127 | 316 | 189 | 42.5 | 134 | – |
| 1990 | 38890 | 33.8 | 11096 | (224) | (109) | 115 | 40 | 137 | – |
| 1991 | 38127 | 31.8 | 10763 | (502) | (415) | 87 | 37.5 | 123 | 268 |
| 1992 | 45984 | 31.2 | 12545 | (202) | (78) | 124 | 35 | 161 | 257 |
| 1993 | *4911* | 32.1 | 13731 | 53 | 129 | 76 | 32.5 | 175 | 289 |
| 1994 | – | – | – | 327 | 474 | 147 | 30.0 | – | 315 |
| 1995 | – | – | – | 343 | 434 | 91 | 27.5 | – | 293 |
| 1996 | 63260 | 27.1 | 10240 | 351 | 520 | 169 | 25.0 | – | 267 |
| 1997 | – | – | – | 344 | 518 | 174 | 22.5 | – | 235 |
| 1998 | – | – | – | 389 | – | – | – | – | 233 |

*Sources*:  AIA (various years).
*Notes*:
Data in italics are not strictly comparable with those of earlier periods, and should be viewed as indicative only.
a  See text for method of estimation.
–  Not available.

147

models locally produced back to six. However, local production of the car proved to be short-lived. While it was successful in the local market, export sales were disappointing. In two years only 13,000 Vectras were produced, less than half of the initial target, and production of the car ceased at the end of 1999. Toyota began production of a large six-cylinder car – the Avalon – in mid-2000, but it was to replace the Corolla, which was to go out of local production. Since 1985 the number of assembly plants has fallen from eight to four (see Table 8.7). Average production volumes per model varied considerably over the period from 1985 to 1996 – from a low of 24,000 units in 1986 to more than 60,000 from 1994.[14] The recession experienced in Australia in the early 1990s had a severe effect on production and sales in 1991 and 1992, lowering model production volumes considerably. The recession similarly affected one of the measures of productivity reported in Table 8.7 – the average number of hours required to assemble a standard vehicle. At the beginning of the 1990s, by world standards Australian production was characterized by very low levels of plant automation and productivity. The productivity of Australian assembly was then about one-half of United States levels and one-third the levels of Japan.[15] In 1990 the average number of hours to assemble a standard vehicle in Australia actually increased from 41.4 hours per vehicle in 1989 to 52.5 hours as a result of declining sales/production and the failure to adjust employment levels to the changed market conditions (see Table 8.8). While production declined in each of the following years, employment in the industry fell drastically in both 1991 and 1992, causing an improvement in the productivity measure in those two years. Since 1994, in terms of the ratio of the number of cars produced/employees, productivity has remained static. Nevertheless it is instructive to compare the performance of local producers with their counterparts in other countries. In 1996 it took Ford, GM-H and Toyota about 24 to 26 hours to assemble a 'standard' vehicle. This compared favourably with overseas assemblers. For example, in that year the time taken to produce a standard vehicle across all General Motors plants averaged nearly 37 hours, and varied from 20.2 to 74.9 hours. GM-H's figure puts it in the top one-third of GM plants throughout the world.[16] Labour shedding, especially in the period from 1989 to 1992 (direct employment fell by almost 30 per cent in passenger motor vehicle production and almost 15 per cent in the specialist component producer sector of the industry (see Table 8.8)), improved work practices and the introduction of higher levels of automation have all played important parts in improving productivity. Complementing these has been the widespread introduction of 'lean' manufacturing practice in the industry.[17] While further improvements in productivity may be expected in the future, if the last few years are a guide, it is likely that they will be small. At least some of the gap between international best-practice and Australian productivity is attributable to the comparatively small scale of Australian output (assembly plant capacities in Australia are

Table 8.7 Australia – production volumes by passenger motor vehicle model lines, 1985–1998[a]

| Sales volumes | 1985 | 1986 | 1987 | 1988 | 1989 | 1990 | 1991 | 1992 | 1993 | 1994 | 1995 | 1996 | 1997 | 1998[b] |
|---|---|---|---|---|---|---|---|---|---|---|---|---|---|---|
| 0–19,999 | 4 | – | 6 | 2 | 2 | 0 | 1 | 2 | 1 | 1 | 0 | 0 | 0 | 1 |
| 20,000–29,999 | 6 | – | 4 | 4 | 2 | 2 | 2 | 1 | 1 | 1 | 1 | 1 | 1 | 1 |
| 30,000–39,999 | 1 | – | 1 | 1 | 3 | 2 | 2 | 3 | 2 | 0 | 2 | 0 | 1 | 1 |
| 40,000–59,999 | 0 | – | 2 | 3 | 0 | 2 | 2 | 0 | 0 | 2 | 0 | 2 | 1 | 1 |
| 60,000+ | 2 | – | 2 | 3 | 2 | 2 | 1 | 2 | 2 | 2 | 2 | 2 | 2 | 2 |
| Models manufactured in the year | 13 | 13 | 13 | 10 | 9 | 8 | 8 | 8 | 6 | 6 | 5 | 5 | 5 | 6 |
| Models remaining at end of year | 13 | 13 | 10 | 9 | 8 | 8 | 8 | 6 | 6 | 5 | 5 | 5 | 5 | 6 |
| Approx. average annual model output | 27000 | 24000 | 26000 | 34000 | 44000 | 47000 | 36000 | 39000 | 49000 | 66000 | 62000 | 65000 | 64000 | 70000 |
| No. of assembly plants | 8 | 8 | 8 | 8 | 7 | 7 | 7 | 6 | 6 | 4 | 4 | 4 | 4 | 4 |
| Productivity[c] | – | – | – | 40.4 | 41.4 | 52.5 | 44.1 | 39.0 | 34.5 | – | – | 26 | – | – |
| PMU manf.: cars/ employee | – | – | – | – | – | 11.64 | 10.83 | 11.55 | 12.75 | 15.82 | 15.81 | 16.11 | 15.54 | 15.82 |

Sources: PAXUS Corporation Limited, Bulletin – New Motor Vehicle Registrations; AIA (various years).

Notes:

a Includes sales for export.

b The Holden Vectra commenced production towards the end of 1998. Nearly 3,000 units were purchased. The average output omits data for the Vectra.

c Weighted average number of hours to assemble a standard vehicle.

– Not available.

about 100,000 units p.a. or fewer; capacities of comparable plants overseas are typically 150–200,000 and up to 300,000 units). Even so, while productivities of Australian producers have improved and the improvement may continue, it cannot be expected that producers overseas will stand still.

*Investment*

Table 8.9 shows anticipated and actual investment expenditures for nine overlapping four year periods from 1986/89 to 1995/98, both in the year in which the forecast was made (for example the forecast for 1992/95 was made in 1991 A$ and the actual investment data is in 1995 A$), and in constant (1993) dollars. The first period proved to be the investment peak: actual total investment was A$2.3 billion (in 1993A$) and it is only in the last three four-year periods that total investment has exceeded A$2 billion. The late 1980s and

**Table 8.8**   Australia – numbers employed in the automotive industry, 1983–1998

| Year | PMV producer | Specialist component producers | Importer | Total |
|------|------|------|------|------|
| 1983 | 33619 | – | 2902 | – |
| 1984 | 33827 | – | 2657 | – |
| 1985 | 34302 | 23729 | 2750 | 60781 |
| 1986 | 31675 | 26417 | 2263 | 60355 |
| 1987 | 30919 | 25331 | 1931 | 58181 |
| 1988 | 30476 | 26345 | 1937 | 58758 |
| 1989 | 33558 | 26357 | 2190 | 62105 |
| 1990 | 32421 | 22350 | 2210 | 56981 |
| 1991 | 26639 | 24835 | 1774 | 53248 |
| 1992 | 24036 | 22618 | 1777 | 48431 |
| 1993 | 23067 | 21820 | 2247 | 47134 |
| 1994 | 20412 | 22568 | 1559[a] | 44539 |
| 1995 | 19754 | 24023 | 1547[a] | 45324 |
| 1996 | 20213 | 22708 | 1080 | 44001 |
| 1997 | 20540 | 21000[b][c] | 1000[c] | 42500[c] |
| 1998 | 22371 | 22000[b][c] | 1000[c] | 45500[c] |

*Sources*: AIA (various years).
*Notes*:
1983–90 data: employment as at 30 June.
1991–96 data: employment as at 31 December.
[a]   Excludes Mazda.
[b]   Based on ABS data. ASIC2814 Automotive component manufacturing.
[c]   Estimate.
–   Not available.

**Table 8.9**  Australia – comparison of anticipated and actual investment in the automotive industry, 1986/89–1995/97 (A$)

| | **1986–89** | | | |
| | Anticipated (1985 $) | Actual (1988 $) | Anticipated (1993 $) | Actual (1993 $) |
|---|---|---|---|---|
| Product | 1417.7 | 1332.1 | 2013.3 | 1503.3 |
| Capacity | 100.5 | 134.1 | 142.7 | 150.6 |
| Efficiency | 325.1 | 355.1 | 461.7 | 399.9 |
| CM&A | 242.8 | 220.5 | 344.8 | 247.6 |
| Total | 2086.1 | 2042.2 | 2962.5 | 2301.4 |

| | **1988–91** | | | |
| | Anticipated (1987 $) | Actual (1991 $) | Anticipated (1993 $) | Actual (1993 $) |
|---|---|---|---|---|
| Product | 1120.2 | 843.2 | 1275.8 | 891.1 |
| Capacity | 95.7 | 170.7 | 109.0 | 180.4 |
| Efficiency | 242.7 | 327.4 | 276.4 | 346.0 |
| CM&A | 303.3 | 315.8 | 345.4 | 333.8 |
| Total | 1761.9 | 1657.1 | 2006.6 | 1751.3 |

| | **1989–92** | | | |
| | Anticipated (1988 $) | Actual (1992 $) | Anticipated (1993 $) | Actual (1993 $) |
|---|---|---|---|---|
| Product | 1147.3 | 744.5 | 1278.5 | 758.1 |
| Capacity | 285.4 | 146.9 | 318.0 | 149.6 |
| Efficiency | 286.8 | 493.2 | 319.6 | 502.2 |
| CM&A | 359.9 | 330.9 | 401.0 | 336.9 |
| Total | 2115.4 | 175.5 | 2357.3 | 1746.8 |

| | **1990–93** | | | |
| | Anticipated (1989 $) | Actual (1993 $) | Anticipated (1993 $) | Actual (1993 $) |
|---|---|---|---|---|
| Product | 1337.7 | 761.2 | 1490.6 | 761.2 |
| Capacity | 335.4 | 120.5 | 373.7 | 120.5 |
| Efficiency | 594.4 | 692.4 | 662.4 | 692.4 |
| CM&A | 364.4 | 318.7 | 406.1 | 318.7 |
| Total | 2631.9 | 1892.8 | 2932.8 | 1892.8 |

Table 8.9 continued

|            | **1991–94** | | | |
|            | Anticipated (1990 $) | Actual (1994 $) | Anticipated (1993 $) | Actual (1993 $) |
|------------|------------|------------|------------|------------|
| Product    | 1168.1     | 752.2      | 1234.2     | 762.7      |
| Capacity   | 307.4      | 78.0       | 324.8      | 79.1       |
| Efficiency | 581.3      | 686.7      | 614.2      | 696.3      |
| CM&A       | 336.3      | 242.5      | 355.3      | 245.9      |
| Total      | 2393.1     | 1732.4     | 2528.6     | 1756.5     |
|            | **1992–95** | | | |
|            | Anticipated (1991 $) | Actual (1995 $) | Anticipated (1993 $) | Actual (1993 $) |
| Product    | 980.1      | 890.9      | 1035.8     | 914.5      |
| Capacity   | 41.1       | 113.3      | 43.4       | 116.3      |
| Efficiency | 789.7      | 595.1      | 834.6      | 610.9      |
| CM&A       | 365.0      | 173.4      | 385.7      | 178.0      |
| Total      | 2176.7     | 1772.7     | 2300.4     | 1819.7     |
|            | **1993–96** | | | |
|            | Anticipated (1992 $) | Actual (1996 $) | Anticipated (1993 $) | Actual (1993 $) |
| Product    | 1120.0     | 1098.0     | 1140.4     | 1143.8     |
| Capacity   | 49.9       | 141.2      | 50.8       | 147.1      |
| Efficiency | 494.3      | 557.9      | 503.3      | 581.1      |
| CM&A       | 383.8      | 201.9      | 390.8      | 210.3      |
| Total      | 2048.0     | 1999.0     | 2085.4     | 2082.3     |
|            | **1994–97** | | | |
|            | Anticipated (1993 $) | Actual (1997 $) | Anticipated (1993 $) | Actual[a] (1993 $) |
| Product    | 1133.4     | 1292.1     | 1133.4     | 1215.5     |
| Capacity   | 49.5       | 169.9      | 49.5       | 159.8      |
| Efficiency | 346.4      | 435.6      | 346.4      | 409.7      |
| CM&A       | 440.0      | 298.9      | 440.0      | 281.2      |
| Total      | 1969.3     | 2196.5     | 1969.3     | 2066.2     |

Table 8.9 concluded

|  | | 1995–98 | | |
|  | Anticipated (1994 $) | Actual (1995–98 $) | Planner[a] (1993 $) | Actual[a] (1993 $) |
|---|---|---|---|---|
| Product | 1169.9 | 1343.9 | 1086.3 | 1289.7 |
| Capacity | 163.3 | 161.3 | 151.6 | 154.8 |
| Efficiency | 303.8 | 361.4 | 282.1 | 346.8 |
| CM&A | 264.8 | 400.3 | 245.9 | 384.2 |
| Total | 1901.8 | 2266.9 | 1765.9 | 2175.5 |

*Sources*: AIA (various years).
*Note*:
[a]   These data were provided by the AIA in nominal $. These have been deflated using the method described by the AIA in its 1994 Annual Report. However, the data for industrial years were not provided and an average of deflation was used for the three years data. The figures should therefore be viewed as indicative.

early 1990s coincided with heavy losses by PMV producers, and at the time GM-H was evidently considering withdrawing from local production.[18]

Product-related expenditure is the largest component of investment expenditure, accounting for about two-thirds of total expenditure in the peak period, 1986–89. A large part of this was made in introducing the (Ford) EA Falcon and (GM-H) VN Commodore models in 1988, to succeed two basic model lines that had been in production for 10 years. The period 1989–92 was characterized by comparatively minor model changes (though a substantially revised VR/VS Commodore was introduced in 1993). A revised and rebodied (EF/EL) Falcon and new (Mitsubishi) Magna/Verada models were introduced in 1994, while completely new (VT) Commodore and (Toyota) Camry/Vienta models were introduced in 1997. A new model (AU) Falcon began production in mid-1998. Despite this, product investment (in constant 1993 A$) was about 15 per cent lower in 1995–98 than it was in 1986–89, and anticipated product investment of A$1.4 billion (in nominal A$) for the period 1999–2002 is about the same as it was more than a decade ago. Efficiency related expenditures peaked in 1991–94 at nearly A$700 million. The results of this expenditure (and labour shedding) were shown in 1994, with productivity (in terms of the number of cars produced per employee) improving by more than 30 per cent over the average of the previous four years (see Table 8.7). While the initial improvement has been maintained, there has been no further progress in more recent years during which in the last two periods efficiency expenditures have fallen by about 40 per cent compared with the peak.

For the first six of the nine periods, actual investment was below anticipations even when the latter was evaluated at prices five years earlier than the reported actual figures. In constant (1993) dollars the discrepancies ranged from 13 to 35 per cent.[19] Only in the last two periods have anticipations been realized.

*Age of the Australian PMV stock and the environment*

The comparatively high proportion of 'old' vehicles in Australia's stock of motor vehicles has been a problem for more than 60 years. In 1935, for example, the 'extraordinary average age of cars [in Australia] was 10 2/3 years' and in 1939, 55 per cent of cars registered in Australia were more than 8 years old – 'the oldest in the world'.[20] Though the average ages of vehicle stocks in the 1970s and 1980s were far lower than the averages of the 1930s, the most recent figures have deteriorated to be about the same as they were 60 years ago. Compared with average age of the US vehicle stock of 8.5 years, in 1995 the average age of the Australian vehicle fleet was 10.6 years – the same as it was in 1935 – and in 1995 almost 60 per cent of Australian cars were more than 10 years old.[21] The most recent (1997) data suggests the average age has deteriorated still further to 10.7 years.

From the point of view of the environment there are two important and interrelated issues arising from Australia's relatively elderly fleet of vehicles – conservation of a non-renewable fuel resource and pollution.[22] Regarding the former, modern vehicles are far more fuel-efficient than those designed 10 or 15 years ago. For example, a current model six-cylinder Ford Falcon with an engine capacity of 4 litres has about the same rate of fuel consumption as a 1980 four-cylinder 2 litre automatic car.[23] Since 1978 the National Average Fuel Consumption (NAFC) has fallen from 11.5 litres/100 km to 8.8 in 1995, and by 2000 NAFC was scheduled to fall to 8.2 litres/100 km.[24]

Moreover, recently designed vehicles have far higher standards of emissions control, though current Australian standards are less stringent than those of many other countries, particularly the United States. From 1986 new vehicles were required to have catalytic converters and to run on lead-free fuel. Nine years later, in 1995, the number of vehicles using leaded petrol still exceeded the number using unleaded fuel.[25] Only in June 1997 did the Commonwealth government adopt an environmental strategy which incorporates a commitment to terminate the use of leaded fuel by 2010, though it is unlikely this will prove to be a binding constraint. As the stock of cars requiring leaded fuel falls, it is likely that the production of such fuel will become commercially unviable for the oil companies well before 2010, and that any mandate phasing out its use will become redundant.

It should be recognized that some measures to deal with the problems of declining petroleum stocks and vehicle emissions have their own environ-mental costs. The penalty for the use of catalytic converters to lower emissions (and which require lead-free fuel) is increased fuel consumption.[26] As well, there is evidence that the emissions from catalytic converter-equipped cars tend to worsen at a greater rate than pre-catalytic converter vehicles.[27] Alternatives to leaded fuel and to petrol itself have drawbacks. Lead is added to petrol as a lubricant and a measure to increase the octane rating of fuel. An alternative means of increasing octane ratings is to increase the proportion of aromatic compound in the fuel. Currently in Australia the proportion is about 20 per cent. If this were raised to levels common in Europe – about 40 per cent (higher-octane fuels are available in Europe than are typically used in Australia) – there would be increased emissions of these aromatics, one of which is benzene, a known carcinogen. Any improvements in overall emissions using petrol blended with ethanol or methanol are doubtful, while other emissions from these fuels – aldehydes – are just as toxic as those removed. Liquid petroleum gas (LPG) is cheap and provides good engine performance, but fuel consumption is higher than for petrol and there is little net effect on overall emissions. Moreover, if engines are not correctly tuned for LPG, emissions of oxides of nitrogen are likely to be substantially higher than for petrol. Compressed natural gas (CNG) is a 'cleaner' fuel in terms of all the controlled pollutants (for example unburned hydrocarbons, carbon monoxide, NOx), but its major constituent, methane, is a potentially more potent global warming gas than $CO_2$.

Practical electric cars are still many years away. Relatively cheap, lightweight batteries are unlikely to be available for at least a decade. Even if they were, their use involves pollution transfer from cities to the site of the power generation, which if coal- or oil-fuelled still involves the discharge of greenhouse gas emissions; if nuclear-fuelled, the possibility of accident and disposal of nuclear waste are the problems. Fuel cells may provide a more practical and immediate alternative power source. DaimlerChrysler, for example, predicts it will have a fuel cell vehicle on the market by 2004.[28] The principle of the fuel cell was discovered in the mid-nineteenth century by a British scientist, William Groves, and involves releasing electrical energy by combining gaseous hydrogen and atmospheric oxygen.[29] The exhaust gas produced by the fuel cell is water vapour, a global warmer of greater effect than any of the other emissions mentioned, though it remains in the atmosphere for only a few days, compared with methane's 10 years and 100 years for $CO_2$.[30]

There are no easy environmental solutions. Increasing pressure for greenhouse gas and other emission controls, and declining reserves of liquid petroleum which will be felt in the second or third decade of the next century will in turn place pressure on the industry to change the nature of its products and production processes. Australia will not be isolated from the inevitable changes.

## Notes

1. Its primary objectives were to:
   (i)   give the industry time to restructure and modernize;
   (ii)  make it more efficient;
   (iii) hold down the price of cars; and
   (iv)  reduce immediate job losses and provide stable employment.
   The strategy involved:
   (i)   increasing import competition through the gradual reduction of tariffs, and the removal of quantitative restrictions;
   (ii)  pursuing scale economies and increased capacity utilization through industry rationalization encouraged by the minimum production volume provisions of the Plan, and the Export Facilitation Scheme; and
   (iii) improving productivity and product quality through investment in new technology and automation, and improved management, workforce training and organization.
   (AIA, *State of the Australian Automotive Industry* (Canberra, 1989), p. 13)
2. Industry Commission, *The Automotive Industry* (Draft Report) (Canberra, 1990), p. 138.
3. Export facilitation enables producers to earn *additional* duty-free import credit above the automatic 15 per cent allowance.
4. The destination of a very high proportion of Australian automobile exports in 1987 was New Zealand. With the impact of a recession on the New Zealand economy in the early 1990s, for a time these exports came to a virtual stop.
5. The Capri ceased production in Australia in 1994.
6. Department of Industry, Science and Resources, *Key Automotive Statistics, Australia* (Canberra, 1999).
7. Some eligible products and services have not been included in the totals (Industry Commission, *The Automotive Industry*, (1997), p. L9). From 1992, exports to New Zealand no longer attracted export credits.
8. *Sun-Herald*, 22 August 1999, p. 2.
9. Both the EA Falcon and the VN Commodore replaced very long-standing series of models. Both cars (the Falcon in particular) proved to have many teething problems.
10. The lowest number of faults for an Australian car was 1.6; the highest number of faults for an import was 1.7.
11. AIA, *State of the Australian Automotive Industry* (Canberra, 1994), p. 22.
12. *Sydney Morning Herald*, 26 January 2000.
13. *Sydney Morning Herald*, 23 March 2000.
14. The figures are approximations, as the inclusion or exclusion of different types of vehicles (for example utilities and vans) has affected production volumes over time reported by the Automotive Industry Authority.
15. In 1991, the number of vehicles produced per employee was 5.8 in Australia and 11.4 in the United States. In 1988 the corresponding figure for Japan was 16.7 (AIA, *State of the Australian Automotive Industry* (Canberra, 1992), p. 16).
16. IC, *The Automotive Industry* (1997), App. E.
17. AIA, *State of the Australian Automotive Industry* (1994), p. 14. Entailed in the 'lean' approach, pioneered in Japan, is the motivation of employees: communicating to them the firm's goals and performance; investing in new equipment and training; devolving responsibility and authority; and improving working conditions. Targets are set for such things as productivity, quality, material wastage and stock levels, and performance is measured against these targets. The 'pull' system of production is used to reduce wastage, inventory levels and

working capital, and increase factory floor space by ensuring products are manufactured only when they are required. Workforces are organized into self-managing teams with job rotation, multi-skilling and responsibility for their own procedures and work flows. Continuous improvement of work methods and organization ('Kaizen' activities) are integrated into the process. An important element of this is the need for visual control. If workers and managers can see what is happening on the factory floor they can respond quickly to any problems. (See AIA, *The State of the Australian Automotive Industry* (Canberra, 1993), pp. 34–8, for a summary of the 'lean' approach. J.P. Womack, D.T. Jones and D. Roos, *The Machine that Changed the World* (New York, 1991), provides a comprehensive description.)

18. *The Australian*, 22–3 February 1997, pp. 57–8.
19. Part of the explanation for the discrepancies between anticipated and actual investment is likely to be the downturn of sales as the Australian economy slid into recession in 1989/90, discouraging investment that had been planned.
20. *Australian Motorist*, 1 March 1935, reporting census data; AA ACT A461/1 D418/1/6 Part 3.
21. In the mid-1970s about 30 per cent of the vehicle stock was more than 10 years old; in the mid-1980s about 45 per cent (Australian Bureau of Statistics, *Vehicle Census of Australia* (Canberra, 1996) (Cat 9309.0)).
22. Pollution problems associated with the production and disposal of vehicles are not considered here.
23. R. King, 'Driving the Environment, A Case History from Ford Motor Company of Australia', in L. Cato (ed.), *The Business of Ecology* (Melbourne, 1993), p. 100.
24. The Federal Chamber of Automotive Industries subscribes to a voluntary code of practice for reducing the fuel consumption of PMVs (IC, *The Automotive Industry* (1997), pp. J7–J8).
25. Department of Industry, Science and Tourism, *State of the Australian Automotive Industry Report*, 1996 (preliminary) (Canberra, 1998).
26. Ford's submission to the Industry Commission inquiry suggested on the basis of tests conducted at the University of Melbourne that up 10 per cent of gains in fuel economy have been foregone as a result of measures designed to improve air quality (IC, *The Automotive Industry* (Canberra, 1998), p. 189).
27. Federal Office of Road Safety, *Motor Vehicle Pollution in Australia* (Canberra, 1996), p. v.
28. *Sydney Morning Herald*, 8 October 1999.
29. Hydrogen may be stored in pressurized tanks, or may be extracted chemically from methanol or petrol.
30. King, 'Driving the Environment', pp. 99–101.

# 9   A Summing-up

## The 1990s and beyond

During the 1990s the Australian automobile industry improved its performance considerably. The quality of locally produced vehicles improved – particularly over the second half of the decade – and is now comparable with all but the best of imports. Pre-tax prices of large cars (Commodore/Falcon sizes) are about the same as similar cars in the United States, and considerably cheaper than in Britain. Small cars, however, are more expensive here than in the United States, but again tend to be cheaper than in the United Kingdom.[1] However, at least partly the result of the luxury car tax, retail prices of these vehicles in Australia are considerably higher than in the US and UK.[2] The success of Korean imports at the low-priced end of the market in recent years has placed considerable downward pressure on virtually all Australian automobile prices.[3]

The target structure for the industry set in the Button Plan in 1984 – three manufacturing groups, producing a total of six models – was for a short time achieved. The divorce of GM-H and Toyota in their partial joint venture and model-sharing arrangement (United Australian Automotive Industries) in 1996 brought the number of groups back to four. Despite the considerable rationalization of models, production levels of GM-H's Commodore and Ford's Falcon, still the two best-selling models in Australia, each at about 70,000–90,000 units per year, are only a little more than one-half the annual production volumes of the EH model Holden of the middle 1960s.[4] Mitsubishi's output of the competitive Magna/Verada models in 1998 was less than 40,000 units, while Toyota's output of the medium-sized Camry/Vienta was less than 45,000.[5] One can only wonder at the economic viability of bringing into production the Commodore/Falcon-sized Toyota Avalon – a model already superseded in the United States – that was released in mid-2000. While there is some evidence that minimum efficient scale (MES) in the production of motor vehicles will decline in the future, the current output levels of the two largest selling Australian vehicles are considerably below any likely future MES of assembly plants.[6]

In terms of domestic sales for locally produced cars the market has been static at about 270,000 units since 1991 (in 1985 the figure was nearly 400,000 units – see Table 8.1). In these circumstances the future of the industry is tied to success in export markets. For vehicles like the Commodore and Falcon – large, powerful, rear-wheel drive cars – access to world markets is quite restricted, aside from any export limitations imposed on local producers by their overseas parents, or the trade barriers against Australian car exports ruling in many countries, especially in Asia.[7] In many ways these two vehicles are almost unique and of limited appeal in most foreign markets where they would be competing (at least in terms of basic design) with large luxury vehicles such as those produced by BMW and ChryslerDaimler which also have the rear-wheel drive configuration. In recent years export facilitation has brought about increased exports of both CBU vehicles and components, but these exports have been realized at high cost. As well, Australia's future competitiveness both at home and in international markets also depends on maintaining exchange rates favourable to the local industry.

Until recently the improved performance of local producers has generally not been reflected in their financial results. While the industry returned to profitability in 1993 (for the first time since 1989), the overall returns have been low. While Ford and GM-H earned record profits in the mid-1990s, both Mitsubishi and Toyota have experienced significant difficulties in recent years.[8] Ford as well has found sales of its AU model Falcon, introduced in mid-1998, to be disappointing.

In recent years there has been considerable volatility in consumer demand – away from four-cylinder small and medium-sized cars in 1993–95, to large six-cylinder vehicles, mainly fleet sales of Commodores and Falcons; then since 1996–98, back again to small four-cylinder imports. Until well-publicized mechanical problems that may have affected vehicle safety, the small Korean Hyundai Excel had been the third most popular model on the market. The medium car sector (including Mitsubishi Magna and Toyota Camry) tended to be squeezed from both ends, and was a major cause of the problems of Mitsubishi (particularly) and Toyota in Australia in the late 1990s.

Of more immediate concern to local producers is global excess capacity that has emerged as a serious problem for car producers in the 1990s. In particular, recent increases in productive capacity, especially in Korea, have had a significant impact on the Australian market. Indeed, in the mid-1990s the most important change in the sources of CBU imports has been the rise of Korean imports – mainly at the expense of Japanese producers (see Table 9.1). In 1985 Japan provided 83 per cent of Australian imports. From then until 1992 Japanese producers provided about 70 to 80 per cent of the total, but in 1994 (following three years of gradual decline), this fell to 61 per cent, and from 1995 to about 45 per cent of the total. These changes were mirrored in Korean-sourced imports. From 1989 there was a consistent, but gradual increase until 1992, which accelerated in 1993, until in 1996, Korean producers were the source of about one-third of total CBU imports. Since then this proportion has

**Table 9.1**  Australia – sources of imported CBU passenger motor vehicles, 1985–1998

| | 1985 | 1986 | 1987 | 1988 | 1989 | 1990 | 1991 | 1992 | 1993 | 1994 | 1995 | 1996 | 1997 | 1998 |
|---|---|---|---|---|---|---|---|---|---|---|---|---|---|---|
| Japan | 95316 | 53280 | 36003 | 57153 | 97530 | 93437 | 99364 | 113749 | 114445 | 112028 | 98680 | 99425 | 132639 | 139459 |
| Germany | 8876 | 6736 | 5405 | 6443 | 9269 | 7801 | 6678 | 9443 | 9968 | 14159 | 16483 | 17411 | 24700 | 30611 |
| Korea | 3 | 2341 | 4625 | 5135 | 7369 | 6259 | 12982 | 17012 | 27007 | 34658 | 65211 | 78548 | 97334 | 98784 |
| Sweden | 2073 | 1690 | 2051 | 2536 | 3591 | 2099 | 1934 | 3721 | 3335 | 4507 | 3472 | 3053 | 3055 | 2668 |
| UK | 1758 | 1003 | 1158 | 1362 | 2387 | 1222 | 491 | 530 | 461 | 1795 | 4172 | 6409 | 6339 | 5494 |
| Belgium | – | – | 396 | 813 | 1586 | 1142 | 415 | 582 | 1002 | 1417 | 6852 | 7049 | 20564 | 29982 |
| Other | 6499 | 4578 | 3517 | 3679 | 4530 | 2191 | 1844 | 2369 | 2445 | 13692 | 19964 | 20992 | 4553 | 1344 |
| Total | 114525 | 69628 | 52759 | 76311 | 126262 | 115151 | 123708 | 147406 | 158663 | 182256 | 214834 | 233287 | 289184 | 308342 |

*Sources*:  AIA (various years); IC, *The Automotive Industry* (Draft Report) (Canberra, 1997), p. C11.
*Note*:
–  Not available.

remained comparatively stable. Together, Japan and Korea now supply more than three-quarters of passenger motor vehicle imports, with Germany the only other consistently large supplier, while imports from Belgium (mainly the medium-sized Mondeo by Ford and Vectra by GM-H) increased significantly from 1995.

Table 9.2 (a), (b) and (c) provides data for production, registrations and 'exportable surplus' (that is the difference between production and registrations) for Australia, the United States and the three countries currently providing the bulk of Australia's CBU imports, Japan, Germany and Korea. With the United States, the last three countries together produced more than 60 per cent of world PMV output during the 1990s. For Japan, notable are the declines in production (22 per cent over 1991–95) and exportable surplus in the five years prior to 1996, though the 1998 data suggests the industry is recovering as the Japanese economy recovers from its prolonged recession. A large part of any decline in Japanese exports is a result of manufacturers moving production capacity to the USA, substituting local (US) production for exports in an effort to improve market access for their products.

The rise of the Korean industry has been remarkable. From an output of 264,000 units in 1985 (about two-thirds of Australian output in that year), it rose to more than 1.1 million in 1991 and by 1996 that had doubled to more than 2.2 million vehicles.[9] During that time the output of the Australian industry remained at about 250,000 to 320,000 vehicles and indeed, production and sales in all the major PMV producing regions – North America, Japan and Europe – have been static over the period or have declined. As a proportion of world production, Korea has gone from less than 1 per cent to 6.5 per cent of the world total. In 1996, just before the Asian economic crisis, Korea's exportable surplus was about 45 per cent of production. During the crisis, as local sales declined this rose to about 60 per cent.

However, the Korean industry's expansion has not been without problems even before the so-called 'meltdown' of the East Asian economies. In July 1997, Kia (partially owned by Ford) needed bank support and a 'fire sale' of its car stocks to avoid bankruptcy. The fallout from the economic crisis in 1998 saw the number of producers in Korea fall from five to two – Hyundai and Daiwa. In 1997 total Korean PMV production was scheduled to be 6 million vehicles per year by 2002, compared with 1996 domestic sales of 1.2 million vehicles. Not surprisingly, car makers elsewhere viewed the Korean expansion with concern. According to the President of the American Automobile Manufacturers' Association, the Korean producers placed 'virtually all of the world's auto makers at risk'. The President of Toyota stated in 1997 that his firm believed the growth of Korean production had been 'too rapid and the investment has been too large'.[10] Despite this, Nissan, Honda and Mitsubishi either have built, or are building new plants in South East Asia.

Malaysia has also added to world capacity and is pursuing export markets (including Australia).[11] Aside from any effects of the Asian economic crisis, not all of the developing countries' plans have run smoothly. An Indonesian project, the 'Timor' – a joint venture between Kia and a firm controlled by ex-President Suharto's son, and originally aimed mainly at domestic sales – has apparently collapsed. Under the agreement Kia was to produce 60 per cent of the Timor in Indonesia within three years. The first batch of Timors that was fully imported from Korea sold poorly in Indonesia, and more than half were re-exported to third markets. A second 'national' car, designed in Australia, was expected to go into production before the end of the decade, but with the political turmoil in Indonesia since the fall of the Suharto regime, the project has apparently sunk without trace.

**Table 9.2**  Major passenger motor vehicle producer countries – production, registrations, and exportable surplus, 1985, 1990–1996

| | 1985 | 1991 | 1992 | 1993 | 1994 | 1995 | 1996 |
|---|---|---|---|---|---|---|---|
| | | | (a) Production | | | | |
| Japan | 7646 | 9753 | 9378 | 8497 | 7801 | 7612 | 7820 |
| USA | 8186 | 5439 | 5659 | 5988 | 6606 | 6333 | 6053 |
| Germany | 4167 | 4677 | 4864 | 3753 | 4094 | 4362 | 4423 |
| Korea | 264 | 1158 | 1307 | 1593 | 1758 | 2003 | 2260 |
| Australia | 384 | 278 | 259 | 296 | 323 | 312 | 326 |
| World | 29497 | 33550 | 33555 | 32618 | 33569 | 33925 | 35000[a] |
| | | | (b) Registrations | | | | |
| Japan | 3104 | 4868 | 4454 | 4199 | 4210 | 4444 | 4640 |
| USA | 11046 | 8176 | 8211 | 8518 | 8992 | 8636 | 8570 |
| Germany | 2379 | 4159 | 3930 | 3194 | 3209 | 3313 | 3510 |
| Korea | 136 | 773 | 876 | 1037 | 1140 | 1149 | 1220 |
| Australia | 500 | 388 | 402 | 414 | 461 | 488 | 492 |
| | | | (c) Exportable surplus | | | | |
| Japan | 4542 | 4885 | 4924 | 4298 | 3591 | 3168 | 3180 |
| USA | -2860 | -2737 | -2552 | -2530 | -2386 | -2303 | -2517 |
| Germany | 1788 | 518 | 934 | 559 | 885 | 1049 | 913 |
| Korea | 128 | 385 | 431 | 556 | 618 | 854 | 1040 |
| Australia | -116 | -110 | -143 | -118 | -138 | -178 | -166 |

*Sources*: AIA, *State of the Automotive Industry*, (Canberra, 1993, 1995); IC, *The Automotive Industry* (Draft Report) (Canberra, 1997).
*Note*:
[a]  Estimate.

From the point of view of world capacity, the Asian region is not the only area of concern. Existing plants of Ford, Volkswagen and Fiat in Latin America have undergone significant expansion and modernization, and new plants have been, or are being built by a number of companies including DaimlerChrysler, Honda and Toyota. Annual capacity in Latin America is expected to be about 2.5 million vehicles by 2001, twice the capacity of just four or five years earlier. All of this adds to the problem of global excess capacity which in 1996 in North America was estimated to be about 3 to 4 million vehicles per year; in Japan, a similar level; and in Europe 5 to 6 million vehicles – a total of up to 14 million vehicles compared with world production of about 35 million passenger motor vehicles.[12] If the established car makers hope that expanding markets in developing countries are to be their saviours their hopes are unlikely to be realized. As these markets expand, every indication suggests that capacity in these countries will similarly expand with no net gain in solving the problem. The 'new' investment plans announced by the Australian car makers following the government's 1997 decision to extend the period of preferential tariff treatment of PMV production, if realized, will merely add (though minutely) to what at the moment appears on a global scale to be an intractable problem of excess capacity. It calls in question the continued survival of a number of the established car makers, not only in Australia, but throughout the world.

One response of the major car makers to the new competitive environment has been the accelerating takeover/merger/joint venture activity of recent years. Among other instances, Ford now either owns or has ties with Volvo, Jaguar, Aston Martin and Mazda; General Motors with SAAB, Opel, Isuzu and Suzuki; BMW with Rolls Royce and until mid-2000 with Rover;[13] Volkswagen with Audi, Skoda, SEAT and Bentley. In many ways the most important recent change in the industry has been the takeover by Daimler-Benz of the Chrysler Corporation in May 1999. Much of the previous activity has been more the acquisition of desirable 'brand-names' (for example Ford acquiring Aston Martin) to satisfy niche markets. DaimlerChrysler is likely to be the precursor of mergers among the major firms which some industry analysts believe will bring the number of car-making groups to just six by the early twenty-first century. The Japanese industry is likely to be hard-hit. In early 1999 Renault acquired a controlling interest in Nissan which has suffered from falling sales for much of the 1990s.[14] Mitsubishi, Japan's fourth largest producer, is now an obvious candidate for absorption. Since mid-1999 Mitsubishi Motors has had its debt-rating cut to 'junk bond' status and its recently proposed 'alliance' with DaimlerChrysler appears to be its best chance of salvation. Toyota and Honda look to be the only Japanese makers able to face the future with some confidence as stand-alone producers.

Australia is a very small producer indeed. With domestic sales of fewer than 300,000 passenger cars in 1991 (and each year since), any reliance on exports for future growth in a world market already characterized by 40 per cent excess production capacity is likely to be disappointed. If it is true that most of the remaining disparity between Australian productivities and world-best are the result of the sub-optimal scale production in the country, it is hard to avoid the conclusion that with this, poor profits and increasing import competition, one or more of the local producers will have to withdraw or at least restructure their operations. The crucial decisions must come when the next round of replacement models is considered.

## How protection shaped the Australian automotive industry in the twentieth-century

If there has been a central influence on the development of the Australian automobile industry in the twentieth century it is protectionism, and the role of the tariff as a protective barrier has often been crucial. Protection has influenced the products the industry has made – whether motor bodies, chassis or other components – the structure of the industry producing them and the processes used in their production. As the protective structure has changed, so too has the nature of the industry and its products.

In the first few years of the twentieth century while a few 'complete' cars were produced, towards the end of the first decade the growing availability of the cheap and reliable Ford Model T and other mass-produced vehicles from the United States brought any prospect of 'full' local production to a stop. These imports, however, provided a market for locally built bodies (which were subject to protective tariffs) for the chassis of these imported vehicles (which were not). This tariff structure (and the high international transport costs on comparatively bulky and fragile bodies) encouraged the initial development of motor bodybuilding behind high protective barriers using as an 'input', imported chassis that were subject to low revenue duties.

The import restrictions first imposed on motor bodies as a wartime measure in 1917 provided the initial stimulus for the large-scale, post-First World War production of motor bodies. Later, the post-war tariff structure – the Greene tariff – provided a margin of assistance for the local assembly of imported chassis that largely encouraged the entry of Ford and General Motors, primarily as vehicle assemblers. During the 1920s extending the range of chassis components subject to protective tariff rates (both formally by changes to the tariff, and informally by bureaucratic intervention) brought a corresponding broadening of the range of components locally produced. When 'tariff broadening' stopped in the early 1930s, so too did the 'broadening' of local production.

For much of the 1920s and 1930s, the essence of the production process shaped by the protective structure was this. The protective tariffs (and high international transport costs) applying to motor bodies and the low revenue duties on car chassis combined to provide almost prohibitive protection for Australian motor bodybuilders during the period between the two world wars. Moreover the tariff in providing a lower rate on unassembled than on assembled chassis (international transport costs were also lower for unassembled chassis) encouraged their local assembly. The result was an industry that in effect assembled imported CKD chassis, bolted on locally produced bodies, and along the way included a few locally produced peripheral components, the most important of which (in terms of value) were tyres and tubes. Most locally manufactured components – radiators, sparkplugs and the like – were produced as replacement parts. Again the tariff contrived this by charging non-protective rates on some components when imported as original equipment, and protective rates if they were imported as replacement parts.[15]

If the 1920s and early 1930s showed the power of tariffs to encourage the entry of foreign producers and influence the range of local production and the sources of imports,[16] the mid-1930s brought a realization of the limitations of tariffs as a sole means of 'creating' a 'complete' industry. Consumers cannot be completely ignored. The Tariff Board in its 1936–37 inquiry into the industry and the economics of 'full' manufacture recognized this limitation in its report published in 1938.[17] The introduction of the Motor Vehicle Engine Bounty Bill in 1936 was evidence that the government knew it too.

The introduction of the engine bounty proposal was a direct attempt by the government to set up complete automobile manufacture by the payment of subsidies for engine production to an 'Australian' producer. The payments proposed under the Bill (even when they were later increased) were insufficient to attract any local (or for that matter foreign-linked) producer. More was required. 'More' turned out to be providing a potential production monopoly for an Australian company (through the Motor Vehicle Agreement Act) making use of the government's wartime powers under the National Security Act. In adopting these measures there was an implicit recognition that further increases in the already high tariffs applying in the mid-1930s would be counter-productive. The effects of still higher tariffs on automobile prices would so adversely affect sales that local production would be uneconomic.

Neither of these measures, however, was ever implemented. The Bounty and Agreement Acts were repealed in 1945 as conditions for the major pre-war producers setting up 'complete' manufacture of passenger cars. The three major producers with links to the US, Chrysler (CDD), Ford and GM-H, submitted plans for full manufacture, while Nuffield of Britain submitted a plan for more limited production – at least initially. All four firms asked for government assistance of varying degrees of generosity.

GM-H was the first into production and its Holden (48-215) was an immediate success.[18] Despite this, the late 1940s (particularly) and early 1950s were periods where the Australian market was dominated by British cars. A combination of a shortage of production capacity for the Holden, the devaluation of the £ sterling and the dollar shortage that virtually excluded imports from North America, provided British producers with a significant advantage over their competitors in the early post-war years. Once GM-H overcame its production bottlenecks, by 1951 the Holden had overtaken the British-designed Austin A40 as the market leader. By the mid-1950s the British ascendancy had ended and GM-H dominated the market, a dominance it (and the other US-linked local producers) maintained for another quarter of a century.

During all of this period the tariff structure remained, but as a protective device it was largely redundant. In the 1950s the virtually prohibitive protection provided by import licensing, imposed not to protect industry but to conserve foreign exchange, had the predictable effect of encouraging overseas manufacturers to assemble and/or produce a proliferation of models behind the protective barrier.

Once import licensing ended in 1960 the tariff once against became the primary means of protecting local producers. It quickly proved inadequate either to preserve their market share from increasing competitive pressure from imports, or to maintain domestically produced vehicles' local content that had suffered with a surge of imported components in 1962–63.[19] The 'answer' to these problems was the first of the local content 'plans', variations of which applied until the end of the 1980s. In return for prescribed levels of local content, duty concessions were offered for imported components. However, rather than a small range of models with high levels of local content which was the aim, the plans – at least those of the 1960s – encouraged a proliferation of models and small-scale production.

With this legacy, the 1970s proved to be especially difficult for local producers. Inefficiencies in both vehicle and component production resulting from the effects of the local content schemes, increasing import competition, mainly from Japan, and increased oil prices all conspired to bring the industry to crisis. By the end of 1974, the government responded to the industry's problems. It phased out the low production-volume plans which were at the heart of many of the industry's problems (the high volume 85 and 95 per cent local content plans were to remain until 1974), and implemented a 'temporary' market-sharing scheme which reserved by means of import quotas 80 per cent of the market for local producers. Except for a short period in 1976–77 when restrictions were lifted, the 'temporary' measure lasted for the next 10 years. The 1980s brought the most prescriptive arrangements of all. The Button Plan introduced in 1984 aimed to bring the industry into the 1990s with three manufacturers producing no more than six vehicle models.[20] Trade barriers were gradually lowered, exports encouraged (export credits could be used for duty-free imports of both vehicles and components) and for a short time the plan's aims were achieved, at least as far as the number of models and manufacturers were concerned. In the post-Button period, the phased reductions in tariffs over the 1990s[21] brought with them improved product quality, but in the main, low levels of profits for local producers and a considerable loss of market share to imports – and it is likely this will continue.

In all of the changes to the Australian industry in the twentieth century, trade barriers have been the driving influences. The focus of assistance measures for the automobile industry has changed, however. For the first 35 years the focus was almost exclusively on tariffs, but tariffs have had their shortcomings in achieving the sometimes quite specific aims of government policies towards the industry. Since the 1930s, however, they have been used as an important compliment to other, often more prescriptive measures. Subsidies, direct quantitative restrictions, the granting of monopoly production rights, tariff quotas, local content plans and export facilitation schemes have all been tried. Tariffs have been a party to all of these devices. In particular they have played important roles in 'enforcing' the various local content schemes and 'industry plans' of one form or another to which the industry has been subjected for most of the period since the mid-1960s. In essence 'enforcement' has entailed allowing tariff concessions (or duty-free credits) on imports in return for achieving the various schemes' objectives. Those who are unable to achieve the plans' objectives are not given the concessions and are then placed at a competitive disadvantage against those who are.

As government's objectives for the auto industry have changed, tariffs, in combination with other measures, have shaped and reshaped the industry (though rarely for the better). However, tariffs alone have seldom been sufficient to do the job required. The Howard government's 'tariff pause' and its promise of the 'absolute certainty' of tariff support for the industry after 2005 are unlikely to contribute much to mitigating the effects of the many other, more important uncertainties that face the Australian industry at the beginning of the twenty-first century.

## Notes

1. Price comparisons should be made with caution, as vehicle models and specifications may differ. US prices are distorted by government policies which have the effect of raising the prices of large cars and creating artificially low prices for small, fuel efficient cars (AIA, *State of the Australian Automotive Industry* (Canberra, 1992), p. 33).
2. Tariff rates in Australia, the UK and the USA at the time of the comparison in June, 1997 were 22.5 per cent, 10 per cent and 2.5 per cent respectively.

Australian prices included 22 per cent sales tax, the US prices included California sales tax (6 per cent and in some cases 8.25 per cent) and the UK prices, VAT (17.5 per cent).

Some relevant comparisons include:

|  | Australia | UK | US |
|---|---|---|---|
| Hyundai Excel | $13991 | $16204 | $12774 |
| VW Golf CL | $24990 | $26695 | $19797 |
| Commodore/Buick le Sabre/Omega[a] | $33500 | $40289 | $32810 |
| Falcon GLi/Taurus GL[b] | $30311 | – | $27824 |

Notes:

[a] The Commodore and the Buick have similar 3.8 litre engines and similar dimensions. The Omega has a 2 litre engine and is smaller than the Commodore.

[b] Both are base models. The Falcon is larger and is equipped with a larger (4 litre) engine than the Taurus (3 litres).

(Phil Scott, 'Tariff Sound and Fury ... and the Pricetag Reality', *Sydney Morning Herald*, 13 June 1997)

3. The prices of most vehicles in Australia were expected to fall with the replacement of a wholesale sales tax by a goods and services tax (GST) in mid-2000. However, anticipating the introduction of the tax, buyers delayed purchases causing sellers to lower their pre-GST prices to levels comparable with expected post-GST prices.

4. In 1964–65 the EH Holden was produced at annual volumes of about 150,000 units.

5. Department of Industry, Science and Resources, *State of the Automotive Industry* (Canberra, 1998), Appendix Table 3. Mitsubishi's Magna/Verada and Toyota's Camry/Vienta models are front-wheel drive cars. The first mentioned of each of these models produced by the respective companies has a four-cylinder engine, the last, a six-cylinder engine. The four- and six-cylinder models of each of the companies' products share the same body.

6. Studies of minimum efficient scale (the scale at which most economies are exhausted) suggest for final assembly of vehicles, a plant needs an output of 200,000 to 250,000 vehicles. Most of these studies are 10 to 15 years old, however. The International Motor Vehicle Project, coordinated by the Massachusetts Institute of Technology, has argued that with changes in products, and production technology, MES is likely to decline in the future to about 150,000 units (IC, *The Automotive Industry* (Canberra, 1991), p. 198).

7. For example, in 1997 the nominal tariff for CBU vehicles for the Peoples Republic of China were 100 per cent; Chinese Tai Pei, 30–42 per cent; Indonesia, 125 per cent; Malaysia, 140–200 per cent, though many of these high tariffs are soon scheduled to fall. The rate in South Korea was among the lowest of all the Asian countries at 8 per cent.

8. GM-H earned a record after tax profit of A$260 million in 1995 and Ford made a record after tax profit of A$217 million in 1996.

9. Output fell to less than 2 million in 1998 with the economic problems experienced there and in much of East Asia at the time.

10. *Sydney Morning Herald*, 26 August 1997.

11. Malaysia's production was estimated to have increased from 140,000 PMVs in 1995 to 250,000 in 1996 (IC, *The Automotive Industry* (Draft Report) (Canberra, 1997), p. B3).

12. M. Keller, 'Excess Capacity – A Past, Present and Future Constant', *Power Report* (July 1996), pp. 14–16.
13. In May 2000, BMW sold Rover to the Phoenix consortium (mainly made up of businessmen from the British Midlands) for £10. Rover had been making very heavy losses under BMW's ownership. The more successful Land Rover operations were sold to Ford for £3 billion (*Sydney Morning Herald*, 11 and 26 May 2000).
14. Under the new arrangement a number of plants will be closed and more than 20,000 employees shed over the next two or three years.
15. Tariff Board, *Engines and Chassis for Motor Vehicles* (Canberra, 1938), p. 11.
16. The preferential tariff arrangements negotiated in the Ottawa Agreement had the effect of switching car imports towards Britain and away from North America.
17. 'Evidence submitted to the Board was strong enough to convince it that any appreciable increase in the price of popular cars would materially reduce the demand, thus increasing the cost per unit of Australian manufacturers supplying that demand' (Tariff Board, *Engines and Chassis*, p. 20).
18. The final agreement between GM-H and the government allowed imported components to the value of 10 per cent of the ex-factory price (or 5 per cent of the vehicle's weight), required tariff concessions on imported plant and equipment and access to short foreign exchange and the maintenance of the pre-war tariff structure. Ford had asked for increased tariffs and in effect a capital grant in its initial manufacturing proposal.
19. Stubbs, *The Australian Motor Industry* (Sydney, 1972), p. 79.
20. During the operation of the market-sharing arrangements, the three leading local producers, Chrysler, Ford and GM-H, were joined at the government's invitation by Nissan and Toyota as full 'plan producers'. By the beginning of the 1980s Australia had five producers for a market of a size that could probably have supported one producer operating at near optimum scale of output.
21. From 35 per cent in 1992, rates have been reduced by annual decrements of 2.5 percentage points each year, reaching 15 per cent in 2000.

# Bibliography

**ARCHIVE SOURCES**

**Australian Archives (AA)**

**1. Australian Capital Territory (ACT)**

AA ACT 1418/1/6 Part 2.
AA ACT 432/57 40/357
AA ACT A425/1 36/10700
AA ACT A425/1 38/4030
AA ACT A425/1 39/9503
AA ACT A425/127 45/3666
AA ACT A457/1 NA 300/17
AA ACT A461 OP418/1/6 Part 2
AA ACT A461/1
AA ACT A461/1 B418/1/6 Part 2
AA ACT A461/1 D418/1/6 Part 1
AA ACT A461/1 D418/1/6 Part 1
AA ACT A461/1 D418/1/6 Part 2
AA ACT A461/1 D418/1/6 Part 3
AA ACT A461/1 D418/1/6 Part 3
AA ACT A461/1 D418/1/6 Part 4
AA ACT A461/1 D418/1/6 Part 5
AA ACT A461/1 D418/1/6 Part 6
AA ACT A461/1 D418/1/65 Part 3
AA ACT A461/1 D418/1/8 Part 3
AA ACT A461/1 F418/1/6
AA ACT A461/1 I418/1/6 Part 2
AA ACT A461/1 M418/1/6 Part1
AA ACT A461/1 O418/1/6 Part 2
AA ACT A461/1/6 Part 2
AA ACT A461/1/6 U418/1/6
AA ACT A6006/1
AA ACT B1/1 850 Bundle 5

## 2. Victoria (Vic.)

AA Vic. 44/106
AA Vic. CRS B1535 File 931/2/239
AA Vic. IC 44/106
AA Vic. MP1118/2 43/1/225
AA Vic. MP273/1 G1914/13096
AA Vic. MP394 Series 1 5/81/151 Part 2
AA Vic. MP394 Series 1 5/81/15A
AA Vic. MP267/1 3 Number Series 5/81/158
AA Vic. MP394 5/81/15A
AA Vic. MP394 Series 1 5/81/102 Part 2
AA Vic. MP394 Series 1 5/81/107 ATT4.
AA Vic. MP394 Series 1 5/81/14
AA Vic. MP394 Series 1 5/81/151 Part 3
AA Vic. MP394 Series 1 IC 44/106
AA Vic. MP394/1 5/81/107 Part 5
AA Vic. MP394/1 5/81/15
AA Vic. MP730/19 IT20

## 3. Mortlock Library, South Australia, General Motors Archive (Mortlock)

Mortlock BRG 213/65/6
Mortlock BRG 213/65/8
Mortlock BRG 213/65/9
Mortlock MLK 4701 ML MSS 5146 Item 2
Mortlock MLK 4701 ML MSS 5146 Item 5

## Other Archive Sources

Henry Ford Museum Archives and Library, Dearborn, Michigan, Accession 84 Box 2
Henry Ford Museum Archives and Library, Dearborn, Michigan, Accession 96 Box 18
Zentrales Staats Archiv Potsdam, Auswärtiges Amt, Abt. II, Bd. I

## PERIODICALS AND NEWSPAPERS

*Adelaide Advertiser*
*Australasian Coachbuilder and Saddler*
*Australasian Coachbuilder and Wheelwright*
*Australian Motorist*
*Autocar*
*Coach and Motor Builder*
*Sun-Herald*
*Sydney Morning Herald*

*The Age*
*The Australian*
*The Australian Magazine*


## BOOKS, ARTICLES

Bade, W. (1938), *Das Auto Erobert der Welt*, Berlin

Baldwin, C.F. (1929), 'The Automotive Market in Australia', [US] *Trade Information Bulletin*, 611

Bardou, J. P. *et al* (1982), *The Automobile Revolution*, Chapel Hill, NC

Barker, T.C. (1982), 'The Spread of Motor Vehicles before 1914', in C.P. Kindleberger and G. di Tella (eds) *Economics in the Long View*, 3 vols, London, II, Part 1

Baruch, B. (1920), *The Making of the Reparations and the Economic Sections of the Treaty*, New York

Beaven, B. (1993), 'The Growth and Significance of the Coventry Car Component Industry', *Midland History*, XVIII

Berger, M.L. (1979), *The Devil Wagon in God's Country: The Automobile and Social Change in Rural America, 1893–1929*, Hamden, CT

Bergmann, C. (1927), *The History of Reparations*, London

Bladen, V.W. (1962), *Report of the Royal Commission on the Automotive Industry*, Ottawa

Bloomfield, G.T. (1982), 'Motorisation on the New Frontier: The Case of Saskatchewan, Canada, 1906–1934', in T.C. Barker (ed.), *The Economic and Social Effects of the Spread of Motor Vehicles*, London

Brigden, J.B. (1925), 'The Australian Tariff and the Standard of Living', *Economic Record*, I

Butlin, S. (1955), *War Economy, 1939–1942*, Canberra

Capling, A. and Galligan, B. (1992), *Beyond the Protective State*, Cambridge

Castle, H.G. (1950), *Britain's Motor Industry*, London

Caves, R., Ward, I. and Wright, P. (1987), *Australian Industry: Structure, Conduct and Performance*, 2nd edn, Sydney

Cheney, S.A. (1965), *From Horse to Horse Power*, Adelaide

Chrysler, W.P. (1937), *Life of an American Workman*, New York

Church, R. (1979), *Herbert Austin*, London

Conlon, R.M. (1986), *Distance and Duties*, Ottawa

Conlon, R.M. and Perkins, J.A (1996), *The Origins and Interwar Development of the Automobile Industry in Australia and Canada*, School of Economics Discussion Paper, University of New South Wales

Davidson, F.G. and Stewardson, B.R. (1974), *Economics and Australian Industry*, Melbourne

Davis, P. (1987), *Wheels Across Australia*, Sydney

Dixon, D.F. (1972), 'Origins of the Australian Petrol Distribution System', *Australian Economic History Review*, XII, 1

Dyster, B. and Meredith, D. (1990), *Australia in the International Economy in the Twentieth Century*, Cambridge

Everett, L.A. (n.d.), *The Shape of the Motor Car*, London

Ford, H. (1926), 'What I have Learnt about Management in the last 25 years', *System, The Magazine of Business*, January

Forster, C. (1964), *Industrial Development in Australia, 1920–1930*, Canberra

General Motors (1983), *The First Seventy-Five Years of Transportation Products*, Automobile Quarterly in association with the Princeton Institute for Historic Research

Giltrap, T. and M. (1981), *Australian Cars from 1879*, Sydney

Goode, J. (1961), 'Australian Early Car Manufacturers', *Bulletin of the Business Archives Council of Australia*, I, 6

Goode, J. (1969), *Smoke, Smell and Clatter*, Melbourne

Harrison, A.E. (1969), 'The Competitiveness of the British Cycle Industry, 1890–1914', *Economic History Review*, 2nd Series, XXII, 2

Hartnett, L.J. (1963), *Big Wheels and Little Wheels*, Melbourne

Holmes, D. (1963), 'Australia's Early Car Manufacturers: A Note on the Tarrant Engineering Company', *Business Archives and History*, III, 2

Horras, G. (1982), *Die Entwicklung des deutschen Automobilmarktes bis 1914*, Munich

Johnson, H.G. (1963), 'The Bladen Plan for Increased Protection of the Canadian Automotive Industry, *Canadian Journal of Economics*, May

Keller, M. (1966), 'Excess Capacity – A Past, Present and Future Constant', *Power Report*, July

Kennedy, E.D. (1934), *The Automobile Industry*, New York

King, R. (1993), 'Driving the Environment, A Case History from Ford Motor Company of Australia', in L. Cato (ed.), *The Business of Ecology*, Melbourne

Knott, J.W. (1994), 'Speed, Modernity and the Motor Car. The Making of the 1909 *Motor Traffic Act* in New South Wales', *Australian Historical Studies*, XXIV, 103

Kohler, V. (1996), 'Deutsche Personenwagen Fabrikate zwischen 1886 und 1965', *Zeitschrift für Unternehmengeschichte*

Lambert, Z.E. and Wyatt, R.J. (1968), *Lord Austin: The Man*, London

Lamont, T.W. (1921), 'Reparations', in E.M. House and C. Seymour (eds) *What Really Happened At Paris*, New York

Laurent, J. (1994), '"Industry Policy" and the Australian Motor Vehicle Industry, 1920–1942', *Journal of the Royal Australian Historical Society*, LXXX

Laux, J.M. (1966), 'Rochet-Schneider and the French Motor Industry to 1914', *Business History*, VIII, 2

Longstreet, S. (1956), *The Boy in the Model T: A Journey in the Just Gone Past*, New York

Maxcy, G. and Silberston, A. (1959), *The Motor Industry*, London

May, G.S. (1990), 'Jackson Automobile Company' in G. May (ed.), *Encyclopedia of American Business History and Biography* 'The Automobile, 1896–1920', New York

Mills, R.C. (1927), 'The Tariff Board of Australia', *Economic Record*, III, 4

Overy, R.J. (1959), *William Morris: Lord Nuffield*, London

Page, E. (1963), *Truant Surgeon*, Sydney

Pound, A. (1934), *The Turning Wheel*, New York

Pratt, C.E. (1891), 'A Sketch of American Bicycling and Its Founder', *Outing*, XVIII, 4

Rae, J.B. (1959), *American Automobile Manufacturers: The First Forty Years*, Philadelphia

Rhys, D.G. (1976), 'Concentration in the Inter-War Motor Industry', *Journal of Transport History*, New Series, III, 4

Rich, J. (1996), *Hartnett: Portrait of a Technocratic Brigand*, Sydney

Rubinstein, J.M. (1992), *The Changing US Auto Industry: A Geographical Analysis*, New York

Saul, S.B. (1962), 'The Motor Industry in Britain to 1914', *Business History*, V

Seltzer, L.H. (1928), *A Financial History of the American Automobile Industry*, Boston

Stanton, J. (1984), 'Protection, Market Structure and Firm Behavior: Inefficiency in the Early Australian Tyre Industry', *Australian Economic History Review*, XXIV, 2

Stubbs, P. (1972), *The Australian Motor Industry*, Sydney

Swann, P.L. (1972), 'General Motors-Holden's – The Australian Automobile Industry in Economic Perspective', unpublished Ph.D. thesis, Monash University

Thomas, R.P. (1973), 'Style Changes and the Automobile Industry During the Roaring Twenties', in L.P. Cain and P.J. Uselding (eds) *Business Enterprise and Economic Change*, Kent, Ohio

Watson, T.S. (1990), 'Government Policy and Two World Wars – Shapers of the Automotive Industry?', thesis, School of Social Sciences, Deakin University

Weber, A. (1909 in German) *Theory of the Location of Industries* (trans. by C.J. Friedrich, 1929), Chicago

Wilson, C. and Reader, W. (1958), *Men and Machines: A History of D. Napier & Son, Engineers Ltd 1808–1958*, London

Winder, G.H. and MacPherson, C. (1931), *The Delusion of Protection*, Sydney

Winser K. (ed.) (n.d.), *The Story of Australian Motoring*

Womack, J.P., Jones, D.T. and Roos, D. (1990), *The Machine that Changed the World*, New York

Wood, J. (1988), *Wheels of Misfortune: The Rise and Fall of the British Motor Industry*, London

Wright, J. (1998), *The Heart of the Lion*, Sydney

## GOVERNMENT REPORTS AND STATISTICAL SOURCES

Australian Bureau of Census and Statistics (1996), *Vehicle Census of Australia*, Canberra

Australian Bureau of Census and Statistics, *Yearbook of Australia*, Canberra (various years)

Automobile Manufacturers' Association, *Automobile Facts and Figures*, Detroit (various years)

Automotive Industry Authority (AIA), *State of the Australian Automotive Industry*, Canberra (various years)*

Commonwealth Bureau of Census and Statistics, *Official Yearbook of the Commonwealth of Australia*, Canberra (various years)

Commonwealth Bureau of Census and Statistics, *Production Bulletin, 1919–20 to 1938*, Canberra

*Commonwealth Parliamentary Papers*, VII, 1914–17

*Commonwealth Parliamentary Record* (Hansard)

*Commonwealth Record* (1978), 3, 45

Department of Industry, Science and Resources (1998), *State of the Automotive Industry*, Canberra*

Department of Industry, Science and Resources (1999), *Key Automotive Statistics, Australia*, Canberra

Department of Industry, Science and Resources (1999), *State of the Australian Automotive Industry, 1997*, Canberra*

Department of Industry, Science and Tourism (1998), *State of the Australian Automotive Industry Report*, 1996 Canberra*

Department of Statistics (1991), *Official Yearbook of New Zealand*, Wellington

Dominion Bureau of Statistics, *Automobile Statistics for Canada*, Ottawa (various years)

Federal Office of Road Safety (1996), *Motor Vehicle Pollution in Australia*, Canberra
Motor Vehicle Manufacturers' Association, *Facts and Figures of the Automotive Industry*, Toronto (various years)
National Automobile Chamber of Commerce (1931), *Facts and Figures of the Automobile Industry*, New York
PAXUS Corporation, *Bulletin – New Motor Vehicle Registrations* (various years)
Statistics Canada (1983), *Historical Statistics of Canada*, 2nd edition, Series R1-22

\* Note: The publications of the Automotive Industry Authority were subsumed in the late 1990s, first by the Department of Industry, Science and Tourism and then by the Department of Industry, Science and Resources. For simplicity in Tables 8.1–8.9 and 9.1–9.2 where relevant the statistical sources are specified as AIA (various years).

## Reports of the Tariff Board, Industries Assistance Commission (IAC), and Industry Commission (IC)

IAC (1974), *Passenger Motor Vehicles, etc.*, Canberra
IAC (1974), *The Australian Market for Passenger Motor Vehicles*, mimeo
IAC (1981), *Passenger Motor Vehicles and Components – Post-1984 Assistance Arrangements*, Canberra
IC (1990), *The Automotive Industry* (Draft Report), Canberra
IC (1991), *The Automotive Industry*, Canberra
IC (1997), *The Automotive Industry* (Draft Report), Canberra
IC (1998), *The Automotive Industry*, Canberra
Tariff Board (1938), *Engines and Chassis for Motor Vehicles*, Canberra
Tariff Board (1943), *Post-War Reconstruction, Motor Vehicles*, Canberra
Tariff Board (1957), *Report on the Automotive Industry*, Canberra
Tariff Board (1965), *Motor Vehicles and Concessional Admission of Components*, Canberra

# Index

*Adelaide Advertiser* 61
affordability index for cars 141
age distribution of cars 154
agriculture 3, 109
aircraft manufacture 3, 54; *see also*
  Commonwealth Aircraft Corporation
Anthony, H.L. 59, 73
Asian economic crisis (1997) 162
Associated Chamber of Manufacturing
  31
Atkey, Sir Albert 40
attitudes to the car 2, 14–16, 19
Austin, Sir Herbert (later Lord) 11, 40,
  104
Austin (company) 29, 116, 122–4
Australian Association of British
  Manufacturers 104
Australian Automobile Manufacturers'
  Association 29, 50, 54
*Australian Coachbuilder and
  Wheelwright* 19, 21, 23
Australian Consolidated Industries (ACI)
  5–6, 60–74
Australian Motor Industries 129
*Australian Motorist* 33, 38, 52, 85–6,
  102, 108
automation 148–9
automobile industry, definition of 1–2,
  87
Automotive Industry Authority 136

baby cars *see* small cars
Barker, Theo 16
Belgium 161
Bell, Marcus 106–7
Bettle, H.E. 119
bicycle manufacture, dealing and repair
  12–13, 20–1
Bladen, V.W. 89
BMW (company) 163
Bounty Bill (1936) 5, 72–3, 165

bounty payments 5, 29–30, 34, 51–2,
  56–62, 165
Boyd-Carpenter, Sir Archibald 103
British cars 102–10, 122, 166
British Economic Commission 110
British management 106
British Motor Corporation 6, 112, 122–6
Bruce, Stanley 57
Buick (company) 4, 39, 84
Bullock Bicycle Works 13
Butlin, S. 28
Button, John 136
Button Plan 7, 131, 136, 143, 146, 158,
  166
by-law allowances 5, 36–7, 137, 145–6

Cameron, A.G. 66–7
Campbell, Archibald M. 13
Canada 38, 83–97, 107, 109
Capling, A. 126
Capri (model) 140
carriage-building *see* coachbuilding
Casey, R.G. (later Lord) 33–4, 56–7, 65,
  73
catalytic converters 154–5
Chambers of Automotive Industries 31,
  38, 52, 70
Chevrolet (company) 84, 89
Chifley, J.B. 70, 72, 117
Chrysler (company) 6–7, 29, 53, 57, 65,
  73, 84, 87, 123–6, 129; *see also*
  Daimler-Chrysler
Chrysler Dodge 38–9, 50
Chrysler Dodge de Soto (CDD) 116
  plans for complete manufacture
    120–1, 165
Clark, E.N. 127–8
*Coach and Motor Builder* 23
*Coachbuilder and Saddler* 19
coachbuilding trade 18–24, 32
commercial vehicles, ratio of cars to 41

177

Commonwealth Aircraft Corporation 5, 34, 54, 73
compressed natural gas 155
corporatism 35
craftsmanship 23
Curtin, John 60–2, 66–71, 117

Daimler-Benz 7, 163
Daimler-Chrysler 141, 145, 155, 163
Daiwa (company) 161
de Chair, Sir Dudley 104
De Dion (company) 10
Dedman, John 66–8, 72, 118
defence needs see strategic importance of the motor industry
Demco Machinery Company 37
deskilling 23
devaluation of the Australian dollar 129, 136, 141–2
doctors, use of cars by 15
Dodge, John and Horace 12
Dodge (company) 4, 6, 39–40
dollar shortage 116, 118, 122
Duncan and Fraser (company) 21
Durant, William 84
Duryea brothers 12

economies of scale 37–9, 43, 84–5, 89, 96, 138
electric cars 155
emission controls 154–5
employment in motor industry 42
excess capacity 137, 159, 163–4
export facilitation 130, 136–8, 141, 146, 159, 167

Federation of British Industries 103
Fiat (company) 163
finance, sources of 12
Ford, Henry 4, 11, 83, 86
Ford (company) 6–8, 12, 22, 29, 33–4, 38–9, 50, 53–8, 69, 73, 83–92 passim, 111, 116, 123–6, 129–30, 142, 146, 148, 159, 164
    plans for complete manufacture 117–18, 165
Ford Model T 4, 11, 17–18, 22, 39–41, 86, 164
Forde, Frank 56–7
fragmentation of motor industry 5, 50, 72, 128, 130

freight costs 10, 40–1, 84, 91–2, 96
French, H.C. 33, 53–5, 57, 85, 87, 110, 117–18
fuel, choice of 10, 154–5
fuel cell technology 155
fuel consumption 154–5

Galligan, B. 126
General Motors 40–1, 53, 60, 84–5, 92, 108, 165
General Motors-Holden's (GM-H) 5–8, 29, 34, 38–9, 43, 50–61 passim, 67–73, 86–7, 106, 111, 116, 123–30 passim, 146, 148, 158–9, 164–5, 166
    plans for complete manufacture 118–20, 165
Germany 161
Goddard, R.E. 102
government policy, 'active' and 'passive' 28–30, 44
government revenue, need for 28–31
Greene tariff 28–9, 32, 36, 44, 164
Grimwade, E.N. 68
Grimwade, R.R. 106
Groves, William 155
Gullett, Sir Henry 34, 51, 55–6, 58, 87, 108–9

Hacking, Lt Colonel 104
Harrison, H.W. 35, 86
Hartnett, L.J. 34–5, 51–71 passim, 108, 119
hire purchase 41
Holden, Sir Edward 119–20
Holden model 48-215 1–2, 6, 119–20, 165–6
Holden model FJ 122
Holden's (company) 24, 29, 43, 86; see also General Motors-Holden's
Honda (company) 161, 163
Howard, John 129
Hyundai (company) 161

image of the car 15, 39
imperial preference 22, 36, 41, 86–7, 92
import duties see tariffs
import licensing and import restrictions (quantitative) 4, 6–7, 23, 109, 122–5, 129, 166
imports
    of chassis 95, 110–11

market share of 7, 137, 167
  of petroleum 10
  preference for 17
  sources of 23, 160
Indonesia 162
Industries Assistance Commission 130,
  136
Industry Commission 3–4, 136
integration of body and chassis 50
interest groups 28, 31
investment 150–1
  anticipated and actual 151–4

Jackson Automobile Company 83
Japan 7, 127–8, 143, 159–61
Jeffery, Thomas B. 12
joint ventures 146, 158
Jones, D.T. 1
Jones, H.C. 64

Kia (company) 161–2
Knowles, Sir George 69
Korea 159–61

Lawson, J. 60, 62, 64, 66, 112
lead-free fuel 154–5
'lean' manufacturing practice 148
Lewis, Howard 13
licensing of manufacture 11
liquid petroleum gas 155
lobbying 5, 22, 28, 31–5
local content schemes 6–7, 54, 95–7,
  123–30 passim, 136, 138, 166–7
local manufacture
  by British companies 110–12, 116
  by Ford 123
luxury cars 4, 143, 158
Lyons, Joseph 51, 54, 108

McEwan, Sir John 60, 73, 126
McGrath, Charles 126
McLauglin, R. Samuel 83–4, 96
McLauglin, Robert S. 84
MacPherson, C. 28
mail, transportation of 15–16
Malaysia 162
market-sharing arrangements 7, 129–31,
  137, 166
mass production 11, 29, 50
Melba, Nellie 15
Melbourne *Argus* 36

Melbourne Motor Body Company 29,
  43
Menzies, R.G. 34, 54, 58–73 *passim*
Mini Minor 124, 126
Mitsubishi (company) 7–8, 140–6
  *passim*, 158–63 *passim*
model-sharing arrangements 146, 158
models, range of 39, 146–8
monopoly rights 60–7, 73, 167
Morris, H.F. 69
Morris, William 122; *see also*
  Nuffield, Lord
Morris (company) 12, 29, 121–4
motor cycles 41
Motor Vehicle Engine Bounty Act (1939)
  34, 59, 87, 109, 116; *see also* Bounty
  Bill
Motor Vehicle Importers' Association
  43
Motor Vehicle Agreement Act (1940) 5,
  67–72, 116, 165
Motor Vehicles Manufacture Legislation
  Repeal Act (1945) 72
motorization of society 40–2

Napier, Montagu 12
Napier (company) 15
national debt 30
National Security Act 62, 73, 165
New Zealand 41, 87
Nissan (company) 7, 129–30, 146, 161,
  163
Nuffield, Lord 40, 107–8; *see also*
  Morris, William
Nuffield (company) 6, 116
  plans for complete manufacture
  121–2, 165

Oldsmobile (company) 39
Opel (company) 11–13, 50
Ottawa Agreement (1932) 51, 107–8
out-sourcing 37

Packard (company) 11
Page, Earle 31–4, 54–5, 57, 73
Parkhill, Sir Archdale 58
patents 11
petroleum imports 10
Phillips, H.B. 55, 60
Pierce, George N. 12
Playford, Thomas 64

political influence of motor industry 3–4
Pope, Albert A. 12
postal services 15–16
Pressed Metal Corporation 123
prices of cars 37, 40–2, 158
    in relation to other countries 142–3
    in relation to prices and earnings
        141
productivity 7, 148–50, 153
profitability 143–7, 159, 167
protectionism, effects of 164–6; see
    also tariffs

quality of motor products 5, 7, 39, 72,
    143–4, 158
quotas 122, 130–1, 136–7, 166; see also
    import licensing restrictions

ratio of motor vehicles to population 16
rationalization of motor industry 146
registrations of motor vehicles 18, 31,
    41, 105, 125
Renault (company) 12, 15, 163
Richards (company) 29, 39, 43, 111, 120
Rickards, H. 33
Roche, F.B. 10
Rochet-Schneider (company) 11–12
Roos, D. 1
Rootes, W.E. 102–3, 125
Rootes (company) 69, 116
Roper J 72
Royal Agricultural Show 19
running costs of motor vehicles 42, 85
Ruskin's Motor Bodies 29, 43, 111, 123

Scullin Tariff 36
Second World War, effects of 115
Secondary Industries Commission 6, 70,
    74, 115, 118–21
security, national see strategic
    importance of the motor industry
Shearer, David 9, 12
Shepherd, L. 58–9
Simca (model) 124
skilled labour 2–3, 10–11, 119
small cars 6–7, 105–6, 109, 127–8, 158
Smith, Arthur E. 63
Smith, F.J. 66

Smith, W.J. 60–6, 70–4
Standard Motor Company 116, 125
standardization of products 24
states of Australia, interests and rivalries
    of 35
statistics of motor industry, problems
    with 93–4
steam-powered cars 9–10
steel, use of 19, 24, 119
strategic importance of the motor industry
    3, 5, 28–30, 58–61, 73
Stubbs, P. 126
styling of cars 39–40, 43
subsidies 44, 165; see also bounty
    payments
Sydney Morning Herald 70

Tariff Act (1911) 22
Tariff Board 34, 36, 51–9 passim, 64,
    70, 73, 110, 115, 122–7 passim, 165
'tariff touts' 5, 28, 32
tariffs 3–7, 21, 24, 28–38 passim, 41–4,
    50, 85–6, 96, 103–7, 123–31 passim,
    136–7, 164–7
    Canadian 83, 88–9, 93–6
    see also imperial preference
Tarrant, Harley 13
Tarrant Engineering Company 10, 13,
    18
taxi cabs 14–15
technology transfer 42
Thomas, Erwin R. 12
Thompson, Herbert 9, 12
Toyota (company) 7–8, 129–30, 140,
    143, 146, 148, 158–63 passim
trade diversion 29, 44, 51, 87, 94–5,
    108–11
transport costs see freight costs
Tudor Tariff 22

United Australian Automotive Industries
    146, 158

Volkswagen (company) 3, 125, 127, 163

White, T.W. 33, 52–3, 56, 106, 112
Winder, G.H. 28
Womack, J.P. 1